SAME-SEX DOMESTIC VIOLENCE
Strategies for Change

Beth Leventhal
Sandra E. Lundy
Editors

Sage Series on Violence Against Women

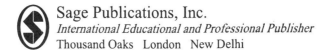
Sage Publications, Inc.
International Educational and Professional Publisher
Thousand Oaks   London   New Delhi

For information:

Sage Publications, Inc.
2455 Teller Road
Thousand Oaks, California 91320
E-mail: order@sagepub.com

Sage Publications Ltd.
6 Bonhill Street
London EC2A 4PU
United Kingdom

Sage Publications India Pvt. Ltd.
M-32 Market
Greater Kailash I
New Delhi 110 048 India

Printed in the United States of America

Library of Congress Cataloging-in-Publication Data

Leventhal, Beth
   Same-sex domestic violence: Strategies for change /
by Beth Leventhal and Sandra E. Lundy.
     p. cm.—(Sage series on violence against women)
   ISBN 0-7619-0322-4 (cloth: alk. paper)
   ISBN 0-7619-0323-2 (pbk.: alk. paper)
    1. Abused lesbians. 2. Lesbian couples. 3. Abused gay men.
4. Gay male couples. I. Lundy, Sandra E. II. Title. III. Series.
HQ75.5 .L84   1999
362.82'92—dc21   99-6399

99 00 01 02 03 04 05 7 6 5 4 3 2 1

Acquiring Editor:	C. Terry Hendrix/Kassie Gavrilis
Production Editor:	Astrid Virding
Editorial Assistant:	Karen Wiley
Typesetter:	Lynn Miyata
Indexer:	Will Ragsdale

SAME-SEX
DOMESTIC
VIOLENCE

reserve!—   Understanding justice
12/4/02—   & introduction To
             idea's —

Sage Series on Violence Against Women

Series Editors

Claire M. Renzetti
St. Joseph's University

Jeffrey L. Edleson
University of Minnesota

In this series . . .

Contents

Introduction

In the 25 or so years of its existence, the battered women's movement has done a wonderful job of bringing the issue of domestic violence in heterosexual relationships to the forefront of public attention. Not long ago there were only a handful of battered women's shelters, arcane laws that sanctioned intrafamily violence, and widespread victim-blaming of those survivors who dared to speak out. Although no one would claim that the problem of heterosexual violence is perfectly understood, the fact remains that we now have a vibrant shelter network, powerful state and national domestic violence coalitions, and even federal laws against spouse abuse. Presentations about dating violence are offered in high schools, courses in violence against women can be found at colleges and graduate schools nationwide, and many police departments and police academies have incorporated training about domestic violence into their standard curricula.

Those of us who have survived or worked with survivors of queer partner abuse, however, have not been quite as fortunate. We often have met with hostility not only in the general public, the mental health professions, and the courts but also within domestic violence organizations and our own queer communities. We have had to shout to be heard. Like poor relatives at a banquet, we have been given scraps of attention and bits and pieces of available resources and have been told we should be grateful. The queer communities have been treated as a monolith, and when the issue of queer domestic violence has been addressed at all, it has generally been in "one size fits all" terms that ignore and disrespect our diversity.

There are signs that things are slowly changing. In recent years, thanks to the tireless efforts of queer activists and survivors who simply would not shut up and go away, many state domestic violence laws have been amended to include victims of same-sex partner abuse. Mental health and community organizations (both queer and straight) are beginning to take the problem of same-sex domestic violence seriously. Most hearteningly, grassroots activists have done an impressive amount of creative work to address issues of queer domestic violence. This book presents some of those efforts in the hope of inspiring more.

Currently, people looking for practical strategies to address same-sex domestic violence find themselves in an informational vacuum. The few available books and articles on queer domestic violence focus primarily on convincing the reader that queer domestic violence exists and that "something" should be done about it. And very little of the work on queer domestic violence has addressed the specific needs of specific queer communities. Thus, the activist, the organizer, the practitioner, and the survivor are constantly reinventing the wheel as they search for antiviolence strategies that fit their unique contexts.

Both of us have worked with survivors of queer domestic violence for many years: Beth as an activist and advocate; Sandy as an activist and attorney. We have initiated and participated in police and court trainings, spoken at schools and to the media, lobbied, and organized. We know firsthand about the dearth of written material to provide guidance and inspiration.

We think it is time to go beyond "Queer Domestic Violence 101" and to offer a book that presents concrete strategies for assessing and stopping the violence in abusive queer relationships. We have compiled a broad range of essays on a variety of issues concerning queer domestic violence. Some of the chapters deal with specific communities (bisexuals, people with AIDS, immigrants), some focus on specific issues (batterer screening, S/M), and some are more general. We have also included the individual stories of survivors. What all of these essays have in common is that they were written by people who have been working on issues of queer domestic violence for many years and who have a wealth of experience to share. We have tried to represent many different queer communities and present a number of different viewpoints. Unlike previous works, which tend to focus either on lesbians or gay men (ignoring bisexuals and transgendered people entirely), we address both woman-to-woman and man-to-man violence. We have also included chapters that address issues of batterer assessment and batterer accountability, two topics that are almost totally ignored in work on queer domestic violence.

Our goal is to provide comprehensive, practical information to the wide range of professionals, lay advocates, and activists who are likely to come into contact with queer people in abusive intimate relationships. We hope to encourage people to address the multi-faceted issue of queer domestic violence not only on the individual level but also on the societal level. If you are looking for a book to convince you that queer domestic violence exists and should be taken seriously, this is not the book for you. If you are interested in effectively addressing the serious issue of queer domestic violence, then you will find a lot of information here to help you do your work.

It would have been impossible for us to compile this edition, or for the individual authors to contribute, if we did not all believe in the possibility of change and in progress. We like to think of this not as a book about violence but a book about *working through* violence in order to promote healthier relationships in our queer communities and beyond. As queer people begin to demand legal recognition of our partnerships, strengthening our commitments to each other becomes an increasingly important endeavor. Although domestic violence may seem like a dreary topic, we believe the contributors to this book offer fresh and hopeful perspectives that are a source of inspiration, not sadness.

Each of us has many people to thank for making this book possible. To list them all would catapult us way over our allotted page limit. Debra Reid has been a steady inspiration to both of us—a model of lesbian courage and survival. The indefatigable Claire Renzetti has been, as always, extremely generous with her support, her time, and her insights and was instrumental in bringing this work to press. The members of Boston's Same-Sex Domestic Violence Coalition, the Network for Battered Lesbians and Bisexual Women, and the Gay Men's Domestic Violence Project are a source of encouragement, good humor, and solidarity. We thank all of the contributors not only for their informative chapters but also for their patience. Sandy would

like to give special thanks to Claire Lundy, Kate Lundy, Ellen Rotters-
mann, Meredith Rottersmann, Rhea Becker, Heidi Holland, and Anna
Baum. Beth would like to give special thanks to Hermine Leventhal,
Deirdre Hunter, and the members of the Network's support group.

PART I

PROLOGUE: HEARING THE PROBLEM

1

Sharing My Story

KJ

I first met J. C. when I was 15 and living on the streets. Living on the streets at the time was safer than living at home because of the violence in my family. J. C. was about four years older than me, and I was comforted that she took me in and took care of me. Then I was sent away to another city to a juvenile home. Six years later I came home for a visit. I was in my early 20s and caught up in the excitement and wonder of "coming out" as a lesbian. I had never forgotten J. C. and had dreams about getting together with her someday. Back then it was difficult to find other Indians who were gay or lesbian.

We finally ran into each other at a party. The intensity and excitement of our interaction were still there. We started seeing each other. At first the relationship was wonderful. We had fun times and gentle moments, and I felt an intensity I had never felt for another. I practically idolized her. She was my "first" relationship with a woman.

The abuse started immediately after I moved in with her. She was still living with her parents. From the beginning, her parents did not approve of our relationship. To get away from them, we would go out partying. At first I was concerned because I began to see that she had a problem with alcohol and drugs. Little did I know that I would get caught up in the addiction myself.

The emotional abuse started gradually. One night we got into an argument at a downtown bar. I didn't want to go to a party with five men she had met because it didn't feel safe to me. Because I refused to go, she started yelling and screaming at me, saying I was a no-good, worthless bitch and that I didn't trust her. Her rage even made her look scary. She gave up trying to convince me to go with her and stormed out, telling me not to bother to come home. I was stunned. I asked a friend next to me if I could stay at her place. She agreed, as long as J. C. didn't find out.

I was a wreck for the next three days. I kept wondering what I had done. I hoped and prayed J. C. was okay and would not stay mad. Against the advice of my friends, I finally went looking for her downtown. When I found her, she acted as if nothing had happened. I noticed she was holding on to one of the guys she partied with. I felt hurt and angry, but she swore it wouldn't happen again. She apologized for getting angry, saying she didn't know what had overcome her.

But the emotional abuse didn't stop. Often, J. C. resorted to put-downs (usually about my race, even though she was part Indian), name-calling, insults, criticism, and threats (usually of hurting me or my family). She often hid my medication from me or deprived me of sleep. Even when I caught her hiding something from me, she was so convincing and had such mind control over me that I *believed* her when she said she didn't do it. She often said that I couldn't do anything right and that I was stupid. Her words hurt and ate away at my self-worth and self-esteem, which were already affected by substance abuse, unresolved child abuse, and family violence. She often told me that I was ugly and no one else would want me, and I believed her. She said I should be grateful for what I had with her.

I am uncertain when J. C. crossed the invisible line, but the verbal abuse eventually led to physical abuse and sexual abuse. She punched me, kicked and choked me, pulled my hair, and threw me around the house. She pulled my hair because she knew I loved my hair, which at the time was very long and thick. She liked to hit me in the face and choke me until I passed out, and then she would kick me all over.

Afterward, she was remorseful, and she cried and promised it would never happen again. She would be tender and loving. I remember thinking, "Maybe this time she really means it." Eventually the remorse disappeared. All that was left was tension and violence.

J. C. also sexually abused me. She started by making suggestive remarks and comments about my body and making accusations of infidelity. If I was five minutes late coming home from work, she said I was messing around with the boss or a coworker. If I smiled at a woman who passed by, or vice versa, she accused me of messing around with her and beat me. She even accused me of messing around with my own family. One of the most painful and humiliating times of my life was when she let a man rape me. In return she got cash and drugs. She acted as if nothing had happened and instead accused me of *liking it*. She also forced me to have sex with her. At this time in the relationship, I cringed when she touched me, but I felt powerless to say anything. Often, she was brutal and seemed to enjoy seeing me obviously in pain.

J. C. had double standards. It was okay for her to do whatever she wanted. It was okay for her to flirt with anyone and go to bed with whoever she wanted. If I told her I didn't like what she was doing, she beat me up. I had to give up a number of friends because she didn't approve of them.

Often, people asked me why I stayed, why didn't I get away, or why I kept going back. I must have left several times and usually stayed with an acquaintance or friend, but J. C. either found me and begged me to come back or threatened me by saying she was going to kill herself if I didn't come back. My self-esteem was so low that I felt that I didn't deserve anyone else. I also kept going back because I felt I had no place else to go. It seems crazy to this day, but at the time I *still* loved her.

I did finally leave the day she almost killed me. I am uncertain how the fight started. I was sleeping, and all of a sudden she got on top of me and was yelling. I pushed her off me and stood up, saying that I had had enough of this. I knew the best way to try to leave was to calm her down first. I tried to, but she started punching me, pulling my hair, and kicking me all over my body. For once, I fought back, or tried to, but this seemed to get her angrier. She pulled out a gun and shot at me. The bullet missed me by inches. After she realized that she had missed me, she tried to shoot me again, but the gun jammed. That was when I escaped by pushing her aside and stumbling up the stairs to the door. I remember thinking, "Please God, don't let her catch me! Don't let her parents stop me!"

I tried to go to my relatives, but they told me, "You made your bed, you lie in it." They said I must have deserved the abuse. J. C. had succeeded in isolating me from my family and friends. I had no one to turn to. I hid for a couple of days behind a hotel in the bushes and then in an abandoned house. I remember jumping at every little noise I heard, thinking it was her.

While I was hiding from her I thought about suicide. I felt so alone, so afraid and worthless. I kept thinking I must have deserved it. I thought about dying, but what kept me alive was that I didn't want to die *alone*. I finally showed up at a friend's house (the same one who let me stay with her after the first argument). When she saw me she didn't recognize me. My face and body were bruised and swollen. She burst into tears. I had to calm *her* down. She then helped me get out of my muddy and bloody clothes. When I looked in a mirror I was horrified. My whole body was covered in bruises. I had dried blood in my hair and my right ear. Both my eyes were almost swollen shut. My ribs hurt, and it was difficult to breathe.

My friend had to convince me to go to the emergency room. I was afraid I would get into trouble with the police, and I was afraid J. C. would find out I was there. After the examination, I found out I had cracked ribs, a shattered eardrum, some internal injuries, and a hair-line fracture under my eye.

It scares me to this day to know that even then I almost went back to her. The constant degradation, put-downs, controlling behavior, and emotional abuse had almost brainwashed me. I believed that I was worthless and ugly, that I wouldn't amount to anything, and that no one else would want me. In J. C.'s eyes, and in mine, I was nothing but a drunken Indian. It took my friend to keep me from going back.

It took a long time to heal emotionally and physically. I was appalled to know that a woman could hurt another woman this way. I struggled with the pain, humiliation, shame, guilt, and fear. I had nightmares about getting shot and woke up when I felt the bullets entering my body. Even to this day I am afraid of the dark. I was lucky to have my friend by my side. She comforted me in my time of fear, grief, and pain. She told me that I didn't deserve the terror and abuse and that it wasn't my fault. Hearing her words and reassurance helped me find the courage deep inside to go on.

Today I am more than a survivor. I have been clean and sober for several years. I am learning more and more about having safe and clear communication with loved ones. I have learned to love others, and myself, unconditionally. I am learning to be more trusting and have had healthier relationships. I continue on my healing journey and take great pride in who I am as an Indian woman and a lesbian. I advocate for women and children who have the right to be safe.

There seems to be resistance and denial in the lesbian, bi, and gay community about same-sex battering We need to hold the abusers accountable. No one deserves abuse of any type. Violence is a form of power and control. If you, the reader, are in an abusive relationship, whether it is emotional, physical, or sexual abuse, please find someone to talk to who will listen and who will be nonjudgmental and empathetic. Often, when we are in abusive, violent relationships we get isolated from family and friends. It is important to reach out. It is important to remember that you are not alone.

2

Rape

Patrick Letellier

I never called it. . . .

His hand on my throat, pressing me into the bed. "Hold still, Patrick, and try not to spoil this." I keep moving away, to get air, to lessen the pain, to make him stop. A punch in the ribs. "Hold still!" The pillow, wet with my tears. I'm trying, but I cannot seem to *not* move. How did he get between my legs so fast? He is being rough deliberately; no, not rough, ferocious. With all my energy I concentrate on not moving. Have you ever tried to remain still when someone is tearing you apart?

I never called it. . . .

He strokes my head, ever so gently. A welcome tenderness. Twenty minutes ago in the kitchen he was punching my face, and blood was dripping from my lips. He unbuttons my shirt, kissing the bruises, scratches. "I'm so sorry. I love you so much." Now he is licking me. "Oh please, God," I think, "not *that*." "I want to make you feel better," he says, pulling my shirt off, pushing me back on the couch, covering my mouth with his. My whole body aches. I'm just so tired. My pants are being unzipped, but I'm too frightened to struggle.

I never called it. . . .

It actually makes me feel sick, but I know I'd better do it. It'll be worse for me if I don't. He insists; he knows I hate this. He tries to make it sound sexy or exciting or erotic in some forbidden way, but his words are mere echoes to me. I'm trying to figure out how to end this quickly. I slap his face. He strokes himself faster, commanding: "Again. Do it again, and do it right." This time I punch the side of his head, but he barely reacts. "Good. More." I slap and punch, head, face, chest, arms, even the one he is using. He gets there right away, grinning. I stagger out of the room, nauseous.

I never called it. . . .

In a workshop, two years after my escape from him. The presenter is talking about violence: "Many gay men and lesbians who are raped in anti-gay assaults feel like damaged goods. Like there is something wrong with them. Like they have been stained." Sitting in my chair, stunned, careening. Was it . . .? No, it couldn't have been. . . . Damaged goods. Three minutes after my hasty exit from that room I'm crying. Body-wracking sobs. "He raped me."

I never called it. . . .

Rape. I called it rough sex. Forcing himself on me. Being selfish and inconsiderate, a beast, a monster. He called it getting what he wanted. What he was entitled to. "I'm giving you what you really want," he would say. How many times, you ask? Not always. But far too many to count them.

For a long time afterward, I felt guilty for "allowing" it to happen. For not stopping him or protecting myself better. For being so profoundly violated. Somehow the rapes permeated my skin, sliced through the barriers of my physical body and sank into my very bones, into the self that lives deep inside. The rapes were attacks against me, my self, my soul. Love contorted, trust obliterated.

As the years tick by, I test the waters and occasionally tell a sexual partner that sex can be difficult for me because I was . . . raped. They almost always furrow their eyebrows. Gay men don't use that word when they talk about themselves. I do.

3

Personal Story

Curt Rogers

I want to start by telling you that my batterer could be a generous, sweet, charming, sensitive man, capable of giving and receiving an intense and fulfilling level of commitment and passion. I say this not to defend him. You are about to read the negative side of our relationship of 3½ years. For you to get a true picture of how this relationship developed, however, you need to know that there was more to it than the abuse. This man could function for long periods of time as a wonderful, caring partner.

Gary grew up in Malden, Massachusetts as one of seven brothers. His brothers were very much into drugs, guns, violence, and crime. He had been clean and sober for three months when we met. He was very honest about his history and his desire to escape that way of life. He wanted to allow himself to be gay, but he suppressed this desire because he had been taught that gay people could not be happy.

I thought Gary was cute. I was very attracted to him. I wanted to spend time with him, especially so I could show him that it was possible to be happy as a gay man. So I did, and we were. We were so happy and it was so satisfying that I fell in love with him. During our first year, Gary stayed sober. He showered me with attention and could always make me smile. Life was wonderful. I finished coming out of the closet because I had finally found someone who meant so much to me that no one else's opinion mattered.

A little over a year into the relationship, Gary started using drugs again. He would try to hide it. That began the unraveling of the trust between us. Over the next four months our relationship quickly deteriorated. Although there were still isolated times of joy, the relationship became a source of constant emotional pain.

I told Gary I couldn't see him anymore. He became hysterical and threatened suicide. I believed him and gave in, although I knew I needed to get out of the relationship.

As I saw his behaviors becoming more risky, I withdrew from some of our sexual practices. It was at this time that he was first violent with me. During an argument, he pushed me so hard into a wall that I caved in the sheetrock. He immediately apologized and swore that it would never happen again.

However, I was soon to learn more about Gary's capacity for violence. Gary and a fellow employee, Eddie, were having an ongoing confrontation. Gary threatened him for several weeks. Then, one Sunday morning, after staying out all night drinking, Gary went over to Eddie's house, rang the bell, and greeted him as he opened the door by beating him with a club. Gary hurt Eddie, but he didn't incapacitate him. Eddie dominated the fight. Later, I met up with Gary—his face badly beaten, cut open, covered in blood—as he was preparing to go back and try again. This occasion convinced me of Gary's potential for violence and his inclination toward it. His threats now carried new weight.

It was during this time that a friend of mine threw a party to which I wanted to go. Gary informed me that if I went without him he would wait outside and shoot me when I came out or crash the party and just start shooting. I believed he was capable of carrying out both of these threats, and I did not go.

Although I felt that we were slowly drifting apart, Gary continually surprised me with a renewed vigor and intensity about the relationship. He would simply forget all the bad things that had happened and expect me to still be in a committed relationship with him. To contradict his perspective was to ask for conflict. Once, as I was reiterating the reasons that I could no longer trust him, he punched me in the face. He immediately apologized and swore it would never happen again.

One Thanksgiving, Gary got very drunk. I helped him into his apartment, and he asked if I would spend the night. I said no. Would I take a shower with him? I said no. Would I just lay down with him for a moment on the bed? I said no. I wanted to get out of there, so I set his alarm clock to wake him up in time to go to work and started putting him to bed. I had gotten his boots off when he just snapped. He threw me on the bed, pinned me down, and said, "If I can't have you, then I can't stand for anyone else to have you. I'm going to kill you." I knew he was serious.

I told him I didn't want that to happen, but he punched me in the face and asked me how it felt to know I was going to die. He told me he was going to kill me with his knife or maybe his gun. But first he was going to rape me. Gary was much stronger than me, and I could not get out of his hold. Even if I did squirm free, the studio apartment was very small with a double lock on the door. By the time I could get the two locks open, he would be on top of me. The only way out, in my mind, was to have Gary let me go.

I could tell by the way he was positioning my hands above my head and trying to hold both with one hand that his next step was to tie them together. I knew that once that happened I would not be physically able to stop him. And emotionally he would have crossed so far over the line that he would not turn back. Every time he tried to hold my hands together, I was able to get one hand free. Instead of fighting back with that hand, I stroked his torso and reassured him with my words. "No, I'm not going to leave you. I love you. Please just lay down with me for a minute." I can't explain exactly how the transition occurred, but with a combination of the distraction of my words, the distraction of my touch, and his desire to be held, I finally broke through Gary's resolve to kill me, and he allowed himself to lay on top of me.

My goal then became to put him to bed so that I could get out. I tried, but he snapped again and pinned me down with renewed determination. A cycle similar to the first occurred, and again I was able to distract him. I realized he was not going to allow me to put him to bed and leave the apartment. I suggested a walk to get cigarettes so that we could talk. He agreed.

I hurriedly put his boots and sweatshirt on him. As we were zipping up his jacket, he snapped for a third time, pinning me up against the wall. Again we went through the struggle. Eventually, I was able to get him to allow us to go outside. Once we got out the front door, I knew I was safe. In Gary's drunken state, I could easily outrun him. From the time I entered his apartment to this point, 3½ hours had gone by. I did not go back to his apartment.

The next day, I packed what I could in my car (including my dog) and left my house for good. I intended to leave the state and move as far away as possible. Gary had allowed himself to almost kill me. Next time I would not be able to stop him.

I was persuaded to stay in the area a few days, hiding out at a coworker's house, so that I could meet with the victim advocate at the local gay/lesbian/bisexual/transgendered health center to explore my options. The victim advocate was very nice and supportive. But all he could offer in addition to goodwill was assistance in pressing charges or taking out a restraining order. Neither choice was an option for me. In my mind, either would have served only to galvanize Gary to search me out and get revenge. There was no way a restraining order would protect me from an angry Gary.

I also discovered that no shelters were available to me. Because I was a gay male victim of domestic violence I was left to fend for myself. My health care provider failed to acknowledge or respond to my needs, which made my situation even more difficult. Gary and I used the same health care center. I told them that I couldn't come into the center for fear of running into Gary. During this time of crisis, I asked, could I meet my therapist outside my center? Or could they assign me to a therapist at another center? No, they said, my only option was to formally change health centers, a process that meant it would take weeks before I got an appointment with a therapist. So there I was: no shelter, no mental health support, no legal options that provided any security. I was on my own at a point of extreme anxiety and crisis.

Luckily, my employer came through with unending support. I was kept on salary for the next month and a half while I was unable to do any work. At the insistence of my employer, I found my own trauma therapist. And when no shelters were available, my employer's parents, virtually strangers to me at this point, provided me with a place to stay. I was fortunate. Without an amazingly understanding and committed employer, I would have fled, alone at a time of crisis when I could not take care of myself.

During this time, I had to disappear from all of my friends. Only my employer and two close friends knew that I was still in Boston. After a month and a half, I got an apartment on the other side of the city and slowly started going back to work. I rented an underground garage space a block away from work so that Gary would not see my car in the lot. I went to work and left an hour early so that if Gary ever checked to see if I was still around he wouldn't catch me coming or going. I sold my car and bought a different kind. My calls were strictly screened at work. Anyone not recognized was told that I no longer worked there.

With every day that went by, I began to feel that staying in Boston might be possible, but living in hiding was wearing on me. I also knew that if I stayed, one day I would eventually run into Gary. The idea that I was hiding from him would make him angry, and that scared me. If I was to stay in Boston, I had to tell Gary that I was doing so. With the help of my therapist, I drafted a letter informing Gary of my decision to stay. It outlined my rules and threatened a restraining order if he tried to contact me.

Over the course of the next year, we had scattered encounters. He became involved with another man, and although I knew I could not allow my barriers to come down, I felt a little safer. Occasionally, we would have conversations, maybe once every two months. The conversations might last for 30 minutes. He would tell me about all the positive things in his life, and I would say that I was happy for him. I was never able to share what was happening in my life.

A little more than a year and a half after I had left, I got a call from Gary. He wanted to get together. I was firm. I said I could not see him. Four days later, his lover called and told me that Gary had hanged himself over the weekend.

A wide range of emotions went through me during the week that followed as I went to his funeral and met the people who had been part of his life over the previous two years. Mostly I found myself overwhelmed with sadness because I was finally able to allow myself to remember the good, the wonderful aspects of Gary that I had buried while he was alive for fear that I would not be able to stay away.

It is because of his death that I am able to tell my story publicly.

PART II

LEGAL PERSPECTIVES

4

Twice Abused

Same-Sex Domestic Violence and the Law

Evan Fray-Witzer

Courts have rarely been hospitable places for battered heterosexual women, much less battered gay men or lesbians. Often dominated by male judges and lawyers, courts routinely minimize and ignore issues of domestic violence. Much has changed in recent years—thanks in large part to the increase in diversity on the bench. Much, however, still needs to be changed. The following study surveys existing domestic violence laws and examines how they meet—or fail to meet—the needs of battered gay men and lesbians. This study also examines how homophobia within the courts and in the ranks of the legal profession has affected battered gay men and lesbians seeking legal protections. Finally, I attempt to provide a modest list of suggestions for those working within the legal community who are grappling (or should be grappling) with the complex and difficult issues surrounding same-sex domestic violence.

Homophobia and Exclusion in Legislation

It is strange to think that the very laws designed to protect victims of domestic violence may actually empower the *batterer,* but in cases of same-sex domestic battering, this is often the case. Batterers often keep their victims trapped in violent relationships by convincing them that no one will take their claims seriously—not the police, not prosecutors, not the courts. Unfortunately, the belief that the legal system does not afford the same (or any) legal protections to battered lesbians or gay men is indeed accurate in many states. An examination of the domestic violence laws of all 50 states reveals that battered lesbians and gay men are often afforded less protection than their heterosexual counterparts or, in some states, no protection at all.[1]

For example, the laws of six states—Alabama, Arizona, Delaware, Michigan, Montana, and North Carolina—intentionally and specifically exclude battered lesbians and gay men from protection by defining domestic violence only as violence between members of the opposite sex. Three other states—Georgia, Illinois, and South Carolina—exclude battered lesbians and gay men from protection by defining domestic violence only as violence occurring between spouses, former spouses, or family members who are related by blood or consanguinity.

Other exclusions are more subtle. For example, Maryland can be added to the list of states that entirely exclude battered gay men and lesbians from coverage because Maryland's domestic violence law requires that an unmarried couple have engaged in sexual relations to fall within the law's protection, but Maryland law also criminalizes all homosexual sexual activities. Michigan's domestic violence law protects unmarried couples who are living together if the couple has consensual sexual relations. Michigan law, however, criminalizes consensual sodomy (defined to include oral sex). Mississippi's laws provide a similar catch-22; they protect unmarried couples only if they are "living together as spouses" but outlaw consensual sodomy (again defined to include oral sex). These statutes are not less problematic for their subtlety: An advocate or lawyer for a victim of same-sex domestic violence must consider the possibility that the client will be confessing to a state-defined "crime" when he or she seeks the protection of the state's domestic violence laws. Even if the state's sodomy laws are rarely enforced, their very existence sends a clear message to the battered gay man or lesbian: Within this court, *you* are the criminal.

In addition, a number of states have domestic violence statutes that offer some protections to battered lesbians and gay men but that offer fewer protections than those afforded to their heterosexual counterparts. For example, Oregon law mandates arrest in cases of heterosexual domestic violence only. Washington and Indiana law both provide for the creation of shelters for battered women but limit the use of such shelters to either heterosexual women (Washington) or spouses and former spouses (Indiana).

A number of states, however, have recently attempted to address these disparities in their laws. In the past few years, New Jersey has eliminated language that limited the scope of domestic violence laws to cases involving members of the opposite sex;[2] California has amended its domestic violence law to eliminate provisions that allowed cases of heterosexual domestic violence to be charged as felonies but relegated domestic violence cases between gay men or lesbians to misdemeanors; and criminal statutes of Arkansas no longer cover cases of wife-battering in the first degree.

On the other hand, other provisions of many statutes contain language that—either intentionally or through ignorance—is simply inadequate to fully protect battered lesbians, gay men, or heterosexuals. For example, in addition to the 12 states that effectively deny protection to all battered gay men and lesbians, 17 other states have statutes that do not cover dating relationships in which the parties are not currently or formerly living together.[3] This, of course, presents a significant limitation in the protections available to victims of both same-sex and heterosexual battering.

Perhaps even more insidious is the widespread existence of restrictive adoption laws that prevent same-sex couples who co-parent from adopting the children of their partner. Batterers often use these laws to their advantage by threatening both biological and nonbiological parents with the loss of their children. When the biological parent is the batterer, he or she can threaten—often correctly—that if the victim leaves, the court will not grant the victim custody or visitation rights and, indeed, the victim may never see the child again. Similarly, when the batterer is the nonbiological parent, he or she can threaten to "out" the biological parent—an act that may very well put the biological parent's custody rights at risk. To understand the validity of this threat, we need look no further than the recent Florida case of *Ward v. Ward* (1996 Fla. App. LEXIS 9130), in which a judge awarded custody to an 11-year-old girl's father, a convicted murderer, rather than the girl's mother, who was a lesbian, on the grounds that the girl should be afforded the opportunity to grow up in a nonlesbian household. (Apparently, violent, indeed homicidal, households are perfectly fine environments for children.)

General Homophobia in the Courts

Perhaps even more of an obstacle than restrictive laws, however, are the courts themselves, which can be hostile environments even when gay or lesbian victims of domestic violence are, at least on paper, entitled to the court's protection. This homophobia, even from the bench, is often overt and unapologetic. For example, in 1988, during the trial of an anti-gay murderer in Broward County, Florida, a judge jokingly asked the prosecutor, "That's a crime now, to beat up a homosexual?" "Yes," the prosecutor replied. "It's also a crime to kill them." "Times really have changed," the judge answered (Minkowitz, 1992, p. 368).

Nor is this an isolated incident. An article in the December 16, 1988 edition of the *Los Angeles Times* reported that in Dallas, Texas, a judge sentenced the killer of two gay men to 30 years in prison and then told the local paper that he had been lenient in sentencing because the victims were homosexual. "These two guys that got killed wouldn't have been killed if they hadn't been cruising the streets picking up teenage boys," the judge commented. "I don't much care for queers cruising the streets picking up teenage boys. . . . These homosexuals, by running around on weekends picking up teenage boys, they're asking for trouble. They really are" ("Killer of Gays Gets 30 Years," 1988, p. 2).

Published legal opinions also reflect the biases of judges against homosexuals. Consider, for example, *Perkins v. North Carolina* (234 F. Supp. 333,339 [W.D.N.C. 1964]), a criminal sodomy case in which a federal judge commented that

> putting Perkins in the North Carolina prison system is a little like putting Brer Rabbit into the briar patch. . . . [P]rison environment, including close, continuous, and exclusive contact with other men, aggravates and strengthens homosexual tendencies and provides unexcelled opportunity for homosexual practices. For the confirmed homosexual, imprisonment can accomplish no rehabilitative function; instead, it provides an outlet for the gratification of sexually deviate desires.

To understand why many gay men and lesbians fear the threat of homophobia in the judicial system, however, we should also consider the case of *Bowers v. Hardwick* (478 U.S. 186 [1986]), in which the U.S. Supreme Court held that the Constitution does not protect consensual homosexual sodomy, even in the privacy of one's own bedroom.

It is important to understand that homophobia within the legal system is much more than an influencing factor by which some gay men and lesbians may be discouraged from *seeking* protection from abuse. It is also a *tool* used by batterers themselves. Many survivors of same-sex battering report that their batterers repeatedly told them that they would not be able to get help from the legal system because they were gay. Every time a judge or a prosecutor or a police officer makes a homophobic statement—or allows one to go unchallenged—he or she gives ammunition to the batterer.

How Have Battered Gay Men and Lesbians Fared in the Legal System?

In addition to understanding the historical fears and concerns born of the generalized homophobia often evident within the legal system, we must understand specifically how victims of domestic abuse have fared before criminal and civil courts.

The Criminal System

To date, battered gay men and lesbians have had mixed results in their dealings with the criminal legal system. At its worst, that system can reinforce the message that the victim's batterer has conveyed all along—that no one will help a battered homosexual. Indeed, the case of Annette Green seems to indicate that battered lesbians who kill their batterers will not find sympathy in the courts even with a sympathetic judge. In Annette Green's case, Judge Tom Waddell became the first judge to allow a battered woman defense to be used by a battered lesbian. In that case, the evidence of abuse was clear. Friends and coworkers testified that they saw Green's partner attack her on various occasions during their 11-year relationship. Hospital records showed that Green suffered broken bones and numerous bruises while living with her abusive partner (Klein, 1989). Judge Waddell allowed Green's counsel to introduce the battered person's defense. Despite the overwhelming evidence of abuse and Judge Waddell's openness, the jury had little sympathy. Robson (1992) notes that the jury took only 2½ hours to return a guilty verdict despite the complications of the case and the fact that potential jurors spoke openly about wanting to serve on the jury in order to "hang that lesbian bitch."

Similarly, Debra Denise Reid (personal communication, winter 1994), a Massachusetts woman convicted of killing her abusive lesbian lover, commented that the district attorney at her trial highlighted her lesbian relationship with the victim but omitted any talk of abuse. "When I heard the DA start to talk . . . focusing on . . . that we shared a bed together, I was like: Am I on trial for being gay, or am I on trial for Jackie's death?" Indeed, Reid's own trial attorney filed a motion to prevent the prosecutor from even mentioning the word "lesbian" during the trial. According to Reid, "That's what made me feel much more ashamed. . . . I had him representing me and he was ashamed to say that we were lovers, and I thought it must be really bad to say that I was gay. If the ground would have opened, I would have gone through it."

At its best, however, the legal system has been an avenue for empowerment and protection for battered lesbians and gay men. For example, in *Ohio v. Hadinger,* the Ohio appeals court held that the Ohio domestic violence law applied equally to same-sex couples and heterosexual couples. In reversing a district court dismissal of misdemeanor domestic violence charges against a lesbian who had battered her lover, the appeals court said,

> Given the language of [the domestic violence statute], this court concludes that the legislature intended that the domestic violence statute provide protection to persons who are cohabiting regardless of their sex. We believe to read the domestic violence statute otherwise would eviscerate the efforts of the legislature to safeguard, regardless of gender, the rights of victims of domestic violence. We decline to adopt such a restrictive position and therefore conclude that [the statute] defining a "person living as a spouse" as a person "who otherwise is cohabiting with the offender" does not in and of itself exclude two persons of the same sex.[4]

Often, the attitude of the judge (and, in criminal cases, the prosecutor as well) sets the tone for the court. Concerned, committed, thoughtful judges can inspire concerned, committed, thoughtful juries. Practitioners can help by educating the courts about the causes and dynamics of same-sex domestic violence, just as they have done with heterosexual domestic violence.

Civil Restraining Orders:
The Tragedy of the Mutual Order

Most victims of domestic violence are not seeking (or defending themselves against) criminal proceedings but, instead, come to the courts seeking a "protective order" or "restraining order." The civil legal system is failing battered gay men and lesbians miserably. Often, courts, not knowing how to deal with same-sex battering cases, have issued mutual restraining orders (that is, orders that restrain both parties from abusing each other under penalty of further civil or criminal sanctions).

At first glance, it may be difficult to see the danger in a mutual order—why, after all, would someone need to worry about being "restrained" from something he or she never intended to do in the first place? These orders, however, present two problems to victims. The first problem is that a mutual order conveys the *perception* that both parties are equally guilty for the abuse. As Robson (1992) notes, "A mutual restraining order apportions responsibility for the violence between the parties. Despite the civil nature of the order, it serves as an adjudication that 'fighting' rather than abuse is occurring" (p. 61).

In addition to the emotional message that a mutual order sends, mutual orders carry with them some very real liabilities. For example, if a victim pushes the abuser in an attempt to flee the abuse, he or she may be found to have violated a no-contact restraining order just as much as the batterer who blocks the door. The victim could then be subject to criminal prosecution or the batterer's constant threats of criminal prosecution. In addition, the victim (now subject to a restraining order) may find him- or herself in a domestic violence registry that becomes part of his or her permanent record.

Indeed, the domestic violence statutes of five states—California, Kentucky, Maine, Massachusetts, and West Virginia—now specifically discourage the practice of issuing mutual restraining orders. For example, the legislative history of Maine's domestic violence statute specifically mentions that mutual orders "undermine the purpose of this chapter" (19 Maine Rev.Stat. 761-A, Section 5 [1996]). The laws of Massachusetts, California, and West Virginia allow mutual orders only if both parties present evidence of domestic violence. In addition, the laws of Massachusetts, Kentucky, and West Virginia all require a judge to make a mutual order detailed enough for police to understand how to respond in case of a violation. These laws, however, are only as effective as their enforcement and will hinge on an understanding of the dynamics of domestic violence in general and same-sex domestic violence in particular. Our knowledge of battering tells us that there is *one* abuser and *one* victim. Our understanding of same-sex domestic violence cases tells us that physical appearance alone cannot tell us which person is which. For any of this to be relevant, however, we need to take the first step and recognize the dangers inherent in mutual orders—both psychological and practical.

What Can Be Done to Save Lives?

If the legal community is truly interested in protecting battered lesbians and gay men, it can take a number of steps. Indeed, many (though not all) of the strategies that have proved to be successful in confronting heterosexual domestic violence can be equally effective in same-sex battering cases. The following is a list of suggestions— which is by no means complete—for judges, lawyers, advocates, and activists that may help move us toward the point at which battering in same-sex relationships is neither ignored nor condoned by the courts.

Education

It is *essential* that all legal personnel who deal with domestic violence—police officers, advocates, prosecutors, defense attorneys, law clerks, and judges—receive training in both same-sex battering and homophobia. Many states now require general domestic violence training for police and court personnel, and some, such as Massachusetts, have begun to incorporate education about homophobia into the training.

Such education serves a twofold purpose. First, it provides judges, prosecutors, and court personnel with more effective ways to deal with same-sex battering. Perhaps even more important, it sends a message to both victims of same-sex domestic violence and the attorneys who represent them that the legal community understands the problem. As the courts get better at addressing same-sex domestic violence, more battered lesbians and gay men will be willing to use them, and of course, the more that battered lesbians and gay men use the courts, the more adept courts will become in handling such cases.

Resources, Referrals, and References

Generalized resource materials that do not acknowledge the existence of same-sex battering do little good (and may do more harm) for a lesbian or gay victim, who is being told implicitly that his or her problems are not understood.

Reference materials that address the issues of same-sex battering must be available. Pamphlets and posters that address same-sex battering and are posted in courthouses, police stations, and shelters will let battered lesbians and gay men know that they are welcome and that their problems are taken seriously. It is also important that police, court-sponsored advocates, and prosecutors know which programs offer services and support groups for battered lesbians and gay men. In the end, when appropriate resources are available they serve a dual purpose: (a) They serve as an educational resource for the battered gay man or lesbian (who may not have understood previously that there was such a thing as same-sex domestic violence), and (b) they serve as a "welcome" sign to the battered person who may otherwise have no reason to believe that any particular member of the legal community understands (or sympathizes with) his or her dilemma.

Take Same-Sex Battering Seriously

Many heterosexual women died at the hands of their batterers while they waited for the courts, legislators, police, and prosecutors to take domestic violence seriously. This is a mistake we should not repeat. It is important that the law not attempt to deny or minimize the violence taking place. Practically speaking, the court's role in ensuring that same-sex battering is taken seriously may manifest itself in writing unbiased laws, issuing and enforcing protective orders, and making sure that the sentences issued in criminal cases arising from domestic violence in same-sex relationships are comparable to the sentences issued in heterosexual cases of the same magnitude.

Avoid Issuing Mutual Orders

One possible reason why judges tend to issue mutual orders in cases of same-sex battering is that—at first glance—it may be more difficult to tell the abuser from the abused.

Although it may be more difficult to distinguish the batterer from the battered in cases of same-sex domestic violence, it is not impossible. According to Professor Claire Renzetti of St. Joseph's University (personal communication, winter 1993), it may take more time and patience to determine who the abuser is in a same-sex battering situation, but by asking the right questions, a judge can often determine who is being abused. "Despite all of the claims," Renzetti says, "you can tell if you listen to their stories. Batterers are very assertive about their rights, victims are confused, almost ashamed." Renzetti suggests that a judge (or any other legal professional who deals with victims of same-domestic violence) ask about the violence itself. "Batterers will say, 'Yes, I was violent but this stuff is a two-way street.' Victims who have fought their batterers in self-defense often feel horribly guilty and ashamed. Sometimes they will even deny they were abused."

Debra Denise Reid's account of her experiences lends credence to these arguments. When asked how police and courts could tell the difference between batterer and battered, Reid commented,

> By the one that's got all the mouth. The one that's always eager to tell you. Say for instance [the police] came in [and said,] "What's the problem here?" [Look to the woman who says] "It's not a problem officer, *we're just*". . . . The one who always comes out first. I think for myself, I was too ashamed to say that a woman was doing this to me, so I wouldn't be the first one to come out and

say, "Okay, she beat me up." (D. Reid, personal communication, winter 1994).

Another tactic that may help judges differentiate the batterer from the battered is one that is already being used by some judges dealing with heterosexual domestic violence. Often, male abusers who are familiar with the system will attempt to get mutual restraining orders by pointing to instances in which the victim fought back in self-defense or yelled at the batterer (batterers often claim that their abuse was justified or mutual because they were being "verbally abused" in response to their physical violence). In response to these claims in heterosexual cases, some judges will ask the man (who has asked for a mutual order) if he is in fear of the victim. Because battering is about controlling the victim, many batterers seem unwilling to say—even for the benefit of a mutual order— that they fear their victim. Once the batterer denies that he is in fear, the order is denied. (In the rare case when a batterer says he is in fear, some judges will ask the person to articulate that fear with greater specificity.)

There is no question that determining who the victim is may be more difficult and time-consuming in a same-sex battering case than in a heterosexual battering case. However, if the goal is to ensure that every person has a right to live free of violence, the additional time expended will prove worthwhile.

**Don't Expect Any More or Less From
a Battered Lesbian or Gay Man**

One of the most frustrating, though understandable, aspects of *all* domestic violence work is victims who return to their batterers a number of times before being able to leave permanently. Because it is no easier for a battered lesbian or gay man to escape a violent relationship than it is for a battered heterosexual woman to do so, this pattern will probably hold true in same-sex battering cases as well. Many judges who deal with domestic violence cases take pains to remind victims that they can always come back to the court, without fear of blame, when they are ready to leave their abuser.

**Use Experience From Heterosexual
Domestic Violence Cases**

Many judges have developed techniques over the years for putting victims of domestic violence at ease in the courtroom. Some judges, for example, allow victims to approach the bench or stand in the witness box so that the victim can talk to the judge without having to expose her personal life to a packed courtroom. For obvious reasons, this technique could work equally well in cases of same-sex battering. Similarly, judicial creativity in crafting a comprehensive protective order can be a vital protection in both heterosexual and same-sex domestic violence cases. For example, in a situation when a batterer has threatened to "out" the victim to his or her family, friends, or employer (an action that can have serious consequences), a court might consider extending a no-contact order to include those parties. Although there is never any guarantee that a batterer will abide by the terms of a restraining order, a batterer may well think twice about terrorizing his or her victim by "outing" him or her if the action holds the possibility of criminal prosecution.

Conclusion

My study of how the legal system deals with, or more often fails to deal with, battered lesbians and gay men is at points discouraging—at least initially. Quite often, individuals at many levels of the system fail victims—from the police to the courts to the advocates themselves. The legal system has been shamefully inadequate. Often, though unfortunately not always, the failures result from ignorance and a lack of understanding of the dynamics involved in same-sex battering situations rather than outright hostility to the issue.

Education is, in my view, the *only* answer. Some of the laws that once excluded battered lesbians and gay men have begun to be rewritten. Training for judges, police, and advocates becomes more common every day. Education and training and awareness must continue if we are to save lives.

Notes

1. Battered lesbians and gay men may, of course, be able to take advantage of general criminal laws (assault, trespass, and the like). However, as experience has shown, these remedies are insufficient to meet the needs of victims of domestic violence. For example, although a battered lesbian or gay many might be able to use a trespassing law, such a law is ineffective when both the batterer and battered have a legal right to be on the premises (or worse yet, when *only* the batterer has a legal interest in the premises). Domestic violence laws, on the other hand, generally provide for a vacate order whereby the victim of abuse can remain on the premises regardless of whose name is on the lease, mortgage, and so forth. Similarly, many domestic violence laws empower police to make immediate warrantless arrests in situations (for example, misdemeanor offenses) in which the police might not otherwise have the power to make an arrest. This, of course, is why we have domestic violence laws.

2. A New Jersey court noted recently that New Jersey's newly revised domestic violence statute "contains no requirement that a cohabitant be a member of the opposite sex or related to the victim. Thus, the 1991 act creates the potential for actions by . . . lesbians and gay men caught in violent relationships." *Bryant v. Burnett,* 264 N.J. Super. 222, 226, n.2 (1993).

3. Kansas, one of the states whose domestic violence law does not provide for protection of couples in a dating relationship, also has a sodomy law, the interpretation of which is so bizarre that it merits separate note. Although the sodomy law of Kansas specifically outlaws consensual sodomy between adults, Kansas courts have limited this definition to include oral sex between two men but not between two women. *Kansas v. Schad,* 247 Kan. 242, 795 P.2d 406 (1990). This presents quite an unusual situation for a battered lesbian in that, although consensual oral sex between women is not a criminal act that the battered lesbian need conceal, *non*consensual oral sex between two women does not appear to be a criminal act and might not, therefore, form the basis for a complaint under the domestic violence laws.

4. 61 Ohio App. 3d 820, 573 N.E. 2d 1191 (1991) at 823, 573 N.E. 2d at 1193. See also *Ohio v. Linner,* 77 Ohio Misc. 2d 22, 665 N.E.2d 1180 (1996); *Ohio v. Yaden,* 1997 Ohio App Lexis 748 (1997).

References

Killer of gays gets 30 years as judge criticizes victims. (1988, December 16). *Los Angeles Times,* p. 2.

Klein, B. (1989, September 7). Lesbian acts out shooting of companion. *St. Petersburg Times,* p. 18.

Minkowitz, D. (1992, March 23). It's still open season on gays: Prosecution of gay bashers. *The Nation,* p. 368.

Robson, R. (1992). *Lesbian (out)law.* Ithaca, NY: Firebrand.

Table 4.1 State-by-State Analysis of Domestic Violence Laws

State	Gender-neutral to victim?	Covers gay and lesbian relationships?	Covers unmarried couples currently living together?	Covers unmarried couples previously living together?	Covers current dating relationships?	Covers prior dating relationships?
Alabama*	Yes	No	Yes, if of the opposite sex and "living as spouses."	Yes, if of the opposite sex.	No	No
Alaska	Yes	Yes	Yes	Yes	Yes	Yes
Arizona	Yes	No	Statutes conflict, but cover only couples of opposite sex in any event.	Statutes conflict, but cover only couples of opposite sex in any event.	No, unless couple has child together or woman is pregnant with man's child.	No, unless couple has child together or woman is pregnant with man's child.
Arkansas**	Yes	Semi	Yes	Yes	No	No
California	Yes	Yes[1]	Yes	Yes	Yes	Yes
Colorado	Yes	Yes	Yes	Yes	Yes	Yes
Connecticut	Yes	Semi	Yes	Yes	No, unless couple has child together.	No, unless couple has child together.

State						
Delaware	Yes	No	Yes, if a male-female couple.	No, unless a man and woman with child in common.	No	No
District of Columbia	Yes	Yes	Yes	Yes	Yes	Yes
Florida	Yes	Unclear	Yes, if "residing together as a family."	Yes, if "residing together as a family."	No, unless couple has child together.	No, unless couple has child together and resided together at some point.
Georgia*	Yes	No	No	No	No	No
Hawaii	Yes	Semi	Yes	Yes	No	No
Idaho	Yes	Semi	Yes	Yes	No, unless couple has child together.	No, unless couple has child together.
Illinois	Yes	Yes	Yes	Yes	Yes	Yes
Indiana	Yes	No[2]	No	No	No	No
Iowa	Yes	Semi	Yes	Yes, if within the last year	No	No
Kansas**	Yes	Semi	Yes	Yes	No	No

(Continued)

Table 4.1 Continued

State	Gender-neutral to victim?	Covers gay and lesbian relationships?	Covers unmarried couples currently living together?	Covers unmarried couples previously living together?	Covers current dating relationships?	Covers prior dating relationships?
Kentucky**	Yes	Semi	Yes	Yes	No, unless couple has child together.	No, unless couple has child together.
Louisiana	Yes	No[3]	No[3]	No[3]	No[3]	No[3]
Maine	Yes	Semi	Yes	Yes	No	No
Maryland**	Yes	Probably no[4]	Yes, if related or engaged in a sexual relationship.	Yes, if there were sexual relations and the couple lived together for 90 days of last 12 months.	No	No
Massachusetts*	Yes	Yes	Yes	Yes	Yes, if a "substantive dating or engagement" relationship as determined by court.	Yes, if a "substantive dating or engagement" relationship as determined by court.

Michigan*	Yes	No	Yes, if opposite sex and consensual sexual relations.	Yes, if opposite sex and consensual sexual relations.	No
Minnesota*	Yes	Probably no[5]	Yes	Yes	No, unless couple has child together.
Mississippi*	Yes	Probably no	Yes, if living together "as spouses."	No	No
Missouri	Yes	Semi	Yes	No	No
Montana	Yes	No	Unclear, but limited to opposite sex in any event.	Unclear, but limited to opposite sex in any event.	Yes, if members of the opposite sex.
Nebraska	Yes	Semi	Yes	Yes	No, unless couple has child together.
Nevada	Unclear[6]	Yes[6]	Yes[6]	Yes[6]	Yes[6]
New Hampshire	Yes	Yes	Yes	Yes	Yes

(Continued)

Table 4.1 Continued

State	Gender-neutral to victim?	Covers gay and lesbian relationships?	Covers unmarried couples currently living together?	Covers unmarried couples previously living together?	Covers current dating relationships?	Covers prior dating relationships?
New Jersey	Yes	Yes	Yes	Yes	Yes	Yes
Mexico	Yes	Yes	Yes	Yes	Yes	Yes, if a continuing personal relationship exists.
New York	Yes	Unclear	Yes, if living together continually or at regular intervals.	Yes, if living together continually or at regular intervals.	Unclear (to be determined by department regulations)	Unclear (to be determined by department regulations)
North Carolina	Yes	No	Only if members of the opposite sex living together "as if married."	Only if members of the opposite sex living together "as if married."	No	No
North Dakota	Yes	Yes	Yes	Yes	Yes, if the court determines the sufficiency of the relationship.	Yes, if the court determines the sufficiency of the relationship.

Ohio	Yes	Semi	Yes, if persons living together as spouses.	Yes, if couple lived together as spouses within last year.	No	No
Oklahoma*	Yes	Yes	Yes	Yes	Yes	Yes
Oregon	Yes	Semi/Lesser[7]	Yes	Yes	Yes, if sexually intimate within the last two years or share a child in common.	Yes, if sexually intimate within the last two years or share a child in common.
Pennsylvania	Yes	Yes	Yes, if living together as spouses.	Yes, if living together as spouses.	Yes, if a sexual or intimate relationship.	Yes, if a sexual or intimate relationship.
Rhode Island	Yes	Yes	Yes	Yes, if couple resided together within last three years.	Yes, if the couple has a child together or is in a substantive dating or engagement relationship as determined by court.	Yes, if the couple has a child together or was in a substantive dating or engagement relationship (within the last six months) as determined by court.
South Carolina	Yes	No	No	No	No	No
South Dakota*	Yes	Semi	Yes	Yes	No, unless couple has child together.	No, unless couple has child together.

(Continued)

Table 4.1 Continued

State	Gender-neutral to victim?	Covers gay and lesbian relationships?	Covers unmarried couples currently living together?	Covers unmarried couples previously living together?	Covers current dating relationships?	Covers prior dating relationships?
Tennessee	Yes	Semi	Yes	No	No, unless couple has child together.	No, unless couple has child together.
Texas	Yes	Semi	Yes	Yes	No, unless couple has child together.	No, unless couple has child together.
Utah	Yes	Semi	Yes	Yes	No, unless couple has child together.	No, unless couple has child together.
Vermont	Yes	Semi	Yes	Yes, if a sexual relationship existed.	No	No
Virginia	Yes	Semi	Yes	Yes, if within last 12 months.	No, unless couple has child together.	No, unless couple has child together.
Washington	Yes	Lesser[8]	Yes	Yes	Yes	Yes
West Virginia	Yes	Yes	Yes	Yes	Yes, if sexual or intimate partners.	Yes, if former sexual or intimate partners.

Wisconsin	Yes	Semi	Yes	Yes	No, unless couple has child together.	No, unless couple has child together.
Wyoming	Yes	Semi	Yes	Yes, if formerly living together as if married.	No, unless couple has child together.	No, unless couple has child together.

NOTES: "Semi" refers to a state whose statutes provide certain protections to same-sex partners but for practical reasons do not benefit all such individuals (for instance, a statute that does not provide coverage for dating relationships).

"Lesser" refers to a state whose statutes specifically give more protection to heterosexual couples than to same-sex couples.

* Indicates a state that criminalizes sexual acts that constitute sodomy between consenting adults regardless of sexual orientation.

** Indicates a state that criminalizes sexual acts that constitute sodomy between consenting adults of the same sex.

1. California has recently amended its domestic violence statutes to remove language that, previously, had allowed only heterosexual domestic violence cases to be prosecuted as felonies. Even so, the resulting legislation appears to provide for stiffer penalties for domestic violence cases between spouses and cohabitants than for cases between noncohabiting dating partners and former spouses.

2. Indiana law provides that domestic violence shelters be established for persons who were victims of domestic violence between spouses or former spouses.

3. Louisiana's domestic violence statute, for the most part, protects only spouses and former spouses. The statute also covers persons living together "as spouses" if there is also a minor child living in the house who is seeking protection under the domestic violence statute.

4. Maryland's domestic violence law covers couples who have a sexual relationship with each other. However, Maryland law outlaws sexual conduct between same-sex couples.

5. Minnesota law provides for coverage of relationships when the parties are engaged in a sexual relationship but then criminalizes consensual sodomy.

6. The Nevada statute refers repeatedly to the perpetrator of domestic violence with male pronouns. Presumably, this is more an oversight than an intentional limitation of the scope of the statute.

7. Oregon law mandates arrest only for domestic violence incidents that occur between members of the opposite sex. Oregon Rev. Stat. 133.055.

8. Washington law provides domestic violence shelters only for victims whose abusers are members of the opposite sex.

Table 4.2 State Statutes Referenced

State	State Statutes Referenced
Alabama	Code of Ala., 15-23-41; 13A-6-65 (1996)
Alaska	Alaska Stat., 18.66.100; 18.65-510, et seq. (1996)
Arizona	Ariz. Rev. Stat., 13-3601; 36-3001 (1997)
Arkansas	Ark. Stat. Ann., 5-26-301, et seq.; 5-14-122 (1995)
California	Cal. Pen. Code, 243 (1996)
Colorado	Colo. Rev. Stat., 14-4-101 (1996)
Connecticut	Conn. Gen. Stat., 46b-38a (1997)
Delaware	Del. Code Ann. 10, 1041 (1996)
District of Columbia	D.C. Code, 16-1001 (1997)
Florida	Fla. Stat., 415.602; 741.28, et seq. (1996)
Georgia	O.C.G.A., 19-13-20; 16-6-2 (1997)
Hawaii	Haw. Code Ann., 586-1; 709-906 (1996)
Idaho	Idaho Code, 39-6303 (1997)
Illinois	720 ILCS 5/45-1; 20 ILCS 2210/1; 725 ILCS 5/112A-3; 750 ILCS 60/103 (1997)
Indiana	Ind. Code. Ann., 12-7-2-70; 12-18-4-12 (1996)
Iowa	Iowa Code, 236.2 (1996)
Kansas	Kan. Stat. Ann., 60-3102; 21-3505 (1996)
Kentucky	Ken. Rev. Stat., 403.720; 403.725; 510.100 (1996)
Louisiana	La. Rev. Stat., 46:2121.1; 46:2132; La. Ch.C. art. 1565 (1997)
Maine	Maine Rev. Stat., Title 19, 761-A, et seq. (1996)
Maryland	Md. Family Law Code Ann., 4-501; art. 27, 554 (1996)
Massachusetts	G.L. c. 209A; c. 272, 34 (1997)
Michigan	Mich. Stat. Ann., 400.1501; 28.355 (1996)
Minnesota	Minn. Stat., 518B.01; 609.293 (1996)
Mississippi	Miss. Code. Ann., 93-21-3; 97-29-59 (1996)

Table 4.2 Continued

State	State Statutes Referenced
Missouri	Rev. Stat. Mo., 455.200 (1996)
Montana	Mont. Code Ann., 45-5-206 (1995)
Nebraska	Rev. Stat., 42-903 (1996)
Nevada	Nev. Rev. Stat. Ann., 33.018, 217.400 (1995)
New Hampshire	Rev. Stat. Ann., 173-B1 (1996)
New Jersey	N.J. Stat., 2C:25-19 (1996)
New Mexico	N.M. Stat. Ann., 40-13-2 (1997)
New York	N.Y. Cos. Laws. Soc. Serv., 459-a (1997)
North Carolina	N.C. Gen. Stat., 50B-1 (1997)
North Dakota	N.D. Cent. Code., 14-07.1-01 (1997)
Ohio	Ohio Rev. Code, 3113.33 (1997)
Oklahoma	Okl. Stat., Title 22, 60.1; Title 21, 886 (1996)
Oregon	Or. Rev. Stat., 133.055; 108.610; 107.705 (1996)
Pennsylvania	Pa. C.S., Title 23, 6102 (1996)
Rhode Island	R.I. Gen. L., 12-29-2 (1996)
South Carolina	S.C. Code Ann., 20-4-20 (1996)
South Dakota	S.D. Cod. L., 25-10-1; 22-22-2 (1997)
Tennessee	Tenn. Code Ann., 36-3-601 (1996)
Texas	Tex. Fam. Code., 71.01 (1997)
Utah	Utah Code Ann., 30-6-1; 77-36-1 (1997)
Vermont	Vt. Stat. Ann., Title 15, Chap. 21, 1101 (1996)
Virginia	Va. Code Ann., 18.2-57.2 (1995)
Washington	Rev. Code Wash., 10.99.020; 26.50.010; 70.123.020 (1996)
West Virginia	W. Va. Code, 48-2A-2 (1997)
Wyoming	Wyo. Stat., 35-21-102 (1997)
Wisconsin	Wisc. Stat., 968.075 (1996)

5

Equal Protection/ Equal Safety

Representing Victims of Same-Sex Partner Abuse in Court

Sandra E. Lundy

As a lawyer, I know from experience that litigating openly queer cases in civil court is never easy. You can be sure that somehow, somewhere, when you least expect it, homophobia will rear its ugly head in the courtroom, derailing your arguments, upsetting your client, making it impossible to be heard.

When the issue is queer domestic violence, the problem of homophobia in the civil justice system is often magnified. Even where state law covers same-sex as well as heterosexual domestic violence, the chances are that the laws are not enforced equally and that same-sex litigants are treated with less dignity, sympathy, and respect than their straight counterparts.

I live in Massachusetts, which has some of the toughest domestic violence laws in the nation. We also have a vocal and effective community of same-sex domestic violence advocates. Many judges, police, and district attorneys across the state have received extensive,

sometimes mandatory, training in issues of same-sex domestic violence. Yet in the years that I have been representing same-sex victims
in Massachusetts civil courts, I have witnessed countless abomina-
tions: the judge who addresses the butch lesbian victim as "sir"; the
county clerk who tells the gay man, erroneously, that the Massachusetts abuse prevention law does not apply to him; the mutual orders
that designate as perpetrators the gay, lesbian, bisexual, or transgendered *victims* who walk into the courtroom seeking protective orders;
the police who refuse to report same-sex domestic violence as domestic violence, who refuse to testify for the victim, who refuse to apply
the mandatory arrest provisions to lesbian and gay batterers who
violate restraining orders; the countless times that battered lesbians,
gay men, bisexuals, and transgendered folks who seek a civil protective
order encounter just one more experience of humiliation and abuse.

Given how difficult it is for out queer people to be treated well in
the civil justice system, particularly when they seek relief from abusive
partners, I understand why some in our community urge queer people
to bypass the court system entirely and instead bring issues of abuse
to friends, private mediators, and counselors. However, the decision
to avoid the courts is, I think, a bad one. First, most empirical research
shows that mediation and joint counseling can often be counterproductive and even dangerous in situations involving domestic abuse.
The batterer is generally no less domineering and manipulative in the
counseling and mediation sessions than he or she is at home. The
unwary counselor, private mediator, or friend can end up validating
the abuse, even unwittingly. Or the batterer will simply terminate the
mediation or counseling session if things do not go his or her way.

Second, much can be accomplished by law that cannot be accomplished by other means. No amount of mediation, friendly intervention, or counseling can force a batterer to surrender guns, or impose
credible, enforceable sanctions against the batterer for disrupting the
victim's work life. No amount of extralegal intervention can assure
that the victim will know exactly when the batterer is released from
jail or that he or she will be able to obtain an order of protection that
the campus police, the building security guard, his or her children's
day care providers, and others are legally bound to recognize and
accept. When we in the queer community turn our backs on the law
enforcement systems that are at least theoretically available to us, we
are removing from same-sex domestic violence victims many real

protections. We are keeping them unsafe, and we are saying to an often hostile system, "You win."

Finally, a very large part of the struggle for queer civil rights is the demand that we be treated equally under the law. Increasingly, queer people are turning to the courts to enforce our rights as parents, partners, and ex-partners. Domestic violence is as much a part of queer family life as it is of straight family life. There is nothing retrograde or demeaning in insisting that domestic violence laws be applied equally for all families.

Although I have seen horrible and upsetting things happen in court in same-sex domestic violence cases, I have also seen wonderful things happen, which is why I keep doing this work. Over and over again, I have seen how empowering it can be for a lesbian, bisexual, or gay survivor of domestic violence to put the abuse on the record, to insist on his or her rights to protection, to feel a little safer at night because, finally, the abuser is being held responsible for his or her actions. I write this chapter with the firm conviction that, with continued hard work and persistence, we can make the civil justice system a genuine source of protection and empowerment for survivors of same-sex domestic violence.

In what follows, I offer some suggestions to lawyers and legal advocates who wish to assist victims of same-sex domestic violence to obtain civil abuse protection orders. These suggestions are based on my own experiences in and out of the courtroom and on the experiences of many colleagues around the United States, but they do not pretend to be comprehensive. Because the abuse prevention laws of every state differ, I have kept my remarks general in the hope of offering guidelines that can be applied in a variety of situations.

The Foundations of Abuse Prevention
Legal Advocacy

Be Informed

Every state has ethical codes that prohibit a lawyer from representing a client in a matter that is beyond the lawyer's competence, knowledge, or skill. Many practitioners who occasionally take cases involving domestic violence seem to feel that their ethical obligation is met simply by reading and applying their state's abuse prevention statutes and the case law relevant to the situation at hand.

Domestic violence, however, is more than a legal fiction bounded by certain rules of evidence. It is a complex, often counterintuitive series of behaviors about which no statute or case law can adequately inform you. Any lawyer or advocate who truly wants to provide adequate legal assistance to victims of domestic violence must take the time to educate him or herself about the dynamics of domestic violence in general, and same-sex domestic violence in particular. The better educated you are about these issues, for instance, the better able you will be to assess whether the person sitting before you is more likely the victim or the perpetrator of domestic violence. Once you have educated yourself about representing domestic violence survivors, you will be less surprised by your client's distrust, self-doubt, and hesitancy; by the amount of effort it takes to get a clear and full picture of the violence; by the fact that, even when you are convinced you have a great case, your client may refuse at the last minute to go forward. The more you know about domestic violence, the more you will also be able to anticipate the batterer's likely defenses and not underestimate his or her fierce opposition. For example, you will have learned to explore with your client very carefully the nature of the abuse and the kinds of vulnerabilities that the batterer most often exploits. You will have learned to anticipate that the batterer will often incorporate this kind of exploitation in his or her legal strategy.

In other words, when dealing with victims of same-sex domestic violence, lawyers (and, I would argue, lay advocates as well) have an ethical obligation to be as fully informed as possible not only about the law of domestic violence but also about its social and psychological contexts. So read books on the subject, talk to advocates at your local battered women's shelter or queer community service center, attend a domestic violence training seminar or conference workshop, or, if these services are not available in your area, create your own panel or workshop with outside speakers to educate yourself and your community. The goal is to gain not just book knowledge of queer domestic violence but also the deeper understanding that allows you to listen sympathetically to your client, deflect the likely mind games of the batterer, and effectively address the homophobia that is sure to show itself somewhere in the course of your case.

Carefully Assess Your Client's Needs and Goals

Once you have determined that your client is in fact a victim of same-sex partner abuse and entitled to civil relief, you need to determine whether, in this particular case, seeking that relief makes sense. If, for instance, your client is in the closet and insists on staying there (a decision you have no right to judge), then you may need to consider other options because you simply cannot assure your client that the proceedings will not be made public or that you can proceed in court without reference to the client's sexual orientation. In fact, you can be sure that the batterer, knowing your client's vulnerability, will do everything he or she can to use the proceedings to "out" your client. In such cases, the most you may be able to do is to contact local police and/or the district attorney's office about the situation, hook the client up with the appropriate counseling and support services, help the client create a safety plan, and let the client know that you are there as a resource in the future if the client changes his or her mind.

You must also discuss with your client the likely effect on the batterer of seeking a civil protection order. In my experience, these orders most effectively act as a deterrent when the batterer is someone who has not been in previous trouble with the law and who is concerned with his or her standing in the community. If, on the other hand, the batterer has an extensive criminal record, he or she is likely to be unfazed by the issuance of a protective order or is just as likely to become so enraged that your client's safety is unreasonably compromised by seeking the order. Remember that your client knows the batterer far better than you ever will, and believe your client when he or she expresses fears about safety if the case goes forward.

Determine whether your client has the emotional and financial resources to carry through with the consequences of an order. If he or she is asking the batterer to vacate the home, does your client have enough money to pay the mortgage and expenses if required? If your client intends to leave, does your client have adequate means of support? If children are involved, can your client care for them without help from the batterer, or can the batterer be ordered to pay child support (as in the case of second-parent adoptions)? If the batterer is the children's sole legal parent, can your client accept that he or she may never be allowed to visit with the children again? Does the client have friends, relatives, a support group to turn to for emotional support? (This is a good time to make it clear to your client that you can provide legal services but that you are not a trained therapist or an "instant friend.")

Even if your client is willing and eager to go forward, you must tell him or her not only what may go right in court but also what may go wrong. If you have an option to proceed in one or more trial courts, explain to the client the benefits and drawbacks of each choice. Explain to your client that he or she may leave court with a restraining order, without a restraining order, or with a mutual order, and be sure your client is aware of the consequences of each scenario.

Explore with your client his or her own vulnerabilities and how they are likely to come out in court. Does your client have a history of drug or alcohol abuse? Is he or she HIV positive? Has he or she recently been fired from a job or written a bad check? Even if these vulnerabilities are wholly unrelated to the abuse, you need to know about them because you can bet that the batterer does. Explain to the client that he or she needs to be prepared to have the abuser make the victim's character an issue—or attempt to. Discuss various ways of responding to such attacks and your client's comfort level for each option.

Throughout this process, never forget that you are working for the client and not the other way around. Listen carefully and never make a significant decision about the case without discussing it with your client and getting his or her approval. As a battered person, the client is probably accustomed to feeling disempowered. It is the lawyer's or advocate's job to make sure that the restraining order process is a step toward empowerment and not just another exercise in coercive control.

Engage in Safety Planning With Your Client

By now we all know that the most dangerous time for someone who is battered is when he or she attempts to leave the relationship. This is the time that the batterer is most likely to get extremely violent, because he or she sees control slipping away. For this reason, the lawyer or advocate representing a victim of same-sex domestic violence must work with the client to create a safety plan to try to ensure that when (or if) the client decides to take the batterer to court, the client won't pay for the decision with his or her life.

Many battered women's shelters and district attorneys' offices have model safety plans that you can use to tailor a plan that fits your client's personal needs. Shelter workers and battered women's advocates should be happy to answer questions you have about safety plans. Do not, of course, leave your client with the impression or guarantee that such a plan will insulate him or her from the partner's violence. But do satisfy yourself that you have given your client some guidelines for keeping safer.

Preparing Your Case

Client Testimony

Victims of same-sex domestic violence, like other victims of domestic violence, often suffer from post-traumatic stress disorder (PTSD), a condition common to people who have been involuntarily held captive and subjected to systematic, random violence. Clients with PTSD can often be difficult. They can be distrustful and hyper-vigilant, minimize or deny the abuse, inappropriately accept blame for the abuse, or change their mind at the last minute. In preparing your client to testify against their abuser, you may come up against any of these defenses or all of them at once, and you may find yourself becoming frustrated or even angry at your client. If you yourself have a history of having been abused as an adult or a child, you may also find yourself being secondarily traumatized by your client's story.

Plan on extra time, patience, and energy in preparing your client. Be aware of your own defenses and stereotypes as they come up. Try to listen carefully and without judgment. Find ways to take care of yourself. Again, this will be easier if you are educated about domestic violence and its manifestations.

Collateral Evidence

Because domestic violence is often a one-on-one crime with no spectators, you may be faced with a situation in which the only evidence of abuse is your client's testimony. Unfortunately, it seems that in same-sex cases a higher burden of proof is implicitly demanded of the plaintiff, and your client's testimony alone may not be enough to meet that burden if an evidentiary hearing is required. If you do not have hospital records, eyewitness testimony, or other normal collateral evidence, you need to be creative and resourceful to find evidence to support your client's testimony.

The client may have pictures of bruises or property damage that could come into evidence. The client may have made "spontaneous utterances" to others about the abuse that could be used to buttress her testimony. Friends and relatives may have seen and heard more than your client is aware of, so it is always important to check these possible sources. School records or employers' records of multiple absences may also be helpful.

The police may be another important source of collateral evidence. Often, in cases in which police are called to respond to instances of same-sex partner violence, they will file sketchy or incomplete police reports that are not listed as "domestics" and are of little use to you in court (or worse, if the report describes the violence as "mutual"). Sometimes, however, it is possible to interview the responding officer at length to get more, and more helpful, information about what the officer actually saw and heard. You may also learn from such interviews that the officer was aware that this was a situation of domestic violence but did not designate it as such in the police report because he or she felt it would be "embarrassing" to the parties to do so. It may be possible to get the police officer to file a supplemental report including the additional significant facts omitted from the first report or to have a superior officer intervene to require that a supplemental report be written. You may be able to enlist the help of your local police department or mayor's lesbian/gay advocate, if one exists, in this effort.

Often, you will find yourself in the position of having to educate the fact finder about the realities of same-sex partner abuse as a means of advocating for your client. If your client has been receiving support services from a battered person's advocacy group or counselor, it may be possible to persuade the counselor or facilitator to testify on your client's behalf. Although this person may not have firsthand knowledge of the abuse, he or she presumably is skilled in assessing whether individuals have been abused and the effects of such abuse. You may also want to consider calling a general battered women's expert or an expert on domestic violence who can testify that your client's account is credible and who may help educate the fact finder about the basics of queer domestic violence. A judge ultimately may not allow such an expert to testify, but that person's presence in the courtroom may be a real advantage to your client. The local battered women's shelter staff and local queer advocacy groups may be good sources for providing or locating such experts.

Know the Batterer

Of course, you also will want to find out as much about the batterer as possible, and often you will not have a lot of time in which to do this. Try to anticipate how the batterer will attempt to destroy your client's credibility. Rely on your client to anticipate which "buttons" the batterer is most likely to push and how best to respond.

Courtroom Advocacy

Do Your Best to Ensure Privacy

Even if your client has obtained ex-parte relief, at some point the client will have to face his or her abuser in court, and the abuser will have a due process right to defend him or herself and confront the accuser. Within every state, and within every courtroom, practices will differ with respect to how such adversarial hearings are conducted. Many judges in Massachusetts, for example, feel strongly that domestic violence cases are private matters that should be heard at sidebar (that is, at the judge's bench and outside of the hearing of the general courtroom public). An equal number of judges seem to feel that the cases should be heard in open court, like any other civil case.

Queer litigants who testify in open court to physical, emotional, and sexual partner abuse are often subtly and sometimes not so subtly subjected to snickers, jeers, or worse by others in the courtroom, even if the judge and the court officers attempt to maintain normal courtroom order. Therefore, it is important for the advocate or lawyer to try to have these cases heard in as private a forum as possible. Many states have codes of courtroom procedure that admonish judges and courtroom personnel to be sensitive to the privacy interests of litigants. All states have some procedures for impounding files or closing courtrooms, although the general bias is in favor of open courtrooms. Do what you can to minimize the public airing of your case—through sidebar hearings, impoundment motions, motions to close the court-room, or any other strategy that might work with your particular judge. The judge may actually be grateful that he or she has the opportunity to assess your case outside of the glare of the courtroom public.

Challenge Courtroom Homophobia

As I stated earlier, homophobia can arise in the courtroom in innumerable ways. The lawyer or advocate for the queer victim of partner abuse must be vigilant to challenge homophobia at every turn, from whatever source, and on the record. The challenge need not be hostile, and in fact it should be pointedly polite: "May I ask the court to state for the record the relevance of questioning the plaintiff about his sexual practices when what he is alleging is that he has been beaten and choked by the defendant?" "Your Honor, I notice that the court officers are snickering to each other as the testimony in this case proceeds. May we have an order that the court officers refrain from such conduct?" "Your Honor, defense counsel's use of the terms 'butch' and 'femme' in this proceeding is irrelevant, highly inflamma-tory, and designed only to prejudice my client. I object to the attempt to discredit my client by means of stereotype and ask that defense counsel be restrained from this line of argument." "Your Honor, you have heard defense counsel state that the battering was not battering at all but just a part of 'normal' gay sex. Coercion and systematic terror are not a part of any normal relationship, gay or straight, and I ask the court to strike from the record this offensive and blatant attempt to minimize the defendant's violence."

If your state has codes of judicial and lawyer conduct that prohibit the use of derogatory remarks about one's sexual orientation, point this out on the record when making your objections. Other portions of your state's various legal codes of ethics and conduct may also be helpful. Even if the judge overrules all of your objections and gets furious with you for pointing up instances of homophobia, you will have made your record for a possible appeal. And you probably will have succeeded in making the offenders a little more cautious.

As a corollary, the lawyer or advocate must also be careful of his or her own use of stereotypes. Is it really necessary, for instance, to point out that the defendant always referred to your client as his or her "wife?" Does it really help your case to emphasize that the defendant is into leather? Many lawyers feel that it is their ethical obligation to use every tool available to represent their clients, including, if necessary, exploiting unsavory cultural stereotypes. This is not the place to engage the question of whether countervailing considerations make such tactics unacceptable. I will point out, though, that every lawyer and advocate who uses these stereotypes is morally accountable for their ripple effects, including their effects on subsequent victims of same-sex partner abuse who are bigger, more butch, richer, more "masculine" than their abusers and who only want a fair hearing. If the facts of the abuse in your case are not strong enough to stand alone without the use of homophobic stereotypes, then I suggest you reconsider the strength of your case.

Finally, you should always keep in mind that this is first and foremost a case about violence. This is not (at least not directly) a "gay rights" case or a case about the validity of your client's sexual orientation. You are not representing all queer people; you are representing one battered individual. Avoid the temptation to grandstand or lecture about general issues; never lose sight—or let anyone else lose sight—of the fact that your client is in danger and in need of the court's protection.

Ask for Everything You Want

In Massachusetts, a person seeking an abuse protection order can ask the court for any relief designed to keep him or her safe. Almost all victims ask for no-contact orders; no-abuse orders; and orders to stay away from the workplace, the home (often through a vacate order), and sometimes a child's day care center or school. But I have also had clients ask the court to require the abuser to surrender car keys and automatic garage door openers (so the abuser cannot ambush the victim in the garage), to return pets, to provide a police escort while the victim moves belongings out of the house, and to require the abuser to pay the costs of replacing locks or of replacing property damaged by the abuser.

I have noticed that in cases of same-sex domestic violence, lawyers representing victims are often so grateful to get plain-vanilla no-contact or no-abuse orders that they do not even present, let alone strongly advocate for, the other kinds of relief that may make their clients safer. This is a mistake. Just as we shouldn't have to beg to be respected in court, we shouldn't have to settle for half a loaf. Ask for everything your client needs (including attorneys' fees if you can!). You will be increasing your client's chances for safety and sending a strong message to the batterer that not only the physical violence but the entire system of control has ended.

Appeal Mutual Orders, if Possible

If you are unlucky enough to walk out of court with a mutual restraining order, strongly consider an appeal. In my state, some judges routinely issue mutual restraining orders in same-sex cases without issuing the statuatorily required written findings of fact. Often, the victims are so dispirited by the mutual order that they do not want to appeal, do not have the money to appeal, or feel that appealing will be dangerous. Explain to your client that the mutual order itself is highly dangerous and that batterers can (and often do) use the order as a basis to take out a criminal complaint against the victim, thus prolonging abusive contact with the victim. Try to enlist the services of a queer legal advocacy group in your area or other attorneys to provide assistance on an appeal on a pro bono basis. I have found that some major law firms in Boston have been eager to offer their pro bono assistance on such appeals, which provide them with community visibility and the chance to participate in shaping new law.

You may determine that an appeal is not possible for any number of reasons. There may be other avenues—such as community organizing or reports to conduct commissions—that your client may wish to pursue. Remember that your client is the person who makes the ultimate decision about what avenue of "appeal," if any, to take.

Leave Wisely

Whether or not you succeed in obtaining a restraining order for your client, you can be sure that the batterer will have some feelings about having had to appear in the courtroom. The end of the court session is a very dangerous time for your client (and for you), a time when the batterer is likely to seek some sort of retribution, regardless of whether the batterer came with counsel. *Never* allow your client and the batterer to leave the court at the same time. Wait 15 to 20 minutes after the batterer leaves to leave with your client or ask the judge to order the batterer to remain in the courtroom for a certain length of time while your client leaves. *Never* let the client leave alone. Leave with your client or make sure that a friend leaves with your client. Make sure that your client has a safety plan in place so that someone close to your client knows his or her whereabouts for the next several days. Ask your client to check in with you by phone for the next several days. Make sure that he or she gives a copy of the restraining order to local police and to anyone else who needs to know about it (employers, day care providers, school officials, relatives, security guards, and so forth).

Conclusion

The civil justice system is just one medium through which to address issues of queer domestic violence—and often it is a frustrating and discouraging medium. Yet knowledgeable, creative advocacy within the civil justice system has the potential to empower not just individual lesbian, gay, bisexual, or transgendered survivors of domestic violence but the entire community of queer people who insist on equal treatment under the law.

6

Creating Courtroom Accessibility

Andrea Cabral
Diane Coffey

Same-sex partner abuse has always existed, but these cases are only now presenting themselves in significant numbers in criminal courtrooms as more gay men and lesbians are willing to come out and as the relationship between the gay communities and law enforcement evolves. However, the criminal courtroom can still be an unsafe place for the same-sex victim not only because of whatever blatant homophobia may exist but also because many law enforcement personnel lack the background and skills to deal with these cases effectively. The authors are, respectively, a prosecutor and a victim witness advocate. In this chapter, we discuss our experiences over the years in representing same-sex victims of domestic violence, and we suggest some ways in which the criminal justice system can be made more sensitive to gay men and lesbians who are seeking protection from partner abuse.

Diane Coffey

In 1989, I was a victim-witness advocate in the Middlesex County (Massachusetts) district attorney's office and was assigned to the

Cambridge district court. My role in the prosecution of cases was to initiate and maintain contact with victims, apprise them of court dates, assess their need for services, provide crisis intervention, and make appropriate referrals to human service agencies. Although I assisted victims of all crimes, the bulk of my time was devoted to advocacy for victims of domestic abuse. In particular, I assisted victims in applying for domestic abuse restraining orders and in the regular court hearings on the issuance of those restraining orders.

Victims in Massachusetts seek restraining orders under Massachusetts General Law Chapter 209A, also known as the Abuse Prevention Act. In 1989, Chapter 209A required that eligible applicants be persons who were currently or had previously been married, were currently living together, were related by blood, or who had a child in common even if they had never been married. It was not until 1990 that the law was amended to afford protection for people in "substantive dating relationships" regardless of whether they ever lived together.

Technically, in 1989, domestic abuse restraining orders were available to gay and lesbian victims so long as they lived, or had formerly lived, with their abusers. Gays and lesbians did not have to disclose the intimate nature of their relationships with restraining order defendants to obtain the restraining order. As a practical matter, however, roommates whose relationships were platonic rarely availed themselves of the process.

For the gay or lesbian victim, the application process was filled with pitfalls. It was common for such plaintiffs to be questioned at length about the nature of their relationship with the defendant. Although restraining order hearings were usually done at sidebar— that is, alongside the judge's bench and out of the hearing of others in the courtroom—sometimes, when the parties were the same sex and certain judges were on the bench, plaintiffs were made to stand outside the bar—some 10 to 15 feet away from the judge—and speak into a microphone. References to the place of the abuse (a gay bar or the single bedroom the "roommates" shared); the language of abuse ("faggot" "dyke" "whore"); or the nature of the abuse (sexual abuse or abuse that typically occurs in the context of an intimate relationship, such as the ripping off of clothing) invited further judicial inquiry. Being "outed" was often the price of seeking the court's protection.

At this time in my career, my sexual orientation was not common knowledge. Frequently I watched gay and lesbian victims and witnesses struggle to decide whether to remain closeted and choose not to seek the protection of the criminal justice system or to courageously come out during a court proceeding. I often thought about and still today painfully remember my own struggle of silence. I prepared victims for the possibility of having to publicly acknowledge their sexual orientation in a forum in which I felt I could not do the same.

In my work as a victim witness advocate, I had opportunities to both assist people seeking restraining orders and observe court proceedings. One such proceeding stands out for me.

Paula[1] came to the Cambridge District Court because her partner, Jan, had been battering and threatening her during the last month of their relationship. Paula and Jan had been living together. Paula was not out and sought help from the court as a last resort. She was seeking a temporary order issued ex parte (without the other side present).

Although I was not the advocate directly assisting her, I was present while she prepared the paperwork and during the court proceeding. I listened as the other advocate discussed the process. She was told that her privacy could not be guaranteed in court. Restraining order hearings were held in a session crowded with lawyers, police officers, clerks, probation officers, witnesses, defendants, and their family members. I felt she was as prepared as she could be for the possibility of having her sexual orientation disclosed. But we could not have predicted, much less prepared for, what actually transpired.

Because this was an ex parte hearing, only Paula was present. I went into the room to observe. Proceedings involving gay and lesbian victims, witnesses, and defendants always drew more people into the courtroom. It was not unusual, in these cases, to hear rumblings of inappropriate, homophobic comments. I thought my presence in the courtroom would provide additional support for Paula. They called her case and Paula and the advocate went to the sidebar.

Paula began her recitation of the abuse by testifying that the abuser, Jan, was her roommate. She then described the abuse that caused her to seek the restraining order, including the battering, fear, and intimidation she had lived with for the past month. She asked that Jan be ordered to vacate the apartment they shared and that Jan be ordered to stop abusing her and to have no further contact with her. She was nervous but spoke in a clear, if low, voice.

When she finished, I expected the judge to ask a few general questions, as I had seen him do in other cases. Paula had clearly testified to facts sufficient to show that Jan's behavior posed a "substantial likelihood of harm," the standard applicable to issuance of domestic violence restraining orders.

Instead, the judge began to question Paula on the exact nature of her relationship with Jan. He wanted to know how long they had known each other, exactly what kind of relationship this was, and whether they were roommates or "more than that." I sat in the courtroom thinking, "This information doesn't matter. She's eligible as a roommate. What's the point of having this woman state in open court that she is a lesbian?" Whether the judge was satisfying some idle curiosity or perhaps something more prurient, he was doing it in a public courtroom at the expense of a woman already humiliated at having to disclose the pain and fear her partner had inflicted.

Paula looked at the advocate and her eyes pleaded for me to help her. It was very important for the order to be issued, so the advocate was not in a position to challenge the judge. Visibly shaking, Paula answered all of the judge's questions. The judge granted the restraining order. Paula could protect herself from her abuser but not from the system to which she entrusted her safety.

Ironically, as a closeted lesbian, I felt unable to do what was routinely required of victims—to disclose to her my sexual orientation.

Andrea Cabral

In 1989, I was a 29-year-old assistant district attorney (ADA) in the Middlesex County district attorney's office at the Cambridge district court. I also handled juvenile cases and, one day a week, was assigned to the jury session. The district attorney for whom I worked encouraged "vertical prosecution," that is, maintaining consistency of victim/witness contact and quality of prosecution by allowing ADAs to follow their own cases up from the district court through to the jury session. At that time, Massachusetts still utilized a trial process known as the *de novo* system, whereby defendants were allowed to choose whether they wanted a bench trial before a judge or a trial before a six-person jury. This system gave defendants who had chosen a bench trial and had been convicted the right to appeal that conviction to the six-person jury session and have the case tried a second time.[2]

This "second bite at the apple" served the defense well. Because the defendant has the right to remain silent and put the Commonwealth to its proof of every element of the case beyond a reasonable doubt, it was not unusual for defendants to routinely choose a bench trial and use it solely to discover, before the eventual jury trial, the exact testimony each Commonwealth witness would offer and how well that testimony would hold up under cross-examination.

Thus, victims and witnesses endured a lengthy and often traumatizing trial only to be told that the defendant's bench conviction was meaningless and that they would have to go through it all again; only this time, the defense would know far more about them and would pounce on any memory failures or other weakness in their testimony. This made bleak the prospect of holding on to victims and witnesses from arraignment through jury verdict.

This system wrought absolute havoc in domestic violence cases. The victims' fear, shame, guilt, and, often, emotional or economic dependence on the defendant combined with a bureaucratic and hostile system to wage war on any chance to hold the defendant legally accountable. The experience of the gay or lesbian domestic violence victim, as in Ben's case, approached the unimaginable.

Ben had been found by the police lying in the lobby of his apartment building. He was bleeding profusely from a number of superficial stab wounds on his body. His face was also bloody and bruised. He was in his early 40s but looked older; short and balding, slightly built with a graying beard. He appeared to be semiconscious but the police could not tell if that was due to his injury or intoxication. The odor of alcohol about him was fairly strong. He was taken to the hospital. He told an officer that his roommate, John, had attacked him.

Back at Ben's apartment building, police followed a trail of blood to his apartment. The door was open, and they followed the trail to the bathroom. The walls and sink were bloodstained, but the bathtub was the worst. This was where the stabbing had taken place and, from the way the blood was smeared all over, it was clear that the victim had fought hard.

John had fled the apartment. He was later arrested at a neighborhood bar. He was in his early 30s, but, like Ben, he appeared older. He was wearing clean clothes and bore no traces of having attacked anyone.

John was charged with assault and battery and assault and battery by means of a dangerous weapon. He had a prior record of driving under the influence of alcohol, traffic violations, and disorderly conduct. He was released after posting a low cash bail, with a warning that he was to have no contact with the victim.

Shortly after the defendant's arraignment, I had my first interview with Ben. He had identified John as his roommate and it had not occurred to me to think otherwise. Because there was evidence of alcohol consumption (at least by the victim), I thought that perhaps an argument had preceded the defendant's attack. Ben's bruises were still fresh, and some of his bandages were visible. He had a quiet, sad voice, and his physical injuries were not the only source of the pain in his eyes. He was very respectful, but he refused to talk about what had happened to him and would not repeat his allegation that John had attacked him.

Nothing I said could dissuade him. I tried to explain (as if he didn't know) how serious this situation was. I told him that the defendant was dangerous and that it was important that he not be allowed to get away with such a brutal attack. He told me he did not want to testify and that he would not change his mind. I let it go. I still had time to convince him before the trial date.

At the pretrial conference date, the defendant chose to skip a trial before a judge and go straight to a jury trial. Although I found this unusual, I thought it would benefit the case because I would have even more time to prepare Ben for trial. John's attorney never asked me what sentence I would recommend if the defendant agreed to plead guilty.

In my second interview with Ben, he was even more steadfast in his refusal to speak about the incident. Nothing I said could change his mind. All of the things that usually persuaded a victim to talk openly about the crime utterly failed with Ben. Subsequent talks were all the same, except I noticed that Ben seemed more and more frightened as the trial date drew near. By the time I realized what he was really afraid of, it was too late. He was gay, he was closeted, and he was not about to come out to me or anyone else in that public courtroom. I now knew why John had opted for the jury trial immediately. He knew that even if Ben could get through a bench trial, he would never be able to undergo cross-examination about his sexual orientation in front of a jury.

On the day of trial, Ben appeared. He was shaking and no longer allowed me to speak to him. There was no question of getting the defendant to plead guilty. He knew the case could not be proven without Ben's testimony. He was right. The case was dismissed. John and Ben left the courthouse together.

Although at the time we in the district attorney's office understood that the gay or lesbian abuse victim had to deal with issues that went far beyond simply challenging the batterer by coming to court, we felt at a loss to effectively deal with them. In 1987, new prosecutors received no special training on the general prosecution of domestic violence cases, much less those requiring heightened sensitivity. Victim-witness advocates did receive training in dealing with gay and lesbian victims of crime, but advocates had little standing to challenge judges and court personnel in the context of civil restraining order hearings.

Prosecutors and advocates generally worked well together, but district court practice seldom allowed the time it took to keep the most fragile victims invested in the process. Even if time was not a factor, attitudes often were. Gays and lesbians in my office were closeted because they feared discrimination. Same-sex domestic violence was grossly underreported, and the cases that actually resulted in criminal complaints were scarce, or so it seemed. Because even the most well-intentioned police officers, advocates, and ADAs used the "don't ask, don't tell" approach to interviewing (believing it a matter of protecting a victim's privacy), it is difficult to know just how many such prosecutable cases existed. At worst, homophobes championed the view that the victim's "lifestyle" was conducive to and therefore to blame for the violence; simple ignorance led others to believe that, because the parties were the same sex, the violence could only be mutual, like a fight between neighbors or a barroom brawl.

Over the next two years, our knowledge and understanding of domestic violence and the politics of sexual orientation in the prosecution of criminal cases evolved. However, the numbers of same-sex domestic violence cases we handled and their ultimate outcome did not change. Domestic violence among gays and lesbians was grossly underreported. In the four years Diane and I worked together in Middlesex County, we handled less than 10 cases. Back then, if any victim of domestic violence appeared in court on the trial date and refused to testify or recanted, we accepted it. They would testify that they freely, willingly, and voluntarily did not wish to testify, would sign papers saying the same, and the case would be dismissed. The irony of asking questions about free, willful, and voluntary decision making by victims in many of these cases did not escape us, we just did not know how else to deal with someone who begged us not to prosecute or just flat-out refused to tell the truth when forced to take the witness stand. When the victim was gay or lesbian and faced being outed during the trial, our concerns about to how to proceed doubled. In this particular category of cases, for reasons having to do less with our obligations as public servants and more with the realities of homophobia, we left it to victims to decide whether the abuser's behavior was criminal and whether they, as victims, cared to avail themselves of the same legal protections as victims who were not intimate with the people who battered them.

By 1991, Diane and I had both left the Middlesex County district attorney's office for the Massachusetts attorney general's office. We spent two years there, and although we were in different offices, we each had experiences working with gay and lesbian victims of assault, including hate crimes, that affected how we would handle future same-sex domestic violence cases. As we worked with victims of gay-bashing and other civil rights violations, we continued to experience homophobic bigotry and indifference on the part of some judges, police, and other court personnel. However, we also had the opportunity to work with other law enforcement officials who took crimes against gay men and lesbians seriously. We also saw that many gay and lesbian victims who chose to pursue their legal rights were empowered by the process of seeking justice, even if they did not get the result they believed was fair. It became increasingly clear to both of us that most prosecutors and other law enforcement personnel, even the most well-meaning, lacked information and basic skills that would have allowed them to represent the interests of gay and lesbian victims of violence as fully as possible, and that this information and these skills could be effectively taught.

The Role of Training

Coincidentally, in 1993, Diane and I both left the attorney general's office to work at the Suffolk County district attorney's office. In 1992, the man who had been Suffolk County's district attorney for 23 years left office, and the governor appointed Ralph C. Martin II to the post. That same year, every district attorney's office in the commonwealth was granted $150,000 to start a specialized unit for domestic violence prosecution. In 1994, Martin won election to the office and became the first African American district attorney in the history of Massachusetts. He appointed me chief of the Domestic Violence Unit and Diane the coordinator of Victim-Witness Advocate Services.

The Domestic Violence Unit was new to Suffolk County, so there were no set paths to follow in establishing and running the unit. We could create a program from scratch. More important, Diane and I both felt that we were finally in positions of authority to educate and empower ADAs and advocates to take strong positions on certain issues and demand that courts treat victims and witnesses with dignity and respect.

First on our agenda was training. We knew that simply setting a policy and providing general training in domestic violence prosecution would not be sufficient to ensure that all victims received appropriate treatment. If ADAs were ever going to be knowledgeable enough to draw for a jury the complete picture of certain violent relationships, we would need to teach them to be sensitive to issues of culture, language, and sexual orientation. Similarly, advocates would also need specialized training to be able to communicate effectively and access the proper services for victims.

In our first training, which we did district court by district court, we added a section on same-sex domestic violence. We highlighted the fears and concerns that victims have about disclosing their sexuality to prosecutors and advocates and about being outed in a public courtroom. Many prosecutors had not realized what a monumental decision it was for many gays and lesbians to declare their sexual orientation so publicly. They simply assumed that the victims' anger at having been victimized and their desire to see justice done would outweigh any concerns that someone might learn their sexual orientation. We discussed various community resources that could be liaisons between the victim and the DA's office and provide a sensitive advocate to accompany the victim to court for extra support.

Most important, we instructed ADAs and advocates that, as representatives of the Commonwealth, they were obligated to set the proper tone for all court proceedings in same-sex domestic violence cases; both by their own behavior and by affirmatively calling attention to it, no prosecutor or advocate should tolerate snickering from the gallery, snide comments of court officers, badgering cross-examinations of defense attorneys, or inappropriate remarks by judges. Although such objections would do little to change the attitudes underlying the behavior, we told them, they would put an immediate stop to the behavior itself and make the victim feel supported. We also made it clear that if homophobic or disrespectful behavior by either advocates or prosecutors was reported it would be dealt with as a serious infraction.

We also incorporated same-sex domestic violence in the trainings we did at the Boston Police Academy and at the many community-based workshops and forums to which we were invited. As part of a working group of domestic violence prosecutors and advocates who plan and present a yearly statewide conference on domestic violence, we made same-sex domestic violence issues a standard workshop on our agenda. The simple but unprecedented inclusion of same-sex domestic violence in all of the trainings we conducted created and reinforced intolerance of homophobia. We exploded myths, identified stereotypes, and affirmed that gay and lesbian relationships were normal and that partner violence made such relationships abnormal.

As time went on, we noticed an increase in the number of same-sex domestic violence cases being reported in Suffolk County either as a result of police involvement or as referrals from community-based advocacy programs. In one of the first such cases, we decided to teach by example.

Ann was a lesbian who had moved to Massachusetts several years ago from California. At the time, she was fleeing an extremely abusive relationship in which her partner had tried to kill her. She had a Ph.D. and worked at a prominent hospital. About nine months prior to coming to our attention, Ann had begun dating

Jane. Jane developed an immediate and unusually controlling attachment to Ann's 9-year-old daughter. Within two months of the relationship, Jane became quite controlling with Ann, dictating where she could go, who she could spend time with, and for how long. Ann was not allowed to associate with any of the friends she had before she started dating Jane.

Within four months of the relationship, Jane began to threaten Ann if she did anything to displease her. Initially, Jane was content with towering over Ann and screaming at her while poking her hard on her chest. That behavior escalated to the point at which the screaming would be accompanied by a shove or a slap. Ann terminated the relationship after an argument during which Ann was threatened, was shoved, and attempted to flee the apartment. Jane refused to allow Ann's daughter to leave and held her inside the apartment, against her will, until Ann called the police for help.

Thereafter, Jane repeatedly telephoned Ann at home and at work, screaming at her and threatening to beat or kill her. If Ann went to a particular club in Boston, Jane would appear. On one occasion, Jane followed her to the bathroom, shoved her up against a wall, and threatened to kill her if she "tried to keep [Jane] from [Ann's daughter]." Jane also flattened Ann's car tires. Ann obtained a restraining order and filed police reports about the incident involving her daughter, the telephone calls, and the incident in the nightclub. The problem was that all of the incidents occurred in separate jurisdictions. Ann's home was in one town, her job in another, the defendant's apartment in another, and the nightclub in still another.

When the case came to us, it was an opportunity to show the district court advocates and prosecutors what we expected of them in similar cases. We viewed the case not as four separate incidents but as a continuing series of acts of harassment and threats that constituted stalking under Massachusetts law, along with charges of assault and battery and malicious destruction of property. Because the appropriate jurisdiction for stalking is where the last incident of harassment or threats takes place, we were able to bring all of the charges in the court that had jurisdiction over the location of the Boston nightclub. Ann would not have to testify in four different trials in four different courts.

Even though it was very difficult for her, Ann stuck with the prosecution. We provided her with ongoing support and assis-

tance. Our positive relationships with agencies serving the gay and lesbian community enabled us to make the appropriate referrals. We created an environment that was safe and nonjudgmental. Once the charges were lodged against Jane, we discovered that three other women had sought and obtained restraining orders against her within the past year. Ironically, some of these same women's names appeared on the defendant's list of witnesses for trial. Jane's criminal record showed arrests for violent offenses, one of them assault with intent to murder, but they had all been dismissed, presumably because the alleged victims had refused to testify.

Ann and the other witnesses appeared on the day of trial ready to testify. When it became apparent that the Commonwealth was ready to proceed to trial, Jane's attorney began asking about the possibility of a plea bargain. Ultimately, with Ann's approval, Jane pleaded guilty to all charges and received a jail sentence, followed by two years of probation with requirements that she attend a program for lesbians who batter and have no contact whatsoever with Ann or her daughter.

Ann made a lengthy and eloquent victim impact statement to the judge prior to sentencing detailing the physical and emotional damage the defendant had done to her and her daughter. The courtroom was crowded with spectators, court officers, police officers, and other court personnel. Because it was clear that the Commonwealth took the case seriously and treated the victim with respect, there was no snickering, no laughter, and no inappropriate comments or references to the sexual orientation of the victim or the defendant. Ann was very pleased with the outcome of the case and with her treatment by the system. She is now part of a panel of trainers that conducts workshops at the Boston Police Academy on same-sex domestic violence.

Conclusion

Our experiences as women, and as advocate and prosecutor, have shaped our goals and our attitudes toward what can be accomplished in cases of same-sex domestic violence prosecution. Ann's experience does not yet typify what happens in these cases, but similar outcomes have been achieved in the district courts since. Her case represents change, which in a process as resistant and impersonal as the criminal justice system, also represents hope for greater change in the future.

Notes

1. All defendant and plaintiff names used in this chapter are fictitious.

2. The option to appeal a conviction and try the case before a jury also applied if the defendant actually pleaded guilty before the judge in the bench session. Defendants were also not prohibited from pleading guilty in the bench session, appealing the conviction, and pleading guilty again in the jury session in an attempt to get a lighter sentence from the jury session judge.

PART III

ORGANIZING COALITIONS/BUILDING COMMUNITIES

7

History, Culture, and Identity

What Makes GLBT Battering Different

Charlene Allen
Beth Leventhal

In the summer of 1997 on the TV show *Ellen*, the first U.S. show to have a gay or lesbian main character, Ellen tells her shy and unassuming father that she's a lesbian. Somehow telling him that she doesn't have a partner is the last straw for him. He explodes in anger and disbelief, shouting, "How the hell can you be gay all by yourself?"

There is important, if unintended, truth in those words. Although you can of course be gay without a partner, there's a sense in which you really *can't* be gay, lesbian, bisexual, or transgendered all by yourself. In a culture as homo/bi/transphobic and heterosexist as ours, people desperately need communities to provide strength, companionship, and identity. Shared culture, shared values, and a

AUTHORS' NOTE: The authors gratefully acknowledge Tina D'Elia and Anne King for their input into this chapter.

sense of community can make life as a gay, lesbian, bisexual, or transgendered (GLBT) person a more full and rich experience. Our communities provide social forums, rites of passage and rituals for celebration, and bodies of art and literature that combat isolation and allow us to explore our full potentials.

It is because we face oppression and because we have built unique communities that battering is different in GLBT relationships than in heterosexual ones. Although the tools that batterers use to maintain control—physical, sexual, economic, and emotional abuse—cut across lines of gender identity and sexual orientation (as they do across race, class, ethnicity, age, and ability), the specific behavior of a particular batterer will always reflect the community in which a couple lives. All batterers exploit vulnerabilities and play on community values and resources (or lack thereof) to their best advantage. As a result, battering in GLBT relationships may look different in some ways from what we expect from male-to-female battering. Understanding these differences is critical to recognizing battering outside its stereotypical heterosexual form.

Context

In heterosexual relationships, men and women have been traditionally apportioned unequal power in marriage or romantic relationships. Legal history teaches us that at the founding of American common law, men had not only the legal right but an accompanying moral responsibility to maintain control of their wives (Bartlett, 1993). The tactics allowed them were many, including physical correction. Although the law no longer supports overt violence against women, the culture continues to uphold these long-established relationship dynamics. It is no longer expected that a man should beat his wife when the dinner is late, but it may well be accepted that he show outrage about it. It may not be expected that a woman remain at home with her children, but a man is likely to be supported in insisting that she work fewer hours or maintain primary responsibility for child care. Because the power is unequal, it is easy to accept the man's insistence that the woman fulfill her socially defined obligations. Battering comes into play when men take the not-so-large leap from a self-righteous insistence to enforcement through physical, emotional, economic, or sexually abusive means.

⤬ Unequal power between men and women is the context in which heterosexual battering exists. It is also the context in which most Americans grow up. A relationship model in which one party holds greater power and control therefore provides the foundation for GLBT battering as well. The cultural differences, however, shaped by both the multiple layers of oppression GLBT people face and by the particulars—both positive and negative—of the subcultures we have developed, make for a profoundly different context in which battering is able to thrive. For example, although a straight batterer threatens to call social services because his partner is "a lousy mother who's never home with her kids," a gay batterer might threaten her partner on the basis of her partner's lesbianism. The straight batterer plays on the value of "attentive motherhood" in his culture, and the lesbian batterer uses the homophobic social services institution to meet her ends. Both are attempts to gain control through fear and both will cause intense emotional pain, but each attack is effective because it is designed to hit where it hurts the most, depending on the culture of the victim. ⤬

Most of us are not raised with a positive sense of queer identity, history, or wisdom passed down through generations about how to cope with gay oppression (and experience in coping with other oppressions doesn't necessarily translate). Negative messages about ourselves as GLBT people therefore have free rein in which to instill shame, fear, and self-hatred. GLBT people learn and live with societal hatred, fear, and disgust directed at us, even before we come out.

We face threats or acts of verbal, physical, and sexual violence from strangers on the street and, many times, from family members or acquaintances. Many of us have been disowned by families of origin after coming out to them.

The institutions that serve as cultural gatekeepers have been active participants in our oppression. Many mainstream religious institutions teach that nonheterosexual people and relationships are immoral, unnatural, sinful, or—more insidiously—that heterosexual (and *only* heterosexual) family life is synonymous with godliness.

The legal system historically has been one of the largest perpetrators and supporters of violence against us. Many of us have lost custody of or visitation rights to our children because of heterosexist courts. Police have routinely raided gay bars and raped and beaten both the men and women found there. Although in some major cities the police now have liaisons to the gay community, police violence against GLBT people (as well as against communities of color and undocumented people) remains an issue. It is only relatively recently that some police departments and courts have begun to take queer-bashing seriously. Legislatively, anti-GLBT oppression has been mani-fested through sodomy laws (upheld in 1986 by the Supreme Court in *Bowers v. Hardwick*) and through anti-gay legislation such as the so-called Defense of Marriage Act, which denied access to marriage to same-sex couples. When GLBT people seek basic human rights such as housing and employment, we are falsely accused of demanding "special rights," against which communities have then tried to legis-late.

The domestic violence within our communities has everything to do with the hostility and condemnation directed against them. Such a climate encourages self-loathing, separates us from one another and from the straight world, creates a false sense of safety and security within the confines of our communities, and leaves us in fear of the consequences of "airing our dirty laundry" in public. GLBT batterers can use the conditions created by homo/bi/transphobia and heterosex-ism to wield highly effective weapons against their partners. The following is a discussion of how GLBT battering reflects the culture of our communities as they exist within the context of this oppression.

Batterer Tactics

Isolation

One of the reasons why batterers are able to maintain control over their partners is that they isolate them from people and activities that could either refute the batterers' messages—that the battered partner is stupid, worthless, incompetent, crazy, oversensitive, impossible to be involved with, ugly, a bad parent, and lucky that the batterer puts up with him or her—or offer such tangible support as shelter, financial assistance, or transportation. The dominant culture assists the GLBT batterer by doing much of his or her work of isolation ahead of time.

For instance, resources used by many battered heterosexual women, such as the legal system and battered women's shelters, often are not available to battered GLBT people. Because of the legal system's history of (and, in most areas, current) violence against us, many GLBT people do not even consider accessing the system as a source of protection against battering. They may fear being ridiculed or being arrested themselves, particularly if they are immigrants, whether legal or undocumented. They may fear having the nature of their relationship become a matter of public record, especially if either one of them holds the type of job in which GLBT people have been especially unwelcome (for instance, teachers, members of the military, and others). They may fear that the police will beat the batterer once they arrest him or her, or that they will not intervene if the batterer is attacked for being queer while in jail. (Most people who are battered do not want their batterers to be hurt or get into trouble—they just want them to stop battering.) And although we are not aware of comprehensive research on the issue, anecdotally it appears that police are more likely to make no arrest or dual arrests in cases of GLBT battering, and courts are more likely to issue no restraining orders at all or mutual orders.

Battered women's programs by and large have been hetero-sexually focused in their services, outreach materials, and staff train-ings. As programs for women, most do not work with gay or bisexual men or transgendered (TG) people (whom they usually define as men, regardless of how the individual battered TG person identifies him- or herself or lives his or her life). Many programs also have refused to serve openly lesbian or bisexual women, or they have not done the work necessary to create an environment safe enough for lesbians or bisexual women to participate in services (for example, developing nondiscrimination policies, confronting anti-GLBT comments or ac-tions within the organization or among service participants, providing staff training on homo/bi/transphobia and GLBT battering, imple-menting policies and procedures to prevent batterers from accessing services or working in the program, and hiring formerly battered lesbians or bisexual women). All of these institutional forces contrib-ute to the especially acute isolation of GLBT people and to the enhanced power of GLBT batterers.

In addition to lack of access to formal services, if the battered partner is not out to family, friends, or coworkers, he or she is by definition isolated. If no one in your everyday life knows that you're in a relationship, it is not possible to ask them if they think that what's going on with your partner is normal. Nor can you ask to stay with them if you decide to leave your batterer. If the battered partner has come out to family and been disowned, he or she will obviously not be able to turn to them for support. If he or she has not been disowned but has still met with homo/bi/transphobia from family, friends, or co-workers, he or she may feel compelled to present a picture-perfect image of the relationship to disprove negative stereotypes. In addition, if the batterer is the only other GLBT person that the battered partner knows, then, ironically, leaving the batterer may mean leaving the only sense of identity he or she has, the only mirror that can reflect back a sense of having a place in the world.

All of these factors leave the person being battered with few or no places to turn for validation and safety. In this context of culturally imposed isolation, typical batterer comments such as "So-and-so doesn't like me, I don't want us/you to see them anymore" or "No one else will ever love you like I do" or "Who's going to believe you?" carry different meaning and increased weight.

Blaming the Victim for the Abuse/
Undermining Pride and Identity

All batterers try to destroy the sense of self and self-worth of their partners; not only will battered partners be more inclined to accept whatever the batterer does to them, but they also will be less likely to feel they can or deserve to leave the batterer. GLBT batterers have at their disposal the weapons of their own and their partner's internalized oppression to help erase their partner's sense of pride in being queer (and therefore, any pride in simply being). For example, a batterer may tell his gay male partner he doesn't deserve any better because "you're nothing but a fucking faggot." Another batterer might declare to her bi or lesbian partner that "this is just how relationships between women are—if you don't like it, why don't you just go back to men?" Still another might tell his or her TG partner that it doesn't matter if he or she calls the cops, "Do you think they're going to help a freak like you?"

Blaming the victim may also look like absolute denial of the abuse. For example, the batterer of a TG person may tell them that they bruise easily or are oversensitive because of the hormones they are taking. This common form of abuse simultaneously denies any wrongdoing by the batterer and blames the victim for "overreacting," whether physically or emotionally.

The threat of or actual verbal, physical, and sexual violence we face from strangers on the street or from family members or acquaintances can also leave us vulnerable to feeling responsible for abuse in our relationships. Because violence against us is sanctioned, it may be difficult for those in our communities who are battered not to internalize blame for it.

Being battered as a GLBT person also can lead to long-lasting questions of identity and pride. The fact that we exist on the fringe of society in and of itself undermines a positive formation of pride and identity. When a batterer exploits the very vulnerabilities created by oppression, the victim may not be able to find respite from abuse. How, particularly if you are battered in your first relationship after coming out, do you separate the experience of being queer from the experience of being battered? How do you celebrate Pride Day—the one day we are supposed to be able to walk the streets relatively unafraid—when you need to hide not from the violence of straight people but from a member of your own community who is stalking you? How do you feel proud of who you are when you carry scars on your body and soul from your partner?

Community/Cultural Norms

Norms within our own subcultures support battering and isolate victims as well. For instance, many GLBT people believe that if domestic violence exists in our communities, it takes the form of mutual fighting and does not reflect the same power and control dynamic as heterosexual battering. Among many men, the notion that one guy would hit another is not considered unusual—men get into fights and it's no big deal. Men are supposed to be able to defend themselves from other men's violence, they are not supposed to be victims. The idea that violence within a relationship might be part of a larger dynamic of power and control is only just beginning to be recognized in GLBT communities. When we do acknowledge that there may be a power differential in our relationships, misconceptions and stereotypes can lead to harmful conclusions.

Sexual violence within relationships between men has been particularly difficult to acknowledge. Gay culture often holds that men are supposed to want and enjoy sex pretty much whenever it is available from someone they are attracted to. So if sex is forced, is it rape, or is it just bad sex? The community offers very little support to a man who identifies as a survivor of rape by another queer man, particularly his date or partner. In fact, the culture is so out of touch with the concept of sexual assault between men that the word "rape" is commonly used to describe initiating a relationship or making the first move; for example, "I couldn't tell if he wanted me to leave him alone or rape him."

In the women's community, attitudes toward butch/femme roles can lead to unintended support for batterers in either role. Femmes who batter can claim that they are "weaker," or "gentler," and play on the misconception (both within and outside GLBT communities) that being butch is the same as being male, that butches are therefore stronger, more powerful. When the community buys into these stereotypes, we obscure the possibility of abuse and make it far more difficult for the battered partner to get support. For example, a femme batterer can abuse her butch partner by forcing sexual activity that her partner does not want. Because "modesty" about sexuality is supposed to be a feminine trait, the batterer can deflect responsibility for her sexual abusiveness by saying that the battered partner just isn't butch enough.

A corresponding set of stereotypes can come into play when a butch partner is a batterer. In this instance, the belief that the butch partner is the "real lesbian" can allow both the battered partner and the community in general to sympathize with the batterer and be reluctant to hold her accountable because, as a butch woman, she gets treated so poorly by society at large as a more visible, more "out" lesbian. Community members may also falsely define or overlook her abusiveness as just part of being butch.

GLBT people can also easily dismiss battering as a problem for some other part of the community. A radical gay male activist, for example, can say that battering happens only among those assimilated men who try to emulate heterosexuals. The "straight-acting and appearing" man, meanwhile, can blame those "sissy faggots" for being too effeminate and therefore victimlike. Among women, feminists can say battering happens to those who are not politically aware enough to not "play the victim." Those who criticize role-playing can relegate battering to butch/femme relationships. Separatists can blame the S/M community. The effect of such thinking is both to deny the possibility of abuse in one's own segment of the community as well as to deflect responsibility for addressing the problem as the community-wide issue that it is.

The lack of awareness of or, in some cases, refusal to acknowledge domestic violence as it exists *throughout* our communities makes it very difficult for those who are battered to remain comfortable as a part of the community. We need to understand that anyone with the desire to control his or her partner and the willingness to do whatever it takes to achieve, consolidate, and maintain that control can batter.

Conclusion

It is essential to remember both the similarities and differences between heterosexual and GLBT battering. Although the same dynamics of coercion and control are evident no matter who the partners are, the sexual orientation and gender identity of the partners strongly influence exactly how the batterer will achieve that control, how the battering will affect the battered partner, and whether there will be any resources for safety and support. The more we learn about the different ways that battering looks, the more we will be able to recognize it in *all* of our communities, and the more we will be able to build overall and community-specific strategies to end domestic violence.

Reference

Bartlett, K. T. (1993). *Gender and the law: Theory, doctrine, and commentary*. Boston: Little, Brown.

8

Lesbians Organizing
Lesbians Against Battering

Ann Russo

Lesbian battering is not often recognized as a significant social issue, despite the efforts of lesbian activists over the past 15 years to make it one.[1] The battered women's movement in the United States mostly has ignored, minimized, or marginalized lesbian battering. The movement has primarily used the heterosexual lens of gender inequality and male dominance to understand and respond to violence against women. In this framework, men are always the perpetrators of violence and women are always the victims. To discuss women as perpetrators of abuse and violence disrupts this analysis and complicates the picture, and thus many feminists tend to shy away from taking on the issue.

Similarly, the lesbian and gay rights movement focuses primarily on hate crimes perpetrated and condoned by heterosexuals and the heterosexist society. Same-sex battering confounds a discourse that sees lesbians and gay men primarily as victims, rather than perpetrators, of violence. Moreover, to discuss lesbians and gay men as

AUTHOR'S NOTE: Very special thanks to Lourdes Torres, Cindy Jenefsky, Barbara Schulman, Suzi Hart, Mary Bertin, Sandy Lundy, and Beth Kelly, Frida Furman, and Teresia Hinga of the BFW writing group for their support, insights, questions, and suggestions.

83

perpetrators of violence seemingly contradicts efforts to dismantle the heterosexist myth of sexual and physical aggression that often is displaced onto queer identities. In this chapter, I reframe the approach to lesbian battering in the hope of encouraging broader lesbian interest and involvement in helping to stop it.

In an effort to gain legitimacy for the problem of lesbian battering within the (heterosexual) battered women's movement, lesbian activists and our allies sought to establish that lesbian battering is just as serious as heterosexual battering—just as violent, hurtful, life threatening, manipulative, damaging. To challenge the myths that minimize, trivialize, or deny the brutality of lesbian battering, and the ideology of women's passivity and nonviolence (Lobel, 1986; Lundy, 1994; Russo, 1991, 1992), we have argued that abuse is abuse no matter what the gender, race, and class identities of the victim and the perpetrator (Lobel, 1986; Renzetti, 1992). We have shown the similarities between heterosexual and lesbian batterers' methods and strategies of control, and heterosexual and lesbian victims' experiences of powerlessness and victimization. The differences between lesbian and heterosexual battering, we have argued, are the homophobic context that lesbian batterers use as an additional strategy of control and domination and the heterosexism of the social institutions (police, courts, social services) that perpetuate battering because they are inaccessible or hostile to lesbians (Lobel, 1986; Lundy, 1994; Russo, 1992).

Although demonstrating the similarities between heterosexual and lesbian battering has helped increase recognition of lesbian battering as a legitimate issue, I am not sure it has been successful in mobilizing lesbians to take on battering as a lesbian issue. Many of the lesbians who I know are active in politics—feminist, gay and lesbian, progressive, left, antiracist organizing. Many have been involved in feminist activism against men's violence against women and against racist and homophobic hate crimes. Yet when I bring up lesbian battering and the need for their support and participation, tension and discomfort rise to the surface and the distance between us begins to take shape.

A few years ago I labeled the primary problem of lesbian resistance to addressing lesbian battering as one of denial (Russo, 1992). The reasons for the denial specific to lesbian battering are shared by many disempowered communities struggling against institutionalized racism, educational and economic inequalities, police brutality, hate crimes, and poverty, in addition to homophobia. They include the fear that addressing lesbian battering in a heterosexist context will increase homophobia as well as sexism, racism, and classism; the feeling that the most significant problems lesbians face as lesbians are homophobia, heterosexism, and bigotry from outside our relationships and groups; the fear that addressing the problem will divide already disempowered and struggling communities; and the fear that it may lead to lesbian despair and disillusionment about being lesbians. Recognizing, understanding, and addressing these fears is essential if lesbian activists want to break down the denial about the violence within our relationships.

After working on lesbian battering for several years, I began to reconsider the strategy of mostly stressing similarities between heterosexual battering and lesbian battering. Much of this reconsideration is connected to the critical analysis offered by feminists of color of the mainstream battered women's movement for its limited relevance to communities of color. For instance, feminists of color often criticize the exclusive focus on male versus female violence; the tendency to analyze men's violence against women exclusively in terms of male domination in an otherwise social, economic, and cultural vacuum; and the uncritical reliance on the criminal justice system as the first line of defense in stopping the violence (e.g., Almeida, 1993; Crenshaw, 1994; Davis, 1981; hooks, 1984, 1989). Socially constructed differences and structural inequalities between white Euro-American women and women of color and between middle-class women and working-class poor women as well as the differences between corresponding groups of men, make the experience of violence and the institutional responses to that violence different. Thus, many call for attention to these differences when addressing the issue at the personal, familial, community, institutional, and political levels. In other words, we need analyses and strategies that are context dependent and are shaped by cultural, historical, linguistic, political, economic, and social factors specific to the communities in which we are organizing.

Similarly, efforts to organize and/or to provide services to lesbians would benefit from context-specific strategies. The context with which I am most familiar is the Boston area with lesbian networks that are mostly, but not exclusively, middle-class, white, urban, and politically involved in lesbian, gay, and feminist activism. This chapter is shaped by my experiences in this context, and I am not presuming that the analysis offered in this chapter would necessarily apply to another context. My argument is that lesbians—individuals and specific groups—might be more likely to connect to the issue of lesbian battering if we talked about it in terms specific to their experiences of lesbian relationships and community. We might incorporate these specifics into the analyses and strategies to challenge and stop mistreatment, abuse, and violence among lesbians in our networks and communities. Drawing on the particulars of lesbian experience in our various contexts might encourage broader lesbian identification and involvement with the efforts to prevent and stop battering.

Considering Lesbian Contexts

My experience has been that lesbian lives are different from those of heterosexual women and men. First of all, the daily lives of self-identified lesbians who are connected with lesbian-identified communities—our sense of self and safety, our social and personal relationships, our activities—often are shaped by lesbian identification. Living in a heterosexist and homophobic society shapes lesbian yearning for love, companionship, acceptance, and community. It influences our personal and social relationships, work, education, religion, recreation. Many of us experience a sense of isolation, social difference, ostracism, or hostility from family and non-lesbigay friends, as well as from the larger society that defines and treats us as deviant, pathological, sick, man-hating, aggressive, and violent, among other things. This hostility compounds the difficulty of facing what we might be doing to each other in our relationships. It is hard to address lesbian battering when many of us are tired of fighting to protect and build personal and social relationships in a hostile, homophobic society. Acknowledging mistreatment, abuse, and violence, even among ourselves, may feel like a reinforcement of what dominant cultures say about us. Many lesbians struggle with the basics of survival—feeding ourselves and our children, keeping a roof over our heads, creating a life for ourselves and our friends and lovers. Moreover, many of us have been hurt by homophobia, racial and class discrimination, sexual assault, and battering. Directly addressing abuse by members of our own communities often brings to the surface the pain of betrayal, hurt, anger, and loss that many of us have experienced, and many would rather avoid such feelings. As activists, we do a disservice to lesbians when we minimize these fears and difficulties.

In our efforts to draw lesbian attention to lesbian battering, activists and service providers must not reinforce self-hatred, blame, and internalized homophobia. Political analyses and strategies against lesbian battering should affirm lesbian lives, lesbian friendships, lesbian sexual and intimate relationships, and lesbian communities in all of their rich diversity while at the same time confronting the mistreatment, abuse, battering, and assault that continue to hurt and destroy lesbians.

Although some of us have had to rethink the idea of lesbian utopia because of experiences or knowledge of battering, as organizers we must not communicate hopelessness with regard to lesbian relationships. When we document and publicize how lesbians can and do mistreat, abuse, or batter other lesbians, we must not equate these behaviors with lesbian identities. We need to talk about the benefits of challenging the attitudes and behaviors that hurt and sometimes destroy us. To do this, we must communicate a faith that lesbians have the capacity to stop the violence and that we will all benefit positively from doing so.

Because dominant social and cultural institutions define lesbians as deviant and abnormal, the language we use to describe lesbians and the problems lesbians face is very important. Although the label "battered lesbian" has helped those victimized to name and recognize the harm of battering, it can be stifling as an identity of transformation and self-determination. It does not offer a positive and forward-moving identity. Many lesbians are uncomfortable with the label because it does not accurately reflect our self-conceptions, despite experiences of abuse and violence. bell hooks (1989) suggests that many women do not accept the label "battered woman" because it "appears to strip us of dignity, to deny that there has been any integrity in the relationships that we are in" (p. 88). Although hooks recognizes that "we are indeed often scarred, often damaged in ways that do set us apart from those who have not experienced a similar wounding," she suggests that part of healing is removing the scar. She writes, "This is an empowering process that should not be diminished by labels that imply this wounding experience is the most significant aspect of identity" (p. 89). The danger of conceptualizing lesbians who have been battered solely in terms of victimization, hurt, and damage is that it reinforces how social and cultural institutions have constructed lesbians in general—as fucked-up women who are abusive and violent or who have become lesbians because of histories of abuse and violence.

I am not suggesting that we ignore the victimization, the isolation, the lack of support, the pain of betrayal, or the despair of battering. Speaking out about the harm done and labeling the experiences as battering, rape, incestuous assault, or attempted murder are essential components of healing and self-determination. However, identifying lesbians who have experienced abuse as only victims and survivors of violence eventually reinforces our status as victims by reducing us to what someone else did to us. When we only describe the individual damage done, it can lead to depression and despair. This strategy within the broader feminist movement against violence contributes to its inability to sustain a broad spectrum of support and active engagement (hooks, 1989).

The lives of lesbians are not simplistic, nor are they stagnant. I have seen tremendous courage, power, endurance, and strength in women, myself included, who have struggled to change or leave abusive relationships. Reclaiming our rights to control our own minds and bodies is a liberating experience, to say the least. When we move from an exclusive focus on victimization to one that includes self-determination and personal power, we expand our vision of change to more than providing validation for the harm done. I believe we will be able to grow in numbers and strength when we emphasize the ways in which work against lesbian battering encourages lesbians to improve and change our lives and our relationships.

One way to do this would be to explore, draw on, and publicize the strengths of lesbians who have experienced, survived, resisted, and challenged violence. We all, in different ways and at different times, have actively sought to change our lives. Why not label ourselves lesbians who can and have left, escaped, fought back, resisted, survived, and thrived? Why not present ourselves and our efforts against battering as lesbians who are actively improving lesbian lives, relationships, and communities? Imagine going to a speak-out on battering and hearing lesbians talk about the pain of the battering, the isolation and the lack of support, and what enabled us to leave the perpetrators, to fight back, and to regain control of our bodies and our lives. Such stories would not only document the abuse and show the strengths of women who have been able to change their lives, but they would also offer concrete examples of what assisted them in their struggles and triumphs.

Lesbian activists might want to publicize success stories of lesbians who refused or resisted abuse and violence. We could promote support groups as places where lesbians get together, share stories, regain autonomy and strength, and change the condition of their lives. When we think about writing testimonies, placards for demonstrations, and pamphlets, why not celebrate lesbian resisters—lesbians who don't take shit from anyone, lesbians who have left batterers or stood up to harassers or bullies, lesbians who don't tolerate abuse in any form, lesbians who challenge lesbians to think creatively about how to refuse any form of complicity with others whose behavior is abusive or violent? Locating our strengths, our courage, and our power and recognizing what makes them possible are essential to sustaining involvement in a movement for social change. In our efforts to break down denial about the abuse, we must also publicize the possibilities for and benefits of change.

When we offer hope for change, we invite involvement. Creating change in ourselves and in our relationships is possible, and such changes increase the potential for us to come together as stronger communities in the face of increasingly hostile forces in this country. We need to build a movement that enables lesbians to make the changes necessary to challenge and fight back against victimization and mistreatment in all of its many forms.

In our efforts to mobilize lesbians as lesbians, we might want to draw on some lesbian-specific traditions and histories. When lesbian activists against battering emphasize the similarities between lesbian and heterosexual relationships, we minimize the historical and social differences between us. Although it is true that lesbians, and women in general, can and do abuse power and control in ways similar to men, this does not mean that lesbians, even lesbian batterers, are the equivalent of heterosexual men, or that lesbians in general exist in relationships that mimic heterosexual relations and dynamics. Lesbians who batter, unlike heterosexual men, do not have the backing of the legal and social establishment. This does not mean that they should not be held accountable or that their violence should not be stopped but that the differences are meaningful. For instance, the reasons for police indifference to battering are different for lesbian than for heterosexual couples. The police do not support the right of one

lesbian to beat up her lover nor do they honor the right of familial
privacy, which may be factors in their nonintervention in heterosexual
partnerships. It is more likely that the police do not care if a lesbian
beats up her partner, or that they assume that violence is just part of
lesbian culture, or that they do not take the violence seriously because
it is two women and no man is involved. The differences are significant
in terms of how battering and its prevention are talked about both
within the mainstream criminal justice system and in lesbian communities.

Contemporary lesbians as a social group do not have a distinct
historical or legal tradition that mandates monogamous, "till death do
us part," marriage-type relations. Rather than perceiving the lack of
"marriage" among lesbians as a deficiency, lesbian organizers against
lesbian battering might frame it in a positive light. Because of this
history, lesbians may actively encourage each other to leave relationships that are unsatisfactory or destructive or to get assistance to
actively change the dynamics of the relationship. Similarly, lesbians
are less likely than heterosexual women to be in a relationship of
complete economic dependence. Why not encourage economic independence as a preventative measure against illegitimate power
between lesbians in a social and economic context in which money
equals power?

Contemporary lesbians in the United States also do not have a
distinct and established tradition of one lesbian assuming an inherent
right to control and own another lesbian. We do not have a lesbian-
specific tradition of stigmatizing and ostracizing those lesbians who
leave relationships. We do not have a lesbian-specific established
religion that encourages us to accept mistreatment or abuse. In fact,
lesbians have a tradition of resistance to compulsory heterosexuality
in this society. Lesbian activists against lesbian battering might draw
on the historical struggles for autonomy and independence that many
lesbians have waged in a (hetero)sexist world as models for refusing
and resisting abuse at the hands of others, including other lesbians. I
am not claiming these traditions as absolutes for every lesbian or every
lesbian community. I am suggesting that lesbian activists might draw
on the distinctive aspects of lesbian living that could be used to
challenge negative, abusive, or violent behavior and to encourage
lesbians to envision, create, and insist on relationships that are rich,
complex, and grounded in mutual respect and dignity. Some of these
redefined strengths might be incorporated into outreach efforts,

pamphlets, and public presentations as a way to connect more specifically with lesbians.

Rethinking "Battering"

One recurring issue that has been raised about lesbian battering has been confusion about what behavior constitutes battering. There seems to be an underlying fear that the label might be used too broadly when applied to lesbians. In *Naming the Violence,* Barbara Hart (1986) carefully and concretely defines lesbian battering as

> that pattern of violent and coercive behaviors whereby a lesbian seeks to control the thoughts, beliefs, or conduct of her intimate partner or to punish the intimate for resisting the perpetrator's control over her. . . . Lesbian battering is the pattern of intimidation, coercion, terrorism or violence, the sum of all past acts of violence and the promises of future violence, that achieves enhanced power and control for the perpetrator over her partner. (pp. 173-177)

In my discussions with lesbian friends and acquaintances, however, this kind of clarity does not exist. "Battering" is used to describe a variety of behaviors and contexts. It is used to describe many different behaviors, including emotional and verbal abuse, physical or sexual assaults that happen only one time, and physical battery and torture. It is used to refer to a variety of relational structures from intimate couples to friends to acquaintances to coworkers to those characterized more formally by inequality, such as employee/employer or therapist/client relations.

Yet there are differences between mistreatment, abusive behavior, battering, sexual assault, torture, attempted murder, and murder; all abuse is not the same, even though it all may be connected in a person's experience. Moreover, the sources of the problem and ultimately the solution may vary depending on the relational structure. This is not to minimize the significance of the hurt or pain caused by "lesser" or "greater" forms of mistreatment or abuse. But the experiences may be qualitatively different and thus may need qualitatively different responses. We can include all forms of abuse and relational structures in our discussions, but indiscriminately lumping them all under one

label—"battering"—may discourage rather than encourage an exploration of the options available to address particular situations.

One result of these confusions about the term "battering" is that
many lesbians simply steer away from the discussion of intralesbian
violence. I believe it is useful to make distinctions between the kinds
of violence in an effort to clarify the range of options that a lesbian
might have for dealing with the issue, either individually or collectively. If activists were to address the varieties of violence as well as
options, we might encourage more lesbians to be open to a discussion.
For instance, lesbians who are being mistreated but do not see it as
battering might more readily label the treatment as unacceptable and
worthy of change despite the fact that it is not labeled full-fledged
"battering." Lesbians who are being physically beaten on a routine
basis might be able to define more clearly that what they are experiencing is not mistreatment but something more systematic, which, if
not addressed, could be (or will be) lethal. The variety of definitions
may be helpful to lesbians, both in and out of abusive relationships,
to find themselves along a continuum and from that vantage point,
make decisions about the need for change.

Confronting Lesbian Batterers

Many lesbians with whom I have spoken are uncomfortable with
the idea that some lesbians are labeled as batterers. They feel that this
labeling divides our communities rather than strengthens them. As a
white antiracist activist, I often hear similar arguments from white
middle-class lesbians and feminists. Resistance to addressing existing
divisions is based on a belief that the only way to "protect" a community is to be uncritical and supportive. It is always easier to talk
about accountability and personal responsibility when the perpetrator
is not one of "our" own. It is easier to point the finger at right-wing
Republicans for their racism and classism than to address practices
of exclusion and bigotry when perpetrated by lesbians or feminists
in our own social groups. Similarly, it has been easier to join the
heterosexual battered women's movement and decry heterosexual
men for their violence against women but much more difficult to decry
women engaged in similar behavior against their children or their
lesbian partners.

However, the refusal to confront battering and batterers ultimately allows the violence to continue unquestioned. Meanwhile, the lesbian who is being battered remains isolated. It seems to me that lesbians who mistreat, abuse, and batter other lesbians should be called on to stop their behavior by other lesbians who are connected to the women involved. We need to encourage lesbians in our social groups, networks, and communities to intervene when we know that mistreatment or abuse is occurring. Personal responsibility and the accountability of batterers must be contextually and collectively determined. These discussions are often fraught with tension and mistrust.

When the issue of accountability is raised, some argue that lesbians who batter are in need of our support as lesbians. For instance, Melanie Kaye/Kantrowitz (1992) criticizes what she perceives as a strategy of ostracizing or excluding batterers from events, forums, or general communities. In response to potential exclusion, she asks,

> Why is this? So our communities remain pure? Do we think we can shove wrongdoers "out there," like garbage, for someone else to clean up? Where are they supposed to go? Who will deal with our abusers, our shadow, our difficult and dangerous ones, if we don't? (p. 37)

Kaye/Kantrowitz's questions sidestep the issue of accountability and erase the life of the lesbian being battered, who in many cases is being treated like "garbage" by this "difficult and dangerous one." Yet the strategies of handling batterers do need to be discussed more thoroughly within lesbian groups and networks.

Within the heterosexual battered women's movement, a major assumption has been that heterosexual male batterers are mostly incapable of change. Perpetrators are demonized, and criminalization is often seen as the most effective solution to battering. Many seem to believe that stronger, more consistent punishment is the goal, and thus they sometimes seem to give up on the possibilities for broad-based social, cultural, and political change. In a society quick to criminalize lesbians and the violent behavior of anyone associated with the "underclass," it is important that we not contribute to the demonization of lesbians or envision criminalization as the primary solution to battering. That is not to say that lesbians who are being beaten, threatened, stalked, and tortured should be discouraged from seeking assistance from the criminal justice system. It is to say that in a movement for social justice, legal action against batterers is a limited goal because it frames the issue as one of individual pathology rather than one grounded in social and community relations. Our public discourse that constructs batterers as inherently violent criminals who are incapable of change seems antithetical to liberation politics. As an activist committed to social change, I believe we must emphasize the need to collectively change the contexts of our lives so that violence is not so endemic. This means recognizing that lesbians who are abusive or violent can and should stop their behaviors. If we do not believe that men and women, whether heterosexual, gay, lesbian, or bisexual, have the capacity to change, then I am not sure why we perceive ourselves as being engaged in a movement for social change.

I do not believe the long-term strategy to preventing battering is to simply get rid of those labeled as abusers and batterers. This method assumes that the problem lies with individuals, not with the social relations in a community. If we agree that abuse emanates from and takes place within social, political, and cultural contexts, then the burden does not simply lie with the individual. Families, friends, social groups, networks, and communities who participate in violence as passive bystanders or who actively minimize or rationalize the behaviors are also responsible. This is a social problem, not an individual one, in which we must all seek to take some responsibility. If we want to stop battering in our specific communities, we must go beyond simply indicting individual lesbians as batterers, although in the immediacy of circumstances, this is a necessary first step. It is essential, on the one hand, that we understand that battering is not mutual, that it is systemic control and power exerted by one over another, and that it must be made an unacceptable practice in our communities. But on the other hand, we must understand that people who batter are neither inherently nor inevitably batterers who are incapable of change. As members of families, groups, and networks, we are also responsible for the perpetuation of the problem when we do not address it until it is too late.

Conclusion

The purpose of this chapter has been to encourage a reframing of mistreatment, abuse, and violence in lesbian relationships. The idea is to shift the approach from a mainstream heterosexual approach to one that is lesbian specific, and furthermore, one that is sensitive to the particularities of the context in which the organizing is taking place. The specificity is essential if our desire is to address the particular, and often different, needs, concerns, and issues that lesbians face within our particular locations. Moreover, given the larger context of homophobia and heterosexism, lesbian activists and service providers must offer lesbians ways to address the problems without exacerbating internalized self-hate and homophobia and with an eye toward improved relationships and communities. Our efforts against mistreatment and abuse must be grounded in an appreciation of the strengths, traditions, and positive aspects of lesbian relationships and communities. In this way, we can draw on our strengths rather than our weaknesses in our organizing efforts. This shift in perspective might broaden lesbian involvement and motivation to work to prevent and stop the mistreatment and abuse in lesbian relationships. And finally, I am seeking to make the issue a community issue rather than an individual one. As I see it, the possibilities for real and substantial improvement depend on changes within our respective communities and in the broader society.

Note

1. For the purposes of this chapter, when I use the term "lesbian," I am referring to lesbians who self-identify as lesbians or gay and who have some connection with lesbian/gay communities. For those who do not identify with this label or with a lesbian/gay community, other organizing analyses and strategies will have to be developed.

References

Almeida, R. V. (1993). Unexamined assumptions and service delivery systems: Feminist theory and racial exclusions. *Journal of Feminist Family Therapy, 5*(1), 3-23.
Crenshaw, K. W. (1994). Mapping the margins: Intersectionality and violence. In M. Fineman & R. Mykitiuk (Eds.), *The public nature of private violence* (pp. 93-118). New York: Routledge.
Davis, A. (1981). *Women, race and class.* New York: Random House.
Hart, B. (1986). Lesbian battering: An examination. In K. Lobel (Ed.), *Naming the violence: Speaking out about lesbian battering* (pp. 173-189). Seattle, WA: Seal Press.
hooks, b. (1984). *Feminist theory: From margin to center.* Boston: South End Press.

hooks, b. (1989). *Talking back: Thinking feminist, thinking black.* Boston: South End Press.

Kaye/Kantrowitz, M. (1992). *The issue is power: Essays on women, Jews, violence, and resistance.* San Francisco: Aunt Lute Books.

Lobel, K. (Ed.). (1986). *Naming the violence: Speaking out about lesbian battering.* Seattle, WA: Seal Press.

Lundy, S. (1994). Abuse that dare not speak its name: Assisting victims of lesbian and gay domestic violence in Massachusetts. *New England Law Review, 28*(2), 273-311.

Renzetti, C. (1992). *Violent betrayal: Partner abuse in lesbian relationships.* Newbury Park, CA: Sage.

Russo, A. (1991). If not now, when: Fighting violence against women. Part I. *Sojourner, 17*(3), 16-18 and Part II, *Sojourner, 17*(4), 13-15.

Russo, A. (1992). A battered lesbian fights for recognition. *Sojourner, 17*(9), 14-17.

9

HIV and Same-Sex Domestic Violence

Bea Hanson
Terry Maroney

The AIDS crisis has added a new dimension to domestic violence—for survivors, batterers, gay and lesbian communities, and service providers. A 1992 national survey conducted by the National Association of People with AIDS (NAPWA, 1992, p. 6) found that 12.3% of the respondents nationwide experienced violence at the hands of their partners. Significantly, 10% of the gay men and 23.7% of the bisexual men surveyed reported such violence. Women respondents, however, were not identified by sexual orientation (pp. 6, 26-27). Brand and Kidd (1986) and Island and Letellier (1991) estimate that the incidence of domestic violence in gay and lesbian relationships is the same as in heterosexual relationships. There is no indication that the incidence of domestic violence is any less in same-sex relationships in which one or both partners are HIV infected. In fact, such violence could be even more frequent given the added physical, psychological, and emotional stressors accompanying HIV.

Most HIV/AIDS service providers find that the energy required to continuously respond to an individual patient or client's physical and psychological needs makes domestic violence seem incidental. Most domestic violence service providers perceive HIV/AIDS to be a nonissue, and they do not consider whether clients are HIV infected. Most gay men and lesbians still believe the myth that domestic violence does not exist in our communities, and many lesbians still feel they are at no risk for contracting HIV. For many gay men and lesbians living with HIV, domestic violence is a reality and the barriers to service seem insurmountable.

In this chapter, we examine some of the unique issues facing gay men and lesbians with HIV or AIDS who are victims of domestic violence, how batterers use HIV or AIDS as a weapon to control their partners, barriers to service for HIV-positive survivors, and ways for community activists and service providers to break down these barriers and create necessary services for survivors.

Much of the information for this chapter comes from our experiences at the New York City Gay and Lesbian Anti-Violence Project (AVP). In 1990, AVP created the HIV-Related Violence Program, the country's first and only program that specifically documents violence against people with HIV/AIDS; provides comprehensive counseling and advocacy services to individual victims; and offers training programs, resource manuals, and other information to a wide variety of social service providers, people living with HIV/AIDS, and gay and lesbian communities. We describe recurrent problems that we have seen in our client population over the past six years in the hope that the stories we tell will spur further action and research on behalf of HIV-positive victims of domestic violence.

The Backdrop: Disability and
Domestic Violence

Many persons with disabilities live within supportive and loving family environments. However, it has been documented (Waxman, 1992) that disabled persons frequently experience higher levels of family violence than persons without disabilities. Such abuse may start in the biological family, where a disabled child may be neglected or provided with a lower level of care than his or her nondisabled siblings. Disabled children and adults who are placed in institutional settings are also frequently neglected and abused by their caretakers; indeed, homes for the disabled have gained such an abysmal reputation that many have been closed. Finally, disabled persons are roughly one and a half times more likely to be victims of sexual violence than nondisabled persons of the same sex and age (p. 5).

Abuse of the disabled in the family and public spheres creates a climate within which such mistreatment may be replicated in intimate relationships. A disabled person may internalize messages that he or she is not entitled to affection, that he or she is responsible for creating tension within the couple, that he or she is indebted to his or her partner for "putting up with" his or her disability, or that he or she is sexually undesirable. In turn, the partner may regard the disability as a burden on the relationship and displace frustrations on the disabled person. Although the existence of such a dynamic will not necessarily lead to domestic violence, it is not hard to see a parallel to a dynamic commonly found in violent relationships. Batterers frequently feel that the victim is making unreasonable demands, and both the batterer and the victim attribute relational problems and assign blame for violence to the victim. The victim, for his or her part, often internalizes a low self-image and feels responsible for his or her own victimization. A framework in which a disabled partner stands on a less than equal footing proves a ready fit with the dynamics of abuse.

Should such abuse develop, the victim's disability will, depending on its nature, provide a batterer with potent weapons. Because of the widespread social degradation of persons with mental illness, for example, a person with such an illness may be especially vulnerable to ridicule. A victim who is physically dependent on his or her batterer— to go to the bathroom, to leave the apartment, to access services—will have a heightened vulnerability to abandonment and neglect.

It is against this backdrop that an exploration of the relationship between HIV and domestic violence begins. Because HIV disease is a disability that is both progressive and accompanied by tremendous social stigma, persons with HIV may be at particular risk.

HIV as a Tool of Abuse

The same range of abuse that occurs in any relationship in which there is domestic violence can occur in relationships in which HIV/AIDS is an issue.[1] The manifestations of abuse include physical, psychological, emotional, sexual, and economic abuse; threats; intimidation; isolation or the restriction of freedom; using children; and, for gay men and lesbians, heterosexist control. A significant additional factor, however, is the potential for "HIV-related abuse." The nature of HIV as a highly stigmatized disability makes it an especially effective tool of abuse. In addition, HIV-positive status will create additional obstacles for the victim and may aggravate the consequences of such abuse.

HIV—like many other factors, such as alcoholism—can be a trigger for violence, but acting violently is always the batterer's choice and responsibility. Abuse can be more devastating, both physically and mentally, for a person who is ill than for a person who is not ill. Persons with HIV who are weak or disabled are more vulnerable to physical abuse and neglect. Persons already struggling with HIV-related stress, grief, and low self-esteem are more vulnerable to emotional abuse. A person who is ill, disabled, or struggling financially may be dependent on the batterer for shelter and economic and emotional support and may feel incapable of surviving independently.

In the same way that many domestic violence service providers have modified the well-known power and control wheel to incorporate the use of "heterosexist control" as a dynamic of same-sex domestic violence, "HIV/AIDS-related control" can be incorporated into the theoretical framework. Each spoke of the wheel will have particular ramifications for a survivor with HIV disease.

Physical abuse and neglect includes inflicting or threatening physical harm without a weapon, general neglect, and refusing to assist a person when he or she is sick or disabled—"taking advantage" of the person's disability. For people with compromised immune systems or those who are frail, physical abuse does not need to be very brutal in order to do severe damage—an assault without the use of a weapon can be just as debilitating as an assault with a weapon on a healthy person. In addition to aggravated injuries, persons with HIV may experience a sharp decline in their general health after experiencing physical assault.

Isolation or restricting freedom includes controlling a partner's access to work, school, or support systems—such as friends and family—as well as participation in support groups, counseling, medical care, and social services. Access to personal and professional support systems is essential to maintaining emotional, psychological, and physical health for persons living with HIV and AIDS, as well as for those in abusive relationships. Isolation from such services can hasten disease progression and foster depression and dependency.

Psychological and emotional abuse includes insulting, criticizing, blaming, and degrading a person for being HIV-positive, or telling a person that they deserve to have HIV. In blaming the victim and his or her HIV status for the violence, the batterer projects onto his or her partner our society's negative attitudes about people living with HIV/AIDS. Batterers use blame as a justification for violence in a number of ways. In relationships in which one or both partners is HIV positive, disputes over who brought HIV into the relationship are common and can escalate into major confrontations. Accusations such as, "If you hadn't had sex with so many men in your past, we wouldn't be dealing with this now," or "If you hadn't had that affair . . .," or "If you hadn't done drugs . . . " may be used, so that the batterer can make the victim feel responsible for HIV and its impact on the relationship. Because many people with HIV do feel responsible for contracting the virus and for creating any subsequent problems in the relationship, they often feel as if they deserve violence from their partner.

Threats and intimidation include making physical, emotional, economic, or sexual threats or threatening to abandon or neglect the person when he or she is sick. Threatening and intimidating behavior creates a "walking on eggshells" atmosphere in which the victim modifies his or her actions to avoid any actions that may "set off" the batterer.

Economic abuse includes stealing money and/or disability benefits; forbidding a person to apply for disability benefits, thus fostering dependency; forcing a person to use disability benefits to support a batterer; or using money needed to purchase medication, nutritional products, or other health-related supplies for unnecessary expenditures, such as alcohol, drugs, or entertainment.

Sexual abuse includes refusing to practice safer sex, sexually humiliating or degrading a person for having HIV, telling a person that he or she is "dirty" or undesirable, or using the victim's HIV infection as an excuse for going outside the relationship for sex.

Use of children includes threatening to reveal HIV status to children, threatening to have children removed from the home, accusing a person of being an unfit parent because of his or her HIV status, or blaming a person for the HIV-positive status of children.

Property destruction includes destroying medical records, medication, proof of benefits, immigration documents, identification, or any property necessary to cope with a disabling condition—for example, a cane, a wheelchair, or medical equipment.

"AIDS-phobic control" includes disclosing ("outing") or threatening to disclose an individual's HIV status to any person who could then hurt the victim, such as family, neighbors, employers, ex-lovers, friends, or city, state, or federal employees; accusing a person of being HIV-positive; forcing a person to submit to an HIV antibody test; or accusing a person of infecting or "posing a threat" to others.

Because the threat of outing an HIV-positive victim has never been addressed in the literature, it bears some extended elaboration here.

Employment. People with HIV and AIDS are often rightly concerned that a disclosure of their status may cost them their jobs. Indeed, 26.1% of the NAPWA survey respondents indicated that they had suffered employment discrimination because of their HIV status (NAPWA, 1992, pp. 27-28). Even at this late stage in the epidemic, there is debate over whether people with HIV should be excluded from certain jobs, such as nursing. The U.S. military excludes any hopeful recruit who tests positive and may soon start discharging persons with HIV.

Many states have passed statutes prohibiting such discrimination, and national programs of workplace AIDS education have made important headway. Additionally, the passage of the sweeping Americans with Disabilities Act in 1990—which includes HIV in its definition—has provided broad-based protections. However, like all legal rights, the right to be free from HIV-related discrimination is meaningful only when it is enforced. Many persons with HIV and AIDS are not aware of their rights or lack the resources to pursue a civil case. Also, employers who know the proscriptions against discrimination may resort to tactics of harassment and sabotage to compel their employees with HIV to leave "voluntarily." Outing may, therefore, have very significant consequences.

Immigration status. Immigrants may share a parallel concern that disclosure to police, social service workers, medical personnel, or the Immigration and Naturalization Service (INS) will result in loss of benefits, detention, or deportation. Unfortunately, the federal and state governments are becoming increasingly hostile to immigrants of all sorts, even those with legal permanent residency. However, even given a national immigration policy that renders people with HIV "excludable" (National Lawyers Guild and San Francisco AIDS Foundation, 1994), the INS seldom investigates private reports of "illegal" residents, focusing instead on those who come into custody through workplace raids, the courts, and border crossings. Still, an HIV-positive immigrant who is being abused by one's partner may feel the threat of outing to be a real and daunting one. Should such people need to leave the country temporarily for their own safety, they may have trouble returning. Should they apply for legal permanent residency, they may be denied and forced into continued reliance on the batterer. Especially because most immigrants are not aware of their rights, fear of immigration authorities deters many HIV-positive victims from approaching both the police and medical services.

Police and the criminal justice system. Fear of being reported to the police is another common concern voiced by survivors with HIV. Because many states—27 in 1994—have statutes that criminalize the knowing transmission of HIV (Gostin et al., 1994, p. 1440), batterers frequently threaten to have their partners arrested and prosecuted. If the victim has had any unsafe sex with the batterer—which is frequently the case if the victim is recently diagnosed or if the batterer refuses safer sex—he or she may be quite afraid that such a charge could be brought as retaliation. Such a threat often comes at a point at which the victim is considering using the police for protection and is designed to dissuade the victim from reporting the batterer's abusive behavior. It is significant that AVP has seen cases like this even though New York has no statute criminalizing HIV transmission.

Even if a threat of arrest is not made, a victim may still rightly fear either discrimination or abuse from the police should the batterer disclose his or her status. Police officers are seldom targeted by AIDS education campaigns and frequently are concerned about becoming infected in the course of their jobs. This combination of worry and ignorance can lead to mistreatment of crime victims (and accused criminals) who police know or suspect to be HIV positive.

Community. Finally, an abusive partner may threaten to out the victim's HIV status to neighbors and landlords. Such an outing may expose the victim to harassment, ostracism, eviction, or assault because of bias (NAPWA, 1992, p. 13) By threatening to reveal the partner's HIV status to community residents, a batterer invokes the specter of HIV bias violence. Victims may refrain from seeking help and confine their victimization to what they experience within the relationship rather than be exposed to potential violence from their community as a whole.

Barriers to Service

The realities of living with HIV infection may present significant barriers to leaving an abusive relationship and accessing necessary services.

Medical Needs

A person at an advanced stage of disease may need medical supplies—for example, he or she may need a wheelchair or an intravenous drip—that are unavailable in a battered women's or homeless shelter. Those settings are themselves inhospitable to persons with HIV; not only do survivors face the health risks inherent in any group setting, many survivors have also reported being harassed by other residents because of sexual orientation and HIV status. Men's homeless shelters, often the only recourse for battered gay men, are particularly dangerous settings in which violence and theft are commonplace (Coalition for the Homeless, 1989). For a person who is ill, physical injury or theft of essential goods—such as medication—is of paramount concern. As a result of such dangers, people with HIV will often resist shelter placement, even in an emergency.

The fatigue and exhaustion associated with HIV disease may mean that a victim simply lacks the energy to confront the many problems associated with domestic violence. This is particularly true if a victim needs to attend multiple appointments, wait in lines, testify in court, and run the gauntlet of obligations that various systems impose on victims.

Finally, the abuse itself takes a serious toll on an HIV-positive person's physical health. Although the impact of physical injury on a person whose immune system is compromised is clear, it is equally important to consider the health effects of elevated stress associated with living in constant fear of abuse. Stress is generally regarded as a significant co-factor in HIV disease progression (Kidd & Huber, 1991). People with HIV/AIDS in abusive relationships are often quick to see this connection; for example, a typical AVP client once reported, "Since the abuse started, my T-cell count has dropped 200 points, my shingles came back, I'm losing weight, and I can't sleep." Making a direct link between abuse and a decline in health can be an excellent tool for assisting a client to see the importance of safety and self-protection.

Economic Barriers

Because so many persons with HIV are dependent on government benefits for income and housing support, they are unlikely to have other convenient, supportive housing options if they are being abused in the home (NAPWA, 1992, p. 10). In the absence of a viable shelter alternative, many victims will be stuck in an unsafe living environment. They will be unable to pay a security deposit on a new apartment, reconnect utilities, pay a mover, and incur all the other expenses associated with a move. They may have their benefits tied to a particular apartment and need permission from the city, state, or federal government to move. Then they will have to wait for new public or subsidized housing to become available.

Economic barriers may also keep HIV-positive victims from competent therapy services. Many such services have sliding scales that don't slide low enough for a person living on a disability check and many refuse to accept Medicaid. In the absence of appropriate support, a victim may never even reach the point of formulating a safety plan.

Emotional Barriers

In addition to concrete barriers, people with HIV/AIDS frequently encounter a host of emotional and psychological barriers to leaving an abusive relationship beyond those encountered by most victims. These barriers center on the stigma associated with HIV/AIDS, the episodic physical dependency often caused by various opportunistic infections, and the emotional trauma associated with a life-threatening illness.

Many batterers capitalize on negative societal views of persons with HIV by blaming their partners for contracting HIV and telling them that they will be socially and sexually rejected by others. Victims regularly report comments from their batterers such as "You're dirty, nobody else will ever want you" or "Who's going to want a sick old fairy like you?" or "You're lucky to have me with the nasty disease you've got." The subsequent internalization of these messages leads to low self-esteem, self-blame, feelings of isolation from social supports, and it fosters further dependency on the batterer.

Most people with HIV and AIDS are also quite conscious of the fact that at some point in their lives they might need someone to physically take care of them. For most gay men and lesbians with HIV/AIDS, family support is not an option because of rejection based on their sexual orientation, HIV-positive status, or both. As a result, gay men and lesbians with HIV/AIDS are frequently dependent on friends and lovers for assistance and fear having no one around when they do become dependent. If the one person who might provide that care is also abusive, the survivor may feel that he or she has no other option but to stay with that abusive partner.

Additionally, a person with HIV/AIDS may feel emotionally incapable of losing one's partner, even though the partner is abusive. Although acknowledging the abuse, survivors frequently say, "I don't want to die alone," or "I know that it's bad, but he's all I've got," or "I'll never meet anyone else, I can't get out of bed, and I have a T-cell count of two." While being abused, the survivor may also be dealing with serious mortality issues and may not be capable of making any difficult changes in his or her life, especially a major change such as leaving a relationship.

Lack of Service Integration

Service providers frequently concentrate either on HIV or domestic violence; it is rare that one finds a provider capable of handling both issues. Many domestic violence professionals remain uninformed about both HIV and same-sex domestic violence. By the same token, HIV professionals may not be sensitive to violence issues at all, let alone those faced by lesbians and gay men. Because of these gaps, an HIV-positive survivor of same-sex domestic violence runs the risk of being either misunderstood, mishandled, or simply overlooked when accessing services.

Policy and Service Recommendations

The task for service providers is to bridge the gap between HIV/AIDS and domestic violence services and to offer necessary information, resources, and support to specifically address the special needs of survivors living with HIV/AIDS.

Service Provider and Police Trainings

The first step toward bridging this service gap is cross-training between HIV/AIDS and domestic violence service providers. HIV/AIDS service agencies need trainings to ensure that staff and volunteers understand the dynamics of domestic violence; domestic violence service agencies need trainings on HIV transmission and the special needs of domestic violence survivors with HIV/AIDS. We recommend that local HIV and domestic violence providers host each other for meetings and offer trainings for each other's staff. Get to know what services the other side provides. Consider starting a joint support group. Create a protocol for prioritized referrals between agencies.

Because of the importance of nonbiased police responses to survivors, we also advise working with local police departments to devise a curriculum of AIDS education and sensitivity training. Our experience with the appalling level of ignorance among officers in New York City precincts, where we have conducted many trainings, and our frustrations with the inadequate time given for such training, indicate that police must prioritize and give adequate organizational backing to such programs for any real progress to be made.

Service Provision

The second step is to incorporate changes into agencies. HIV/AIDS service providers need to routinely ask questions about domestic violence during client intake and assessment; domestic violence service providers need to assess the impact of HIV/AIDS on a survivor's physical health and safety and incorporate this information into development of a safety plan. All providers must respect the survivor's right to make his or her own decision about staying in or leaving an abusive relationship.

When providing services to survivors of domestic violence, we recommend an integration of counseling and advocacy with good linkages to other HIV/AIDS service providers. Counseling should be focused on the effects and dynamics of domestic violence; effects on the individual's health, including HIV-related conditions; development of a workable safety plan that incorporates any health-related concerns; and the integration of domestic violence issues into HIV-related physical and mental health concerns.

The following counseling goals incorporate many of the needs of domestic violence survivors living with HIV/AIDS:

1. Confirm and emphasize that violence is unacceptable behavior and that no one deserves to be abused for any reason.
2. Let the survivor know that he or she is not alone and that other gay men, lesbians, and people with HIV/AIDS have experienced and survived similar situations.
3. Help the survivor name the forms of abuse he or she has endured and validate those experiences. Use the wheel to identify specific HIV-related forms of abuse he or she may have experienced.
4. Explore available options and advocate for the survivor's safety. Be realistic about these options, including their potential impact on stress levels and on physical health.
5. Build on the survivor's strengths. Avoid blaming the victim for his or her situation, his or her HIV status, or the abuse.
6. Respect the survivor's right to make his or her own decisions, even if he or she decides to remain with an abusive partner.

In addition, advocacy is an important and necessary service for any survivor of domestic violence. For people in poor health, the obstacles to escape and recovery may seem insurmountable and advocacy and accompaniment services may be essential to achieve safety. When discussing options, it is important to realistically discuss the amount of time and energy needed from the client and the length of time required to complete a process, such as court proceedings.

Advocacy may take various forms: calling police precincts and arranging for home visits to report a crime; urging a district attorney to expedite prosecution of a case or issuance of an order of protection because of the survivor's frail health; petitioning for emergency housing transfers; accompanying a client to an HIV/AIDS service organization to receive services for the first time or to identify ways to incorporate a focus on domestic violence into services he or she already receives; filing for crime victims' compensation; and expediting issuance of benefits. Advocacy services should be developed based on both the service capabilities of the agency and the needs of the individual, keeping in mind any health-related concerns. Consider joining forces with other providers to force policy changes—for example, lobbying the public housing authority to make emergency transfers available to both male and female victims of domestic violence and to all disabled crime victims.

Immigration Advocacy

Because of the difficult situation faced by HIV-positive immigrant victims, it is essential to forge coalitions with legal service providers. Many legal providers for persons with HIV have also become expert in immigration law and can often help persons with HIV gain legal status by, for example, filing for a "voluntary departure," which will buy additional time in the United States. It is also essential that community activists and providers pressure their local governments to enact ordinances that prohibit providers—police, hospitals, and benefits offices, in particular—from revealing the immigration status of persons seeking their services. Find out what your local policy is on this.

Employment Protections

People with HIV can make use of numerous statutes, most notably the Americans with Disabilities Act (ADA), in battling employment discrimination that may follow a disclosure. Find out who in your area is working with the ADA. You can contact the Department of Justice, the Equal Employment Opportunities Commission, or a local disability services provider for referrals. Additionally, city and state human rights commissions will take such reports.

Conclusion

Gay and lesbian people with HIV, already suffering from a progressive disease accompanied by enormous social stigma, are also suffering at the hands of their partners. Their needs can be met only when HIV service providers, domestic violence professionals, and gay and lesbian communities recognize their existence. Such recognition, however, is but the first step. Together we must formulate strategies, design programs, educate one another, and advocate for institutional change. Finally, we must send a strong message that every gay and lesbian person with HIV—indeed, every person—deserves love, support, and respect, not abuse.

Note

1. Although the issue is beyond the scope of this chapter, our communities must also engage in a discussion about HIV-positive partners as perpetrators of domestic violence. It is our experience that HIV (like job stress or loss, alcohol, drugs, or victim behavior) is sometimes used as an excuse for violence. As a batterer becomes sicker and perceives a loss of power in the relationship, he or she may escalate the violence in an attempt to regain a sense of control. Many victims, although they realize the partner's behavior is abusive, refuse to leave the relationship because they feel guilty about "abandoning" the batterer in a time of need. This dynamic, in which the victim feels directly responsible for the batterer's well-being, presents complex issues and requires further study.

References

Brand, P. A., & Kidd, A. H. (1986). Frequency of physical aggression in heterosexual and female homosexual dyads. *Psychological Report, 59,* 1307-1313.

Coalition for the Homeless. (1989, October). *A false sense: A study of safety and security issues in New York City's municipal shelters for men.* New York: Author.

Gostin et al. (1994). HIV Testing, counseling and prophylaxis after sexual assault. *Journal of the American Medical Association, 271,* 1440.

Island, D., & Letellier, P. (1991). *Men who beat the men who love them.* New York: Harrington Park Press.

Kidd, P. M., & Huber, W. (1991). *Living with the AIDS virus.* Berkeley, CA: HK Biomedical.

National Association of People with AIDS (NAPWA). (1992). *HIV in America: A profile of the challenges facing Americans living with HIV.* Washington, DC: Author.

National Lawyers Guild and the San Francisco AIDS Foundation. (1994). *HIV and immigration: A manual for AIDS service providers.* San Francisco: Author.

Waxman, B. (1992). Hate. *The Disability Rag, 13*(3), 5.

10

Six Steps

Organizing Support Services and Safe-Home Networks for Battered Gay Men

Curt Rogers

On Thanksgiving night, 1992, my partner of three and a half years tried to kill me. I found myself with no shelter, no mental health support, and no legal options that provided any glimpse of security. I was on my own at a time of extreme anxiety and crisis. That experience led me to initiate the Gay Men's Domestic Violence Project in 1994. Our goal is to educate and motivate the community to acknowledge and respond to the problem of same-sex domestic violence and to coordinate services to meet the needs of gay male victims.

This chapter is about the nuts and bolts of actually *organizing* services for battered gay men, a road map that I hope will save time and energy and help other organizations get off the ground.

Six Steps

As I see it, starting a support service/safe-home network for gay men is a six-step program.

1. Recognize

When I was leaving my batterer, I recognized my own dilemma of having no support and no shelter. But later, as my life began to level out, I recognized that all gay men attempting to leave violent relationships experience this dilemma. Although society was actively trying to address the needs of heterosexual victims of domestic violence, gay/lesbian/bisexual/transgender (GLBT) victims were being ignored.

2. Organize

Once you've recognized the problem and have decided to take action, organize your thoughts and approach.

Evaluate which services are most urgently needed in your area and do not duplicate efforts. For instance, you may find that legal services are already available through a local gay or lesbian bar association. Crisis therapy may be available through a gay or lesbian health clinic. You can be more effective in the beginning if you prioritize services and focus on the ones that are most needed.

Lay out your administrative structure once you have determined the services you want to provide. Do not waste valuable time and energy reinventing the wheel. Administrative structures, policies, screening procedures, training curricula, and most everything you need on paper to run a support organization for victims of domestic violence already exist. Approach a same-sex domestic violence program in a city near you or use materials from a heterosexual program and alter them to be same-sex appropriate. For instance, when the Gay Men's Domestic Violence Project was initially exploring how to set up the many facets of a safe-home program, our most valuable information came from the *Park Slope Safe Homes Project Technical Assistance Manual: How to Set Up a Community-Based Program for Battered Women and Their Families* (Kiebert & Schechter, 1980). This excellent, in-depth manual is written for heterosexual programs but can easily be adapted to be same-sex appropriate.

Create a time line for the projected growth of your organization and pay close attention to the order in which specific services are offered. You will never adhere to this time line, but the clarity of vision the process provides is invaluable. When we were drawing up our time line and list of proposed services, we envisioned a "one-stop shopping" model that would take care of all of the needs of victims and coordinate the services as well. This model allows a client in crisis to focus his attention on decisions regarding his abusive relationship rather than expend energy trying to pull together all the aspects of a support network to survive.

Our first goal was to establish an administrative coalition and a foundation of volunteer support. From there we chose to work on providing the following services in order of priority: case managers and peer support; safe-home network; hotline; crisis therapy; legal advocacy; support group; assistance in obtaining health care for clients without coverage; food and essentials for clients in crisis; transportation assistance for clients who decide to relocate to another city or state; creation of a national network of gay male domestic violence organizations; referral to lawyers willing to provide pro bono representation; campaign to increase public awareness; and campaign for equal rights and equal access to services for gay male victims.

Over time, our priority list remained pretty much the same, except that the campaign to increase public awareness moved to the top of the list. When we thought we were ready to start screening and training potential volunteers and safe-home providers, no one responded to our outreach. I had failed to realize that a great deal of community education would have to take place before volunteers would come forward.

When you plan your organization's development, be sure that you have appropriate support in place before you activate larger services. If you promise safe-home providers that the survivors placed in their homes will have daily encounters with a peer support person, make sure that you have a peer support system up and running before activating the safe-home network.

Where does fund-raising fit in? Is your group going to be a grassroots organization administered and staffed completely by volunteers? Or are you going to spend your initial energy attempting to raise funds despite the strong possibility that after months of hard work you may end up with nothing to show for your effort? Or do you begin as a grassroots organization (to establish services and credibility) and then, as human resources allow, pursue funding?

Our initial approach to funding was that we could not afford to spend valuable start-up time chasing money that might not materialize. It was our hope that as the organization's volunteer pool grew, a fund-raiser would come forward. In the meantime, we felt that our goals were achievable through a volunteer grassroots approach.

Three things happened that made us look at fund-raising differently. First, we realized that motivating volunteers required community education and that an effective campaign required money. Second, it did not seem that a volunteer fund-raiser would be walking through our door any time soon. And third, our local business community turned out to be more responsive to our efforts than we initially thought—with very little effort, we found ourselves being offered contributions of computer hardware and office supplies. Given these factors, we decided to invest time in creating proposals to raise funds for a community education campaign.

Decide whether to incorporate your organization. Incorporation is a lengthy process, and I strongly suggest you begin it as soon as possible. Many funders will not contribute to unincorporated associations or organizations that do not have charitable exemptions. Delaying incorporation because you think your organization will not be doing fund-raising and then finding yourself treading water when asked to present a funding proposal is deeply frustrating.

Incorporation can have other advantages. Establishing a board of trustees can be a way to involve diverse members of your community; to engage individuals who may have the financial means to contribute to the organization; and to obtain wisdom, advice, and guidance. A strong and respected board can lend credibility to a young organization.

Consider insurance. You are about to enter the world of direct client services and need to protect yourself should someone attempt to sue. You should at least explore insurance for directors and officers, professional liability insurance, general liability insurance, and workers' compensation to see if and when they are appropriate. Because of the expense of liability insurance, we decided to delay providing direct client services—and focus solely on community education—until we were funded.

3. Network

Once you have the blueprint for your organization, meet the other people in your community who are working with domestic violence and/or GLBT issues. Two rules apply for networking: Meet everyone and listen.

You should first seek out a lesbian support group in your area if one exists. The lesbian community is years ahead of the gay male community in addressing same-sex domestic violence. If you have access to such a group they will be an invaluable resource. Listen to them. You may not want to hear what they have to say. You may think you have all the answers and fresh new ideas. But they will be speaking from experience and can save you time, energy, and frustration if you listen to them. I remember my first meeting with the coordinator of Boston's Network for Battered Lesbians and Bisexual Women. Although she emphasized that the Gay Men's Domestic Violence Project should grow however *I* wanted it to, she also strongly hinted that (a) I would not accomplish a safe-home network on my 12-month time line, and (b) I might be jumping ahead by focusing on a safe-home network before addressing community education. She proved to be correct on both counts, and I could have made my life simpler and more productive if I had believed her.

You should also meet with the coordinators in your area of heterosexual support programs and shelters. However, you should be prepared for some of them to be suspicious of you at first and for some to never trust you. Some may not open up to you because of homophobia. Others will not be able to let go of their definition that domestic violence is exclusively male violence against women. Understand that heterosexual domestic violence activists encounter countless men who are unwilling to take battering seriously. To educate society of the reality and severity of domestic violence, these activists have had to continually insist that their perception of the issue is accurate, often to unsupportive, confrontational, or hostile audiences. Consequently, these advocates may not be open to hear arguments that run counter to their beliefs, especially when presented by a man. It is a delicate situation. You need to balance the respect you have for the accomplishments of the domestic violence movement with a strong intolerance for defining domestic violence in heterosexist terms.

You also need to contact district attorneys' offices, police departments, politicians, GLBT groups, batterers' programs, public health departments, and hospital social work departments.

4. Educate

Although community education may not be one of the priorities of your organization, it is essential to the development of other services. The idea of same-sex domestic violence has never occurred to most people. Before volunteers, funders, safe-home providers, board members, or survivors will come forward, they need to be educated.

Education will take time. And, in truth, your job as a community educator will never be finished. You will have to use several educational tactics and people will need to be presented with information repeatedly before they absorb it. Articles in newspapers (gay or straight) are a good beginning. If you can't get an article printed, try submitting letters to the editor. Try to be a guest on a radio talk show or make your presence known as a caller. Brochures and flyers can also help get information out on a mass scale. A recent survey that we did on attitudes of the gay and lesbian communities in Boston toward same-sex domestic violence, for instance, generated a lot of interest in the local press and was the basis for a lengthy story on National Public Radio that in turn generated a considerable amount of interest in the topic nationwide.

Of all the media for teaching about same-sex domestic violence, I have found the most effective to be personal interaction—sharing my own experience. This can be accomplished in a forum or panel discussion open to the general public, or your group could solicit speaking opportunities and professional trainings at various legal, social service, health care, and community organizations.

Speaking opportunities at organizations are relatively straightforward. You have a captive audience and need only consider the content of the presentation. Creating a forum to which you invite either the general public or specific individuals adds another time-consuming element. Generating an interest and motivation to attend requires inventiveness and persistence. Media outlets, letters, and flyers are critical; however, your most important tool is the telephone. Make contact with your intended audience before the event and get commitments to attend. Follow up with reminder cards. Make sure that you have a crowd large enough to fill your space. A full room can give your forum the additional energy it needs to make it memorable and effective. A poor turnout can cause those in your audience to wonder why they are there because apparently no one else in the community thinks the issue is worthy of their time.

I cannot stress enough the importance of personal survivor stories. They have the ability to bring an audience to a common ground of empathy for the devastation and abuse the survivor has experienced. As a result, the discussion can move beyond being a debate on the reality and severity of the issue to a more productive dialogue about actions to address the situation.

However, I need to also stress that a survivor must be properly prepared and supported both before and after a presentation. Ensure that this is an appropriate activity for the survivor. Is he emotionally ready to share his experience publicly? Is he placing himself in danger of retaliation? Is he likely to experience any positive emotional benefit from telling his story—or has he agreed to come forward to help others out of a sense of guilt? Although a public relations disaster can occur when a forum flounders because of an inappropriate speaker, the real tragedy is the revictimization of the survivor. It is your responsibility to make sure the survivor has a solid understanding of battering, an emotional stability to withstand such a situation, and a strong support system in place to help him process and rebound from a potentially harsh experience.

If you are a survivor and decide to tell your story, give thought to what you are going to say beforehand. Work with someone who is familiar with same-sex domestic violence issues who can help you decide how best to illustrate the points you want to get across. Prepare for the strong possibility that this will be an emotional event for you. I have been telling my story for over three years and still take a script of what I am going to say. If the emotions become too great or I become too overwhelmed to think on my feet, the script will convey my message and keep me from rambling.

I also do not tell my story unless another same-sex domestic violence professional is part of the presentation. One reason is so that the subject does not become too sensationalized. But my primary concern is that once I have labeled myself a survivor, no matter what my other experience, I can become a target for a hostile "professional" in the audience. For instance, a mental health professional once stated that my pattern of behavior in the relationship indicated "codependency" and that both my partner and I were responsible for the violence in the relationship. Another panelist, a fellow same-sex domestic violence professional, responded by illustrating the clear signs and patterns of primary aggression on the part of the batterer and that the batterer *chose* to be violent. Those same words coming from me might not have been so convincing because I could be perceived as being defensive and less educated on the issue. Without the intervention of my fellow panelist, I could have lost the audience, and in addition, I could have been revictimized.

No matter what medium you use to teach your community, one of the most important questions to ask yourself is "What does my audience already know?" Some people will have a wealth of knowledge and experience in gay or lesbian issues but lack awareness of the issues surrounding domestic violence. Others will be the reverse. And in both situations, you need to be wary of people who believe they know the facts when in reality they are operating on the basis of myths and misconceptions.

A wonderful by-product of educating your community is that you will also be reaching battered gay men. Society presents a myriad of obstacles that prevent battered gay men from coming forward. Unsupportive families; disbelieving friends; stereotypes that men need to be strong; homophobic police, legal, and health care systems—all are unfortunate realities that will take years to turn around. The one obstacle you can have an immediate effect on is the victim's perception of what he is experiencing. Through education you can provide him with the knowledge necessary to identify his situation and begin to remove himself from his abusive relationship.

5. Motivate

Education alone won't get your program off the ground. You must also motivate your community to contribute time, energy, wisdom, and money. The two groups most likely to respond are the domestic violence community and the GLBT community.

I have found the domestic violence community to be understaffed, underfunded, and overworked. The most I hope for from anyone working on domestic violence is that they be supportive and willing to work shoulder to shoulder in addressing the issue. That leaves the GLBT community.

I was caught completely off guard about how difficult it is to motivate the GLBT community to come forward and address same-sex domestic violence. First, I mistakenly thought everyone was aware of domestic violence. Second, I thought that surely the community would come forward to help protect their own. They had come forward to deal with AIDS when society initially ignored the crisis because of a belief that it was exclusive to gay men. Here was another example of gay men's needs being neglected. I thought motivating the gay community would be a quick and simple proposition. I was wrong.

To begin to understand some of the dynamics at play in motivating our community to respond to same-sex domestic violence, we should consider (a) the concept of marketing, (b) the marketing of heterosexual domestic violence, and (c) the factors that motivate the gay or lesbian community to respond to AIDS.

The concept of marketing. I personally think in terms of marketing not only because I come from a business background but because I believe it is the quickest and most effective way to motivate my community. I ask those of you who may have a negative reaction to the term marketing to reconsider what it means, what its place is in our society, and how it is relevant to your work. For the purpose of this chapter, I define marketing as motivating the public to take a specific action or to feel a specific way. I choose the term marketing because it has an aggressive edge to it. I choose it because for me it implies an evaluation of the target population and a planned course of implementation. If you include education in your marketing campaign, the public can become aware of the seriousness of the issue and be proud of the actions it is persuaded to undertake.

The marketing of heterosexual domestic violence. Heterosexual domestic violence is, in many ways, an "easier sell" (easier to motivate people to take action) than same-sex domestic violence. In organizing against heterosexual domestic violence, advocates often use the image of the strong taking advantage of the weak. People are more easily motivated to help if they perceive an underdog and a bully, even though not all male batterers are physically bigger than their female victims. In same-sex situations, many people incorrectly assume that domestic violence is a confrontation of equals, both in terms of physical strength and in terms of societal privileges and resources.

Heterosexual domestic violence advocates can also use an "us" versus "them" strategy to motivate women, who not surprisingly make up the overwhelming majority of people who are working on heterosexual domestic violence. With a gender-based theory, they can point to a clearly defined enemy. Also, when a woman believes the gender-based theory, she can define herself as a person not capable of violence.

By comparison, same-sex domestic violence has no such quickly identifiable "us" and "them." It is much harder to motivate the community when the enemy is among us. Also, recognizing the reality of same-sex domestic violence does not endow you with the illusion that you belong to a "naturally" nonviolent group; rather, it requires that you come to grips with the fact that members of your own community are brutalizing their same-sex partners—not quite as attractive as a rally call.

The factors that motivated the gay or lesbian community to respond to AIDS. The "enemy among us" rhetoric is also a distinguishable difference between motivating the lesbian and gay community around domestic violence and motivating them around AIDS. The slogan "Fight AIDS, not people with AIDS" illustrates this point. AIDS can be turned into an "us" versus "it" cause. The disease is the bad guy. Everyone can agree to hate the disease. And the effects of the disease are undeniable within our community.

With domestic violence, the bad guy is sometimes an otherwise charming and charismatic person, someone known within the community. Not everyone will agree that the batterer is a bad guy. Also, the effects of same-sex domestic violence are often hidden both because victims are not currently coming forward and because when we as a community see warning signs (a) we are not aware of what they mean or (b) we choose to look the other way.

From my experience, there are three identifiable obstacles to motivating the lesbian and gay community to respond to same-sex domestic violence: indifference, HIV burnout, and denial. Indifference comes from the lack of attention to the issue, including little or no media coverage, which creates the illusion that the issue does not exist. Survivors most often have nowhere to go for services, and consequently, the majority never have their experiences documented. This silence creates a void in which our community can assume that the problem does not exist. One person who stands up and says that this is a paramount crisis that demands immediate attention will not suddenly overturn years of silence.

The second obstacle is HIV burnout. Quite simply, our community is emotionally drained from the effort it has put forth to address AIDS. Whether they have worked on this issue or not, many individuals feel that the community has done more than its share and that they deserve a vacation from social causes. This explanation may be oversimplified and grossly off the mark for many members of our community; however, I have encountered individuals who use this argument as a reason for not getting involved.

The third obstacle is denial. Who would want to deny that same-sex domestic violence exists? More people than you might think. Let's start with the strictly gender-based theorists. This group is not limited to heterosexuals (nor is it limited to women). Many activists who are working on domestic violence strongly connect their work on battering with their commitment to end male oppression of women. This becomes a problem when it does not allow them to see domestic violence as a power issue that can happen in any relationship.

Another group that is helping to keep the community in denial is the gay media. Many gay newspapers avoid covering the issue because they perceive it as giving the gay community bad publicity. Their attitude that same-sex domestic violence does not sell papers can cripple the effort to raise community awareness. However, over the past year, the gay papers in Boston have begun to give the issue considerable coverage. This can be partially credited to society's increased attention to domestic violence, but it is also the result of several years of active outreach and education by same-sex domestic violence programs in the city.

Community organizations may try to silence your message as well. When I approached a leading Boston organization about having same-sex domestic violence as a topic at their monthly dinner meeting, the person in charge initially responded negatively, saying that the organization "was not about furthering the image of the homosexual as a victim."

The primary group that benefits from the silence and denial are batterers. Most experts agree that somewhere around one-fourth of all same-sex relationships are abusive. If that is true, a great number of batterers are in our community—and they don't wear name tags. Given the number of batterers in the community, we are sure to encounter many during our efforts to raise awareness.

Motivating the community to address same-sex domestic violence has been by far the most challenging aspect of my work to establish services. It is an overwhelming task that consumes the majority of our current efforts. Recently, with the endorsement and support of Rev. Kim Crawford Harvie of Arlington Street Church, a prominent community leader, we co-hosted a "Community Leaders" meeting of social groups, service organizations, sports leagues, religious groups, and the media. Over 40 leaders of the gay and lesbian community in the greater Boston area gathered to brainstorm about how to over-come the challenge of motivating the community. A similar event was held for community businesses. These events were successful in not only generating a level of awareness and interest in the issue but also in developing a sense of ownership of the problem.

Other efforts to motivate the community include grant-writing to local foundations and corporations. In 3 months, we raised half of the funds needed for a 12-month community education program. We relentlessly pursue speaking engagements and have slowly made in-roads into organizations that at first appeared to be closed to us. I also personally go out, meet individuals in the community, and present them with the issue and the struggle.

Motivating your community will take creativity, new ideas, a tremendous amount of work, and perseverance. Every community will be different and will have its own unique resources and obstacles. As with an individual, you can successfully motivate a community only when you have a knowledge of what factors influence their decisions.

6. Coordinate

Unfortunately, I can't write very much about coordinating serv-ices. The Gay Men's Domestic Violence Project has not progressed to that point in its development. However, we plan to take advantage of several resources when we do get there. Experiences from heterosex-ual shelters and gay or lesbian social service organizations combined with the varied experiences of the Gay Men's Domestic Violence Project's Board of Trustees will all contribute to the evolution of a process by which we will coordinate services.

This final step is fundamentally different from the previous ones. The steps leading to this point all deal with creation; this step deals with the tangible day-to-day management of your organization.

Conclusion

As we work to get the Gay Men's Domestic Violence Project off the ground and established, I often get frustrated. I wonder if the vast amount of time we are devoting to this issue will ever reap the tangible results we seek: shelter and support for gay male victims. I get little solace from the knowledge that we are at least raising awareness. I know too well that many gay men are living with fear and violence every day; awareness alone will not change that. However, my frustration fades when I think of what has been accomplished. Our community, the media, funding sources, the mainstream domestic violence movement, and our state government are all beginning to respond to the issue. With patience and persistence, these responses can be transformed into services for gay male victims.

Reference

Kiebert, I., & Schechter, S. (1980). *Park Slope Safe Homes Project technical assistance manual: How to set up a community-based program for battered women and their families.* Brooklyn, NY: Park Slope Safe Homes Project.

11

Lesbians and Bisexual Women Working Cooperatively to End Domestic Violence

Beth Crane
Jeannie LaFrance
Gillian Leichtling
Brooks Nelson
Erika Silver

I tell this story for all lesbians who have lived the violence in silent fear. I tell this story for those of us who named the house in memory of Sharon Bradley and Pam Angle, who died, and for all of us who have yet to live.

—Bonnie, 1978

Background

Bradley-Angle House is a feminist, social change domestic violence intervention agency in Portland, Oregon. We began in 1971 as Prescott House, primarily a shelter for women who were coming out

EDITOR'S NOTE: All of the authors are associated with Bradley-Angle House.

of prison and women who were prostituted and/or in the gay bar scene. Many who started the house were working-class lesbians or dyke feminists who were involved with the street community. In 1975, the shelter was renamed in memory of two lesbians whose lives included a lot of violence. The focus shifted toward support for women escaping violence in intimate relationships. The founders chose this direction because no services for women leaving domestic violence were available.

The agency started very informally and was grassroots based. We have grown to a staff of 18. We provide a 24-hour hotline, a shelter, a children's program, support groups, transitional services, community education, and technical assistance on family violence issues. This chapter focuses on the specific services that we provide to lesbians, bisexual women, and other members of sexual minority communities.

Evolution of the Program

In 1986, one of the shelter staff, a lesbian, was approached by a classmate who began talking about battering in her lesbian relationship and asked if she could stay at the shelter. Even though shelter staff had been through antihomophobia training, there was a lot of denial among staff members about lesbian battering. The woman came to the shelter and struggled with whether or not to be out. Some lesbian and nonlesbian staff began seriously discussing how to address lesbian battering more effectively. They decided that we could do a support group for and by lesbians, and they submitted a proposal to the executive director and the board to start a battered lesbian support group. The idea elicited homophobia from many different people, including board members, staff, and volunteers. Nonlesbian and lesbian staff had a hard time accepting the reality of lesbian battering.

Despite initial resistance, the group eventually started and has continued for 11 years. Outreach proved to be the key to the group's success. Advertisements were placed in local queer papers, and flyers were posted throughout the community. Beginning in 1992, Bradley-Angle sent representatives to several nationwide conferences on domestic violence and/or lesbian issues, where we presented workshops, lobbied for the inclusion of lesbian battering on various agendas, and worked in coalition with many lesbians of color. We developed brochures specifically for lesbians who were being battered. Since that time we have also linked with other grassroots groups organizing against the religious right to develop outreach strategies, discuss internalized sexism and homophobia, and build bridges in lesbian community organizations to recognize and take lesbian violence seriously.

One of the groups with which we have built bridges was the local sadomasochistic (S/M) community. In spring 1992, a local lesbian and gay S/M organization planned a fund-raiser for Bradley-Angle called "In the Erotic Garden." Communication between Bradley-Angle and the sponsoring organization was not coordinated, and the event was controversial among staff and the community. The agency's position on S/M was (and is) that our services are available to all women, including lesbian, bisexual, and straight women who are participants in the S/M community. However, conflict arose from stereotypes that both the domestic violence (DV) movement and the S/M community held about the other. Some individuals in the S/M community viewed the DV movement as judgmental and inaccessible by the S/M community. Some domestic violence movement workers viewed S/M as an unhealthy and violent behavior. We were not prepared for the negative publicity our neutral, open-door position garnered from the "lesbian police" on both sides of the S/M issue.

We dedicated the proceeds from the event to four community forums that focused on lesbian battering and S/M. The topics were: Basic DV in Lesbian Relationships, Oppressions in Lesbian Relationships, Dialog on DV and S/M, and Healthy Relationships–Healthy Community. The workshops were extremely well attended. Many issues were hotly debated, including the definition of abuse, how oppression and abuse interact and affect relationships, the ability of abuse survivors to make consensual S/M decisions, and sexualized violence and racism in an S/M context. The workshops created relationships within the lesbian, S/M, and antiviolence communities that were not present before.

In 1993, the lesbian caucus identified a need for a separate agency to help lesbians to stop battering their partners. We approached our local queer counseling agency. They worked with us to develop program assumptions and design, and the group for lesbian batterers was created.

Structure of the
Lesbian Support Group

We know that not all women battered by women in intimate relationships identify as lesbian. However, providing services for lesbians survivors of abuse that use lesbian support group facilitators and staff has been a major component of our work. Our current practice is to ask women during the first call about how they self-identify—lesbian, bi, or heterosexual—and then refer them to the appropriate intake worker. The lesbian and bisexual caucuses also offer limited one-on-one peer counseling to women battered by women who do not identify as lesbian.

Our lesbian support group meets weekly and is facilitated by lesbians for lesbians who are dealing with same-sex domestic violence. The group is ongoing and has a 12-week cycle. Generally, the group discusses a topic for the first 45 minutes to an hour, then takes a short break and begins "share time."

The topics give information regarding domestic violence or surviving the effects of abuse; for example, the dynamics of abusive relationships, specific safety barriers for lesbians, safety planning, and resources in the local area. Sometimes, the group generates needs that facilitators choose as a discussion topic. Two such topics that our group addresses fairly often are boundaries and different aspects of healing. Participants also get information about the intersections of oppression. Facilitators work to create a safe place for all women in the group and to interrupt oppressive behaviors.

"Share time" is a place to talk, to break the silence of the violence. Women can use this time to get support or input about specific issues they are dealing with. The facilitators ask the participants before they start their share time if they want feedback; sometimes, women just need to get stuff out and that's okay. New members of the group often use this time to share the story of their survival.

The intake procedure for members of the lesbian group are more involved than they are for members of the general domestic violence support groups. In an effort to get beyond the "snapshot" view of relationships we gather information about the dynamics of the relationship as a whole. We use a checklist to have a better understanding of who did what, who started it, who escalated it, and if there was self-defense. We need this kind of information to keep the women in group safe and to screen out batterers.

Safety Concerns

Antioppression work with staff and volunteers is one of the most important steps domestic violence shelters can take to better serve lesbian and bisexual woman survivors and to make the programs more accessible and safer for all women.

In 1991-1992, shelter staff at Bradley-Angle House wanted to better support lesbian survivors and provide antihomophobia education to shelter residents. We reviewed our phone screening process, shelter intake process, children's intake process, and shelter rules. We identified 30 to 40 shelter programs in order to ask them about their shelter rules and materials, drawing from rural and urban areas and from geographic areas with higher concentrations of communities of color. We researched our archives for our original shelter rules. (We found some materials from the earliest days that requested women to find another space to "make love in!").

We developed a revised phone screen that included the question "How do you feel about living with women from different races, classes, religions, or who may be lesbian?" We had already been screening for racism and communal living issues. However, adding the word lesbian (a) let lesbian callers know we take their physical and emotional safety seriously and are advocates for lesbians, (b) let straight women know our expectations about respect, communication, and community living issues, and (c) told all callers that it is safe for battered heterosexual women to reevaluate their sexuality in relation to their battering if they so desire.

We wanted women to feel safe enough to bring out their general feelings, thoughts, and questions. At the time, we were the only shelter in the state that was actively screening all callers for homophobia and compatibility with diversity, and the screening process continues to this day. We feel that it is very important to use specific words—for example, "lesbian or bisexual" rather than the vague "sexual orientation." Callers are not expected to have perfect responses. When issues of oppression—be it racism, classism, or homophobia—come up, staff and volunteers respectfully probe for a willingness to consider accurate information, self-reflection, and personal growth. We make connections between stereotypes about battered women and whatever the other targeted group is.

We also have amended the shelter rules to clarify respect for diversity. Statements that are derogatory toward people of color, welfare recipients, lesbians, or others can be grounds for immediate dismissal. By clearly communicating the shelter's expectations beforehand, we encourage participants to ask for help to reevaluate stereotypes or misinformation. One of two weekly house meetings focuses on issues of oppression and their connection to sexism and domestic violence.

In addition to offering shelter to battered lesbians and their children, we also provide a motel voucher for women who have confidentiality issues connected to domestic violence movement participants, the lesbian community, or concerns about homophobic targeting by other residents. Motel vouchers are also a way to provide shelter to woman-identified transsexuals and transgendered people. Bradley-Angle has begun to discuss policy regarding trans women and as yet vouchers are the best solution we can come up with. We are still working on this issue.

In the volunteer training, we devote much time to unlearning different oppressions. The homophobia/biphobia training is divided; straight women and queer women work separately. Each group is facilitated by pairs that include at least one lesbian or bisexual woman. Lesbian and bisexual women focus on unlearning internalized oppression. Heterosexual women get general training in unlearning homophobia as well as specific tools for shelter and crisis phone work. Something as simple as a phone worker not assigning a sex to the batterer until the caller does makes the program more accessible to sexual minority women.

Agency Caucuses

At present, the agency has a lesbian caucus, a bisexual women's caucus, and a working group of participants from both caucuses and from the community. The agency supports participation of staff and volunteers in the state coalition's Lesbian and Bisexual Women's

Caucus. Staff use paid time to attend agency and state caucuses as a part of fulfilling their job responsibilities.

Bisexual Women and the
Bisexual Women's Caucus

In 1991, a bisexual woman went through the Bradley-Angle volunteer training. At that time, the antihomophobia training was divided into separate sessions for lesbian and straight women so that the different issues of unlearning homophobia and internalized homophobia could be dealt with in a safe environment. The volunteer raised her hand and asked, "Where do the bisexuals go?" The facilitator said, "That's never come up before. I'll leave that up to you." This incident made clear to us that in our agency bisexual women were made invisible. This incident also led us to our current practice of inviting women to join the "unlearning internalized homophobia and biphobia" group.

The volunteer coordinator was responsive and suggested a separate group for the bisexual women. It didn't work because of the complexities of identifying sexual orientation. Around the same time, however, another bisexual woman was hired as outreach coordinator. She expressed interest in either forming a joint lesbian/bisexual women's caucus or joining the work group on lesbian battering. The caucus decided to remain lesbian only. The work group vacillated over the issue. At one point the work group invited bisexual participation, then decided against it. At this time, it was somewhat acceptable to make assumptions and generalizations about bisexuals and their behavior. Women commented that bisexuality did not exist or was perverted or that the process of organizing bisexuals was disrespectful to lesbians.

The two out bisexual women formed their own caucus. Despite a rocky beginning, the caucus slowly gained members. Soon bisexual women from other domestic and sexual violence programs started attending. Currently, the group is oriented toward both social support and specific tasks. The group has spent a lot of time problem-solving around issues of biphobia within the battered women's movement and issues that battered bisexual women face.

During bi caucus discussions, members consider the dynamics of the intersections of internalized homophobia, straight privilege, and external biphobia. Many issues center on specific barriers to bisexual women in same-sex domestic violence relationships, including lack of appropriate services to bisexual women battered by women, disagreement about how these services should be provided, a sense from the lesbian community that it is unethical or even abusive to be a bisexual woman and in a relationship with a lesbian, and exclusion of or failure to acknowledge the work of bisexual women on same-sex domestic violence.

Many of the initial conflicts and oppressive behaviors that the bisexual women's group encountered have greatly improved over time. The bi caucus has tried but not yet succeeded to start a woman-to-woman domestic violence group open to lesbians, bisexual women, and women who do not identify as either. We held the first-ever workshops on bisexuality and domestic violence in our area. We also put together workshops for the state annual conference on domestic violence and local forums on lesbian battering. We worked with the lesbian caucus to change the language in Bradley-Angle forms to be inclusive of bisexuals and did coalition work with the bisexual women's network in Seattle and bisexual members of the Battered Lesbian Intervention Project in Eugene.

Lesbians and Bisexuals
in Alliance

Individuals from both the bi caucus and lesbian caucus took leadership in bringing the groups together. This important process was made possible because each group believed in the goodness of the other, despite a lot of hurt feelings and disagreements. We had the mutual goals of providing respectful services to women battered by women and the vision of an ever-strengthening movement. The more the two caucuses started to interact, the more we were able to identify how our conflicts arose.

For example, bisexual women often identify specific events or beliefs on the part of the lesbian community as biphobic. The lesbian community perceives this identification as homophobia on the part of the bisexual women's community. Both communities respond similarly to each other's reactions and a cycle of mistrust is born. Bisexual women in our agency have wanted the lesbian support group to be open to bisexual women battered by women. Lesbians on staff have felt that it was important to deal with same-sex domestic violence in a lesbian-only space. As a result, bisexual women sometimes have felt excluded, and lesbians sometimes have felt disrespected. Each group feels like the other group's sentiments come from an oppressive place.

Some of the ways we have built a coalition between lesbians and bisexual women are these: joint work projects with equal lesbian and bisexual women participation, a joint lesbian and bisexual women's caucus that meets quarterly, and social time together. The lesbian and bi caucuses work together now to organize our community forums about same-sex domestic violence. Lesbians and bisexuals support each other while resisting becoming invisible in our work together.

Recently, we held another series of forums focusing on accountability and appropriate community response to lesbian battering. We also do person-to-person outreach, train the staff and volunteers of other organizations, do outreach to bartenders at women's bars, and do outreach to barbers within the community.

Agendas for workshops include basic information about abuse, the cycle of violence, and effects of abuse on women and children. We brainstorm on how woman-to-woman violence is different from heterosexual domestic violence; how homophobia silences sexual minority women in healthy relationships and further intensifies their isolation when they are battered; community denial; and how unsafe community space can drive survivors away. We discuss the triple jeopardy of women of color—as women, people of color, and lesbians. We discuss the effects of internalized sexism on women battered by women who often have intense guilt, emotional ties to the abuser, and boundary confusion. We discuss internalized homophobia and its effects on batterers and survivors.

These workshops help us get ideas and feedback and help community members deal with specific situations, set up a dialogue, and hear about successes and failures. Lesbian and bisexual staff members and volunteers bridge the gap between our agency and our community. Queer women can do this only because we count on the agency to be a safe place for us, so we believe that we can offer some measure of safety to other members of our community. That is not to say there are no risks. However, lesbians and bisexual women weigh the risks personally and for our communities.

Two lesbians from another program recently felt that it was necessary to propose statewide antihomophobia training standards to the Oregon Coalition Against Domestic and Sexual Violence. The Bradley-Angle House lesbian caucus worked to develop input for the state coalition lesbian and bisexual women's caucus. The antihomophobia training standards took only two months to pass (the antiracism standards had taken two years!). Now each program is required to provide three hours per year of antihomophobia training for all staff and volunteers. This is a good beginning but certainly not a panacea. Bisexual women helped immensely in getting the antihomophobia training standards passed.

Future Strategies

Future strategies include continuing to foster community intolerance of same-sex domestic violence, providing services for children affected by same-sex family violence, organizing a conference on lesbian family violence, and continuing to work with police and the justice system on lesbian family violence.

Conclusion

This chapter would not have been possible without the dedication of the lesbian, bisexual, and straight women who have committed to providing the highest quality of service and support to battered women. All women have the right to live with dignity and respect and without violence. Many lesbians and bisexual women have taken risks and have provided brilliant analyses that contribute to our work today. These women continue to influence our future directions.

We remember.

12

Coalition Building
'Til It Hurts

*Creating Safety Around
S/M and Battering*

Jennifer Margulies

The bedroom is still dark, but the light of the dawning morning filters in through the drawn shades. She has gotten up to make coffee, and as you hear the liquid starting to percolate and her footsteps coming back toward the room, you sit up in bed and decide that you are going to say something to her.

She walks in and sits down next to you.

"Hey listen. . . ," you start.

"Mmm?" she answers, her lips at your neck. You put your hand in her hair and leave it there, not quite pushing her away but hoping she'll stop so that you can go on. She pulls back and looks at you. You drop your hand.

"The other day, when we were fighting?" You are careful to keep your voice calm. "It really startled me when you hit me. No one's ever done that to me—no lover, I mean. I've been thinking about it a lot."

She says nothing; she doesn't look away. You wonder if you've said anything out loud. You try again.

"It bothered me. It's been bothering me since then."

"Huh," she says. "Hmm. That's funny." Her voice has an edge to it now. "I thought you liked that—aren't you the one that's into that kind of thing?"

Not like that, you think. It had been quick, sharp, and angry: her hand slamming into your face after an hour of taunting you mercilessly. It had been pure rage, nothing playful in it, no concern for your pain, coming out of nowhere, coming out of the gathered frustration of an hour that had turned her into someone else.

But then you remember another time: her hand pinning your wrists to the bed, your arms held above your head, your hips rising to meet hers, your own sharp gasp of pleasure as she spread your legs with the pressure of her knee, grabbing the soft, easily bruised skin of your thigh with her one free hand.

How do you explain the difference?

How can you?

There are many ways to establish the difference between intimate abuse and sex that plays with power and pain, but the simplest way is to chisel the interlocking surfaces of battering and sadomasochism down to one word: *consent.* S/M has it; abuse does not. S/M is a particular kind of sexual activity that takes place in a determined time and place, or "scene," with the limits and roles of each partner clearly defined. Any violence, coercion, or domination in S/M takes place in the context of the consensual scene. Both of the partners agree on a safeword, so either partner can stop the action at any time if she feels that she needs to do so. Some people engage in S/M that extends beyond "scene play" into the exploration of "nonconsensual consensuality" or full-time dominant/submissive relationships that are entered into through the negotiated consent of both parties. Whatever its form, however, S/M is conscious, consensual activity. Battering, on the other hand, is a pattern of violent and/or coercive behaviors that one person uses to maintain control over his or her partner.[1] Battering never takes place in a limited, predefined setting; it permeates an entire relationship, often seeping out to affect daily life outside the relationship. Most important, battering is not consensual; no one asks or agrees to be abused.

Consent is by no means a magic word here. The fact that a simple one-word marker can differentiate S/M and battering does not mean that the issue of S/M is or soon will be a simple one for the movement against domestic violence. After all, there are feminists who question the possibility of true female consent in a patriarchy, who argue that a woman's "yes" is irrelevant in a culture that ignores her "no." It seems to me, however, that in thinking about S/M and battering, we must stand up for both our "yes" and our "no," find a middle ground in the debate that allows us power and pleasure even as we denounce abuse and cry out for safety. To do this might just mean to bring together what we have been working to make separate, to consider S/M and battering in the same breath but not in the same light. It is vital that we in the movement against domestic violence remember the distinction between abuse and S/M, but it is also important that we begin to bridge the distance between the pro-S/M and anti-abuse camps.

The polarization of S/M feminists and anti-S/M domestic violence and sexual assault activists has prevented exploration of the ways in which abuse between intimate partners is always a complex combination of desire and coercion, violence and love. Although this combination is not as striking in all situations as it is in the opening scenario of this chapter, it is a common element of abuse. The abuser's most charming qualities are his or her best weapons; what draws you in keeps you down as well. He or she hurts you with what you desire, be it his or her strength, wit, or sensuality— a tactic that encourages survivors to doubt themselves and question whether they actually did want the abuse. After all, they wanted the abuser, didn't they? This is exactly where the demonization of desire that has been used against S/M gets turned against survivors. Because abusers use this confusion to manipulate, and because gay, lesbian, bisexual, and transgendered survivors of intimate abuse bear enough shame around their sexuality, the movement against domestic violence has a responsibility to more openly address the complexities of S/M as it relates to battering.

The Movement Against Battering

Historically, organizations and service agencies working to end domestic violence have either taken stands against S/M as a form of battering or kept silent about S/M sexual practices and the controversy around them. It may seem counterproductive to reopen community wounds by addressing the topic, but there is nothing to shatter but an illusion of peace by naming problems that are kept quiet. As things stand now, survivors who practice S/M may be provided with inappropriate services that focus on their sexuality as the cause of their problem or with no services at all. Silence always benefits the abusers.

Organizations and service agencies can take several steps to be more inclusive. Considering the amount of anger, pain, and politics contained in the debate over S/M and battering, these "steps" are better understood as directions for change than as stages to be followed sequentially. This is said by way of both invitation and challenge. It is vital that organizations and agencies evaluate their own positions and work toward the level of change that is feasible for them.

Develop a Clear Policy That States That S/M Is a Form of Sexuality, Not a Form of Battering

Have this policy in place before it is needed. This is not to say that abuse does not occur in S/M relationships, nor is it to say that S/M cannot be used as a tool of abuse. Such a policy merely states that S/M is not the cause of abuse any more than, say, a woman's lesbianism is the cause of her abuse. For some organizations, instituting such a policy might mean reversing existing policies or contradicting very deeply held beliefs of long-time advocates and staff. An understanding of S/M as a form of sexuality rather than a form of abuse is the strongest base from which to provide effective services for survivors who also practice S/M. However, there *are* concrete ways to improve services for battered lesbians and bisexual women who practice S/M, even if an organization cannot reconcile itself to a proactive neutral policy on S/M.

Make a Commitment to Serve Survivors
Who Practice S/M

Even if the organization cannot reach a consensus that S/M itself is not abuse, steps can be taken to make services available to women who are abused in S/M relationships. Advertise this commitment. Use an S/M couple as one of several examples in outreach about battering—not to demonize S/M but to demonstrate that abuse is no more normal in S/M communities than it is in others. In literature that states that the organization serves all battered women or all lesbian, gay, bisexual, or transgendered (LGBT) people who are battered in intimate relationships, regardless of ethnicity, race, age, ability, and so forth, include "sexual practices" or "sexual philosophy." Otherwise, given the years of exclusion and debate over their sexuality, many survivors who practice S/M will not assume that feminist or antiviolence organizations will be at all safe for them.

Some people may object that it would be "revictimizing" other survivors to be in support groups or in shelters with survivors who practice S/M. Organizations should be thinking about ways to support both survivors who practice S/M and those who are triggered by it. Organizations with more than one support group, for example, might mark one as S/M-friendly or S/M-neutral. Consider, however, that groups are for working on battering and members are going to be discussing abuse issues, not giving play-by-play descriptions of their sex lives. It is also important to remember that it is not uncommon for a group member to be triggered by another member's experiences, mannerisms, or ideologies, yet no efforts are made to segregate groups around these issues. Rather, the group might discuss ways that the two survivors could be together that would avoid or override the triggering. This is part of the work of creating safety in a group. I am wary of the paternalism implicit in urges to "protect" survivors from other survivors. Such concerns are not only demeaning to survivors of battering, they often serve as a screen for prejudice. Remember that the same reasoning was used to argue against the presence of lesbian and bisexual survivors of battering in shelters with homophobic heterosexual survivors.

Back Up the Commitment to Inclusive Service
With Appropriate Training

In order to offer nonjudgmental support to people in the S/M community who have been battered, advocates and staff will need training in discussing S/M and abuse. Such training could offer a history of the debate around S/M in antiviolence movements and women's communities, but it should always emphasize that the basic principles of advocacy apply to the support of survivors who practice S/M. Whatever a staff member or advocate's personal feelings may be, the person calling the hotline is the focus. As always, survivors must be given the space to figure out for themselves what is abusive in their relationships. The advocate's job is to facilitate this space for a survivor, not to judge the survivor's lifestyle.

A similar training for staff and advocates would be helpful in making the transition to an S/M-neutral policy and in making such a policy work for inclusiveness. Prospective staff members and advocates should be made aware of the policy and asked if they feel they can work within it. Routine advocate trainings should include an explanation of the policy and suggestions about how to deal with issues of S/M in the context of abuse, regardless of the personal viewpoint of the trainee.

Education Must Continue

Whether or not a particular agency is ready to adopt a neutral policy on S/M, service agencies and organizations can encourage more productive discussions of S/M within their own groups. Groups can continue to educate themselves about S/M. If S/M support groups or political action groups exist in the area, domestic violence agencies can contact them and ask if they have speakers who could talk to a group of domestic violence service providers. The National Leather Association has established a national clearinghouse for materials and questions about domestic violence specifically for the leather/fetish community. These resources, including a brochure on domestic violence designed for S/M players, are available to anyone who requests them.[2]

An organization that does have a neutral policy on S/M can serve as a resource to other organizations that are struggling with the issue of S/M. They can let other organizations and agencies know how they arrived at the policy, what they have found the benefits and drawbacks of the policy to be, what community reaction has been, and how they have handled it.

The benefits of a more open approach to S/M extend beyond the increased number of survivors who practice S/M who will contact the organization or agency for services. Separating battering from S/M removes some of the stigma from women who practice S/M, who may be afraid of condemnation as "sick" if they are open about the abuse in their relationships. Efforts to include survivors who practice S/M also begin to present survivors in general with less restrictive and blaming messages about pleasure, which has been an unfortunate gap in many institutions of anti–domestic violence work. In the polarized debate between S/M and anti-S/M feminists, the companion to the stereotype of sadomasochists as fascist and immoral is the image of the anti-S/M domestic violence or sexual assault advocate as uptight and opposed to pleasure. Although neither stereotype deserves reinforcing and nobody could pay me to believe that anti–domestic violence advocates are anti-pleasure, there *is* a history of stigma around the (sexual) pleasure of survivors. From the first heterosexual texts that psychologized the condition of battered women by referring to the "bizarre and puzzling nature of the intimacy between people who live in violence,"[3] to shelter staff that expressly forbid conversation about the positive aspects of the abusive marriages of survivors,[4] the multiple emotional realities of survivors' lives have presented difficulties to a movement that sees only the horror of abuse. S/M is on the extreme end of this scale of disallowed survivor pleasure.

The S/M Community

When I logged on to an S/M computer bulletin board to eavesdrop on what "the S/M community" was saying these days, I found references to "abuse and other vanilla [non-S/M] kinks," as if those who practice S/M have developed sexually and emotionally beyond such unhealthy "vanilla kinks" in favor of fully redeeming S/M sexuality. There is no sexuality that will protect against abuse. People involved with S/M communities have a responsibility to improve understandings about abuse and S/M.

S/M Communities Must Own Battering

This is a difficult sentence to write, because for far too long S/M as an image and the S/M community as a whole have been forced to "own" battering for all of the queer nation. This is not the kind of owning that I mean. Rather, we need to acknowledge that S/M communities are not immune to abuse and that they must be accountable for the battering that does go on inside them. Accountability carries with it the burden of action, the duty to take steps to end the abuse.

Many survivors of color and survivors from various religious and ethnic backgrounds have been similarly reluctant to implicate their already denigrated communities. That survivors who practice S/M have done less than survivors of other minority groups to raise abuse issues in their community and to raise their community's issues in the movement against abuse may have to do with the fact that no other group is as consciously, purposefully, and methodically maligned by the movement itself.

Believe Survivors

Because abuse is so often a misguided charge laid against S/M communities from "the outside," survivors of abuse who identify as S/M players rarely speak out about the issue. And the social structure of S/M communities supports silence about abuse. Social repercussions travel faster and hit harder in small communities with rapid gossip networks. Tops stand to lose their sexual reputations if they admit to being beaten by or losing control to their bottoms; bottoms stand to lose their reputations if they name their abuse for what it is. The attacks on the identities of survivors and the taunts of "You can dish it out but you just can't take it" (directed at tops) or "You're just chickenshit, you're no bottom at all" are especially poisonous because they tend to echo so closely the psychological manipulations of the perpetrators. When survivors do speak out, they *must* be taken seriously.

S/M Insularity Is Not the Cure to All Social Ills

Many S/M communities have the attitude that the community will look out for its own. If a relationship turns abusive or a scene gets out of hand, everyone will know; the abuser will be censured and possibly subject to retaliation. However, the idea of an insular S/M community that can protect its own through a well-maintained gossip chain relies on an old, nearly obsolete idea of community translated directly from the S/M friendship networks of San Francisco and New York City in the 1970s and early 1980s. The community is no longer small enough to make such protective measures effective. Increased publication of S/M materials and the advent of the Internet make the entity labeled "the S/M community" a vast virtual community with none of the strict initiation rituals and customs of the S/M community in its underground days. These days, one might consider oneself S/M without ever having met another S/M person in real life, much less one who will recognize abuse as it develops and step in to help. What is more, the sort of intervention most talked about among community members is of the "ride in to rescue the helpless bottom from the really seriously nasty top" variety. Not only does this perpetuate the myth that abusers are always tops, it also relies on a method of intervention that rarely succeeds. Rescuing does not engage or empower the survivor. Prevention and empowering intervention are much more successful ways of struggling against abuse and assisting survivors, and they require a strong framework of pro-survivor, anti-abuse attitudes. Such attitudes are difficult to find and benefit from in a community that does not discuss abuse openly. Everyone who has ever joined the movement against domestic violence has had to sacrifice some form of insular protection in order to build a larger sense of safety. We all have to move away from old ideas of security in favor of crafting new ones that will provide a much different version of safety. The S/M community can be no exception.

Reach Beyond "the Community"

There are many outside S/M communities who have much to offer abuse survivors who practice S/M. It is important not to shy away from those resources that can actually be useful. Individuals who think that a friend might be abusing or being abused should call and research the local resources for abusers and survivors rather than assume that these groups will be anti-S/M. S/M organizations have a responsibility as community groups to ensure that local abuse resources are educated about S/M and that community groups are informed about abuse. S/M organizations can offer workshops to women's shelter staff, do speaker swaps with the local GLBT antiviolence project, or ask the local victim/witness agency if they will do a joint training for police about survivors who also practice S/M. Just because the marginalized have been denied safety in the mainstream does not mean they do not deserve to be safe.

Creating Safety Out of Risk

In the struggle against abuse there are certainties and gray areas. Certainties come in the form of generalizations: Abuse is wrong; S/M is consensual; no one wants to be abused; no one deserves to be hurt. The territory of the general cannot extend to the full reach of our multiple realities, however. At some point we have to admit that reality gets too personal and too complex. The lines become blurry and our knowledge partial, and this is painful. It is always painful to know that we have only pieces of the truth and not the whole thing. It is always painful to know that we cannot do it alone. So in our organizing we avoid this pain, avoid the personal and the confusing. We work at the battered women's shelter, but we don't admit to our leather orientation or challenge the anti-S/M policy there, even though it prevents some women we know from calling to get the help they need as battered lesbians. We are quick to say that violence against women and LGBT people is wrong, but we are slow to respond to personal attacks in the movement against domestic violence on visible leatherfolk. We are quick to say to perceived outsiders, bigots, and critics that S/M is consensual, but we are slow to acknowledge and protect against the possibility of real abuse in S/M relationships as in all others, reluctant to provide a forum to discuss it, and downright unwilling to approach domestic violence service providers to begin work in our communities. We have struggled together in the clearly marked public spaces of general consensus and have avoided the murkier, more difficult places in the interest of preserving our movement and our communities.

We need to start building coalitions in the gray areas, the individual spaces that are not yet—and may never be—completely clear. We need, on all sides, to recognize the imperfection of our vision. Perhaps it is better called the infinite perfectibility of our vision once we move *toward* rather than away from each other for our safety.[5]

Notes

1. This definition of battering is adapted from B. Hart, "Lesbian battering: An examination" in *Naming the violence: Speaking out about lesbian battering.* (K. Lobel, ed., Seattle, WA: Seal, 1986, pp. 173-177).

2. For more information, contact Safe Link, c/o Domestic Violence Education Project, National Leather Association, 3439 NE Sandy Blvd. #155, Portland, OR 97232. (614) 470-2093. E-mail: nlai@aol.com

3. See L. Walker, *The battered woman.* New York: Harper & Row, 1979.

4. See D. R. Loeske, *The battered woman and shelters: The social construction of wife abuse.* Albany, NY: State University of New York Press, 1992.

5. Califia, P. (1991). A house divided: Violence in the lesbian S/M community. *Brat Attack, 1.*

13

Woman-to-Woman Battering on College Campuses

Tonja Santos

I sat outside the room on a couch with my now-girlfriend, Emily. I debated whether I actually wanted to go to the meeting room or just go back to my dorm room and forget about the whole thing. That was a big temptation back then (and sometimes even now), to just go somewhere where I would be able to forget about it. Emily and I made a safety plan (although I did not call it that at the time, nor did I realize that that was what I had been doing for the past two years). She would sit with me and if I needed to leave the workshop she would leave with me unless I indicated otherwise.

We walked into the room to find five women there. Two were the facilitators and two were from the sponsoring organization. This was the turnout for a workshop on lesbian battering on a campus of 2,000 women with a sizable lesbian and bisexual population. Four women had to be there, and the other was doing a research project of some sort. And then there was me. Why was I there? I was sure I wasn't going to learn anything I didn't already know about lesbian battering. I was also fairly sure that the facilitators were competent and didn't need my input.

What could have possessed me to walk into a room in which I knew every single woman there? None of them knew (or wanted to know) that I was battered, much less that I was battered by a woman they all knew and with whom at least two of them were close. All that kept my batterer from the workshop that day was another engagement. She was a Women's Studies major, dedicated to ending all forms of violence against women, a loyal attendant of Take Back the Night marches, and a batterer. My batterer. And I, a woman who attended those same marches, had gone home to or with my batterer and added daily to my list of things not to do in order to keep the peace.

How do I reconcile the woman I thought, and the world thinks, my batterer is with the way she systematically undermined my independence and happiness? How do I reconcile my own hypocrisy in believing that violence against a woman is never her fault, yet creating and constantly expanding a mental list of things that I should and should not do to make things right, or at least not wrong, to appease my batterer? How do I begin to explain the fact that I was battered for two years on a campus that is supposed to be a protective environment for all women; that no one, myself included, saw or wanted to see what was happening to me; that in coming out as a battered lesbian on that campus I would risk rumors, anger from the queer community, and being called a liar?

Why the Deadly Silence?

Why was it so difficult to recognize the battering happening in my own life when, from an intellectual perspective, I knew so much about the dynamics of battering? There are many reasons. In the general public and in many queer communities, and certainly the queer community on my campus, there is not enough exposure to concepts and words that describe and include what many women experience in abusive lesbian relationships.

Even when patterns of behavior in a relationship feel for some reason "not right," one may still hesitate to use the word "battering." The generally accepted definition of battering is, in and of itself, problematic in identifying battering within our relationships and our communities. To many, "battering" evokes images of physical violence or direct threats of physical violence. To say that this definition is inadequate to describe the abuse that can and does occur in many intimate relationships is an understatement. Threats of violence in my relationship were extremely subtle. She would tell me in vivid detail about violent dreams in which she would "beat the shit out of me." The only time she supposedly had these dreams was after we had argued. Or she would make threats while we were having sex, such as, "Now I understand how someone could rape another person." My batterer rarely struck me, and these instances were always a "mistake" that happened in the course of her throwing something across the room or the like. Had I been able to associate "battering" with the way she made me feel and the control she exercised over me, rather than with the rigid definition that is generally accepted, I may have felt that the word "battered" applied to me as well and analyzed my situation differently.

Ironically, I was also alienated from the term "battered" by the notions of "feminism" that are popular on my campus. I have lived the past three years on a small, all-women's, mainly residential college campus. The sizable queer community is conservative and separatist. Many women on campus subscribe to a "feminism" that holds that "traditional" roles (such as choosing to be a homemaker and/or to raise a family and, in some ways, choosing "butch" and "femme" roles) and "nontraditional" roles (such as sadomasochistic [S/M] sex) limit women's abilities and do not contribute overall to changing the sexist and hierarchical institutions that dominate women. In effect, this perspective circumscribes not only women's ability to define feminism for themselves but also limits women's ability to make decisions that directly affect their own lives.

Many feminists on campus equate or closely associate the words "violent" with "male." This equation serves many purposes in the feminist and queer communities on campus. It allows frustrations and blame for social inequities to fall on men and "their" institutions and allows women to push aside or ignore the identities that constantly separate *women* from forming alliances with one another, such as race, class, nationality, religion, ability (both physical and mental), sexuality, and lifestyle. And with all of these disturbing issues that remain unaddressed or underaddressed, it is easy to add the fact that violence is not an inherently male characteristic, that there are women among our feminist and queer ranks who use violence of all sorts to control other women.

For many queer women on campus, admitting that there is partner violence in our community would force us to recognize the hypocrisies in our lives around issues of violence. We would be forced to acknowl-edge that we have protected batterers with our silence and that what a woman says about violence in a classroom, at a meeting, or at a rally is not necessarily the way she chooses to live her life and interact in her personal relationships. A bit closer to home, it would mean admitting that there is not automatic safety from violence because one is in a relationship with another woman.

There are many stereotypes about same-sex violence and, more specifically, woman-to-woman battering that coupled with the pervad-ing feminist attitude on campus, particularly among the queer women, contribute to the lack of acknowledgment of and dialogue about woman-to-woman battering. Two common misconceptions are (a) that battering most frequently or even happens only in relation-ships in which the women identify as "butch" and "femme" and (b) that battering is either related to, a result of, or a form of S/M sex. The negative attitudes on campus surrounding butch and femme identities and S/M sex have effectively suppressed any dialogue about ways in which people incorporate either or both into their identities and their relationships. As a result, for the woman who needs to do so, it is easy to believe that these phenomenon do not "exist" in her environment and that relationships between women on *her* campus are characterized by an inherent purity and equality.

Another popular stereotype on my campus is that only women who are "apolitical" (if such a thing exists) are involved in battering relationships. Many women have said things to me like "*You?* But you are so politically aware!" when I tell them I was battered. This defensive reaction is dangerous in many ways because we know that any woman is capable of getting involved in a battering relationship. It also results in messages like "Are you stupid?" when women talk about their experiences as battered women. Such reactions further perpetuate the self-blame, isolation, and silence surrounding the issue of woman-to-woman partner violence.

Assumptions about class and race also play into the denial of same-sex battering on campus. One thing that continually amazes me is that the community on campus has, on the whole, convinced itself that our racial, ethnic, religious, and sexual differences make our campus a better place to be but that we all come from middle-class backgrounds. We have made an art of actively ignoring that, for example, the phrase "I have no money" means very different things for different people: For some, it means "I have to run to the bank" or "I have to call my parents," and to others, it means studying in the library every night because they can't afford to buy their course books. We like to pretend that we are all one big happy middle-class diverse family. The media have done a superb job of convincing most people, at least on a subconscious level, that violence and abuse in the home occur only or predominantly in non-white and/or lower-class families and that it is a matter of personal dysfunction. If we all believe that we are a campus of middle-class women and simultaneously associate violence with people who are not "like us," then once again we can ignore the problem in our midst.

Even if there were complete openness about the issue of battering within the queer community on campus, there are logistical problems with the size and nature of the community that make it difficult for women to come out and speak openly about being battered. As battered women, we often hesitate to talk about our experiences in any context. On the small campus on which I live within the small, closely knit, interconnected queer community, practically everyone knows and interacts with everyone else. This makes it difficult for a battered woman to "come out" about her experiences. Chances are that the people who constitute her support network are acquainted with, or even have relationships with, her batterer. Faced with this situation, I usually did not talk to the people I was closest to because they were also my batterer's closest friends (not a coincidence). What if they didn't believe me? What if they passed what I told them on to my batterer? There was also this odd concern I had for not ruining her reputation! If people knew what she was doing to me, what would they think of her? What would they think of me? There was a lot of self-doubt—I wondered sometimes if I was making up the abuse or blowing it all out of proportion. I felt doubtful in part because I did not know any other women who had been in abusive lesbian relationships; I had only read about them. Although reading was reaffirming, I still felt I was alone. I didn't know what was worse: Telling friends and having them say "I saw it happening" or telling people and hearing them tell me "I can't imagine her doing that!"

The situation can get even more claustrophobic if you are a member of another smaller queer community, such as Jewish lesbians and bisexuals or lesbians and bisexual women of color. I am a woman of color and know most of the queer women of color on campus quite well. The one place where I may have been able to open up and discuss the way I felt about the relationship was the support group for queer women of color, which my batterer attended as well.

As a woman of color, I have also found that when I have dated a white woman, my friends of color on some level have disapproved and been disappointed in me. If I were being battered by a white woman, I can imagine that I might find it in some ways even more difficult to discuss my relationship with friends who felt this way. I can imagine becoming defensive about the relationship and hesitant to talk to them under the circumstances. White women being battered by women of color probably would have similar feelings of defensiveness about their abusive relationships, reluctant to do what they may perceive as perpetuating stereotypes by seeking help and talking about the battering in the relationship.

Where to Go From Here:
Some Considerations for a College Campus

As a woman of color interested in organizing around battering and especially woman-to-woman battering on a small women's college campus, I have often felt that I have few options and resources. The group on campus that has in the past dealt with issues of violence against women focuses mainly on rape or solely on male violence. The one attempt this group made to bring attention on campus to the issue of woman-to-woman battering, which I mentioned earlier, was poorly attended. Over the years, the one queer alliance on campus has become mainly a place for very out, white lesbians (and occasionally bisexual women, provided they are not dating men at the time or do not plan on "selling out" in the near future) to go mainly to socialize. Our counseling center, health center, and campus security all claim to provide staff training in diversity issues, including queer issues and lesbian battering, and I believe for the most part that they want to help any woman who needs it. However, something is lost between their intention to help, their ability to deal effectively, and the perceptions of campus women about their effectiveness. What follows are some suggestions for addressing same-sex battering on campuses.

The group on my campus that deals with issues of violence against women has limited resources. However, we are close to other larger schools and organizations in the area, with resources and services that are quite extensive (such as hotlines, speakers bureaus, and advocacy programs). So the best and most effective way to serve the campus might be to form alliances with the organizations and resources at the larger institutions and in the area. Providing competent, complete referrals and education could bring to my small college more attention, discussion, and information about many issues, including lesbian battering.

Queer organizations can also be a resource for queer women who are or have been in battering relationships. The queer organization on my campus, however, provides little more than a social arena for white middle-class women. In order to be more of a resource to students of color, the group needs to address the biphobia, racism, and classism within it as well as the needs and issues of both bisexual women and queer women of color. The queer organization also might act as an effective educational forum by sponsoring events that raise awareness and foster discussion on topics of concern to the queer campus community. If queer organizations such as the one on my campus are to participate in breaking the silence surrounding lesbian battering, they must also do more than address this important issue. They must become a safe place for all members. One necessary component of creating safety is to formulate statements and policies that violence and battering will not be accepted from any group members and set procedures in place to deal with accusations against and between group members.

As for the other resources on campus, such as campus security, the student health facilities, and the counseling services, there is often a great discrepancy between the way these organizations perceive themselves and want the campus community to perceive them and how they are actually seen by the student body. Any facility that is going to provide services for battered and/or formerly battered lesbians and bisexual women must not only be accessible but must also be *perceived* as such. Lesbian and bisexual women who are being or have been battered and who are looking for a resource must feel, among other things, that the resource is sensitive to the needs of queer women and understands the nature of battering relationships. The battered lesbian on campus must feel confident that she and her situation will be taken seriously, that her confidentiality will be respected regarding her sexuality and/or her battered status, and that she will be effectively protected. Battered women of color must also feel confident that they will not be subjected to debilitating stereotypes or unfair treatment based on race.

One way to raise awareness of woman-to-woman partner violence on campus is through the distribution of informational literature. There are few pieces of literature on my campus that address the needs of lesbian and bisexual women, few that address the issue of relationship violence, and none that address woman-to-woman battering. This situation must be remedied if the college truly wants to serve all battered women on campus. An effort must be made to include information on woman-to-woman relationship violence in any place a woman may look for information, support, and services.

A woman on campus also must feel that her confidentiality will be respected. Confidentiality must be kept at all costs, and breaches, whether intentional or not, should be severely punished. On my campus, the dispatcher who receives all emergency calls and calls to campus security sits in a fairly open area. Someone in a waiting room could feasibly overhear a call. This is unacceptable. It is also imperative that the campus administration or anyone providing services be honest with the woman regarding what will and will not be done with any information that she gives and who has access to that information. For example, a woman needs to know that after she has reported a rape or sexual assault to the health center her confidentiality will be kept and that, although the crime may be reported in the college newspaper, her name will not be released to anyone.

Of course, physical safety also is a large issue. A woman being battered or harassed must be able to keep a batterer away from herself. This need may not be effectively addressed on campus. Security on many campuses is such that there are many ways that a batterer can easily find access to a battered woman. For example, when a woman reports that she has lost her keys to her room, campus security may let her into the room without verifying that she has a right to be there. I have been admitted to my room without being asked to produce verification that it was actually my room. This laxity means that a batterer can easily gain entry to a battered woman's room and therefore have access to her. There are other ways that the negligence of campus personnel (including student workers) can compromise a battered woman's safety by allowing other women access to her mail, her personal space, her storage room, or personal information about her. Ironically, a man seeking the same information or access might be immediately suspect. Thus, there needs to be a clearly defined procedure which, as far as possible, secures the safety and privacy of students from all possible intruders. The consequences for intentionally or even negligently violating these procedures should be as severe as they need to be to ensure compliance.

If a woman obtains a restraining order against another student (or staff person), campus security must strictly enforce the terms of the order. Although this seems like a "given," the fact is that some security guards are reluctant to enforce the terms of such an order for a variety of (irrelevant) reasons, including a hostility to restraining orders and a sympathy for the batterer.

The school also should have policies on battering and complaint procedures that are separate from formal legal procedures. If a board is developed to deal with the issue and potential cases, board members must be well trained in the issues of domestic abuse, same-sex battering, and screening. There must be an appropriate, set procedure for dealing with accusations of battering. For example, it is common for students who are having problems with one another to have a mediation with a trained student or a college staff person. The school must recognize, however, that mediation in a battering situation is extremely dangerous because of the power differences in the relationship and the batterer's potential to use the mediation for further abuse. The school must also establish clear disciplinary procedures for batterers, and a battered woman should have some input about what the disciplinary consequences in a particular situation should be.

And the school must address the needs of women and communities of color. It is important to me as a woman of color to see myself reflected in some way in the resources I am looking to for services. The area in which this is most lacking is campus security. There are few women in my campus security department. People of color are routinely hired and fired within a short period of time, and I am unaware of any out lesbian or bisexual women in the department. I generally feel safer with any of the above answering my call than with a straight white man. As a result of our unique experiences, many women of color and a large number of straight and queer women in general exhaust as many other resources as possible before calling campus security to deal, for example, with an issue involving a Black or Latino man or a lesbian batterer. Campus security must develop a positive relationship with the community of color on campus if that segment of the community is to feel that campus security is accessible to them.

Conclusion

On my small, all-women's college campus, many lesbian and bisexual women live daily with the effects of current or past battering relationships, and they are, for the most part, unseen and unheard. In an effort to protect our images of lesbian communities and intimate relationships between women, many of us in the campus feminist community (as well as others on campus) have been protecting batterers and endangering women's lives with our silence. If we truly want women to be safe, we must acknowledge that we cannot protect and help women with our silence, denial, or negligence. The violence within our lesbian and bisexual communities will not end until we as a student body, as service providers, and as a college community are ready to fully acknowledge woman-to-woman battering and dedicate resources and energy to dealing with it effectively.

14

Domestic Violence Among Same-Sex Partners in the Gay, Lesbian, Bisexual, and Transgender Communities in Puerto Rico

Approaching the Issue

José Toro-Alfonso

During the past decade, domestic violence has been recognized as a major social problem in Puerto Rico. In fact, due mostly to the commitment and support of thousands of women, since 1989 domestic violence has been classified as a crime in Puerto Rico by Law #54. Over the years, the women's movement has organized information centers, shelters, and a strong campaign against domestic violence. However, all these efforts have been exclusively around the issue of domestic violence among heterosexual couples. Only recently have we begun to realize that it is time to open another closet: that of violence and psychological abuse among same-sex couples.

The Gay, Lesbian, Bisexual, and
Transgender Communities in Puerto Rico

The invisibility of gay, lesbian, bisexual, and transgender (GLBT) communities in a Latino culture such as the culture in Puerto Rico makes it easy to ignore the problem of domestic violence. The GLBT population in Puerto Rico is a community driven into hiding by patterns of extreme, socially sanctioned forms of repression. As a consequence, it is a community without precise geographic boundaries, without common historical references (folklore or otherwise), without any major circulating media outlets, and with only nascent political organization efforts. As the San Juan HIV/AIDS prevention needs assessment of the U.S. Conference of Mayors (1993) put it, "Homosexuality is still, for the most part, a hidden phenomenon [in Puerto Rico], and prevention efforts targeting gay/bisexual populations must take this into account and create innovative ways to reach this 'hard to reach' and invisible group" (p. 84).

Nonetheless, with the advent of AIDS, the Puerto Rican general public has been introduced to portions of the gay and lesbian population in the context of what was first considered to be a "gay" disease. The notion that homosexuals had peculiar characteristics that made them susceptible to the infection was prevalent on the island for a long time.

The combination of the AIDS epidemic's ravaging of the Puerto Rican GLBT communities, the media's sensationalist, distorted representation of "lifestyles," and institutionalized discrimination prompted segments of these communities to establish stronger links and institutional forums to organize and increase community cohesion. Over the past decade we have seen the establishment of several organizations to serve the social, political, and medical needs of the GLBT communities in Puerto Rico. It is in this context that the need to look at violence among gay and lesbian couples developed. As initial organizing effort began, the Puerto Rican GLBT community emphasized domestic violence (as well as self-esteem, relationships, cultural issues, and community development) as an essential component of community behavior and an issue in preventing the expansion of the HIV epidemic.

The Puerto Rico Gay/Lesbian
Anti-Domestic Violence Project

The Puerto Rico Gay/Lesbian Anti-Domestic Violence Project initiative was born out of organizing efforts to address the growing HIV epidemic. We recognized that in order to develop a strong, organized, and healthy GLBT community in Puerto Rico, we had to examine the issue of violence among same-sex partners. Funding for the project came from the National Latino/a Lesbian and Gay Organization (LLEGO) in Washington, D.C. Although LLEGO's funding is primarily restricted to HIV prevention, we were able to creatively combine the issues of HIV and domestic violence into a successful proposal.

Because naming the issue of same-sex domestic violence is the first step in motivating community leaders and institutions to recognize the problem and confront denial (Hamberger, 1996), we decided that the first phase of the project should address general myths about domestic violence in our community. To generate community interest in the issue, we decided to use the opportunity of a general sexuality conference developed by the University of Puerto Rico and included a small presentation about domestic violence among lesbians. From there we gathered a small group of people who were interested in continuing to examine the topic. We took advantage of the personal networks found in a close community such as ours to carry information from that circle outward.

We organized a working conference for the GLBT community with the following objectives: empowering the GLBT communities in Puerto Rico by providing an open space for discussing health issues; developing a comprehensive perception of health in these communities with emphasis on the development of healthier lifestyles (including mental and physical health); empowering our communities with the development of nonviolent interpersonal relations; and reducing high-risk behaviors that threatened to compromise mental health and put people at risk of HIV infection.

An advisory board made up of GLBT community members developed an agenda and distributed preliminary information. It was difficult to identify speakers for the conference. We decided that for this initial discussion we needed at least one speaker from outside

Puerto Rico. Because the conference included males and females, we invited a woman from the mainland who had done organizing and direct service work on woman-to-woman battering and a man from Puerto Rico who had published work on gay males, masculinity, and violence.

Conference participants developed small group discussions focused on prevalence, etiology, and different manifestations of violence. There was strong agreement about the prevalence of domestic violence among Puerto Rican gay males and lesbians. Issues of gender, power, "machismo," internalized homophobia, and culture were addressed frequently by group participants.

Many of the participants identified themselves during these discussions as both aggressors and victims of violence in some of their previous relationships. The traditional position of rejecting the aggressor and supporting only the victim produced heated discussion, and the group recommended a more in-depth analysis of the issue. Another area of disagreement was the definition of psychological abuse and control. Many participants thought that we should further examine the social construction of love among same-sex partners within the context of oppression. They felt that the manifestation of intense interest in their partners and the need to protect their relationships in a hostile social environment could either be wrongly interpreted as abuse, or conversely, could play into existing issues of power and control.

Gay and Lesbian Domestic Violence Survey

A second phase of the project was a questionnaire developed by the staff of Fundación SIDA following a review of gay and lesbian domestic violence literature. A translation and adaptation of an instrument developed by Nieves-Rosa from the HIV Center of Columbia University in New York (Nieves-Rosa, 1996) led to a final questionnaire addressing issues of same-sex domestic violence in Puerto Rican communities.

The questionnaire was distributed within GLBT communities in Puerto Rico. The sample of 152 consisted of 88 gay males, 63 lesbians, and 1 transgendered person. (Future surveys and studies will have to address bisexual and transgender invisibility.) The sample was self-selected but included participants from different geographical areas of the island. Among this sample, 40% reported being in a permanent monogamous relationship; 83% were currently employed, and 5% were students. The participants reported an average of 16 years of school, and 72% reported an income of less than $19,999 per year. Almost one-fourth (24%) of the participants reported that their fathers were abusive to their mothers and siblings; a similar number reported sibling abuse. A large percentage reported a high amount of alcohol abuse and behavioral obsessions (for example, eating disorders, sexual abuse) by their fathers, siblings, and selves; nearly half the lesbians and one-third of the gay men reported previous or current alcohol abuse.

The findings about domestic violence are similar to those of studies in the United States. From 7% to 13% of all participants reported at least one instance of physical abuse in their relationship; all identified themselves as the victims. (This could be the result of a self-selected sample, which might concentrate a disproportionate number of people who had been victimized by their partners.) Half reported frequent instances of verbal and emotional abuse. One-fourth of abusive partners were under the influence of alcohol during the abusive episodes. Men reported more incidents of disagreement about daily life issues with their partners—friends outside the relationship, money, work, housecleaning, commitment to the relationship, and communication. The main areas of disagreement for women were outside friendships, communication, and children.

Men were asked about coercion for anal penetration without the use of condoms. Nearly one-fourth reported that they let their partners penetrate them without condoms because they felt the need to please them. Approximately 15% of the male participants reported being penetrated without condoms either by force or because they felt pressure to do so or because their partners insisted, saying things that the participants later realized were not meant seriously. Interestingly, 15% of the male participants were HIV positive.

Conclusions and Recommendations

Although the results of the Puerto Rico Gay/Lesbian Anti-Domestic Violence Project survey cannot be generalized to all gay, lesbian, bisexual, and transgendered people in Puerto Rico, it gave us an idea of the magnitude of the problem and the need to address the issue of violence in our communities. The final results of the survey showed a strong correlation between participants being victimized in a relationship and having been a victim of emotional abuse by their fathers. Project members agreed about the need to further study the relationship between gays, lesbians, bisexuals, and transgendered people and their fathers. As Zemsky (1990) states, for violence to occur there must be learning, opportunity, and choice. Like their heterosexual counterparts, same-sex abusers appear to learn to abuse; it is possible that violent behavior is being learned when fathers model emotional and verbal abuse. Homophobia helps create the opportunity for abuse without consequences by isolating the victims and preventing their access to resources (Merrill, 1996). The problem of isolation may be of utmost importance in Puerto Rico, where a "machismo" cultural subtext might encourage homophobia.

Participants in the Anti-Violence Project in Puerto Rico have been learning to take control of their lives and to show commitment and solidarity for all members of our diverse communities. The project was only an initial effort to address the issue of domestic violence among same-sex partners in Puerto Rico and needs to be expanded. There is an urgent need to identify funding for an ongoing antiviolence project in Puerto Rico that might include same-sex violence, sexual coercion, and hate crimes. The gay, lesbian, bisexual, and transgender communities in Puerto Rico have taken the initial steps to develop a well-balanced and healthy community, and we must now focus on creating the institutional support to enable us to continue our work.

References

Hamberger, L. K. (1996). Intervention in gay male intimate violence requires coordinated efforts on multiple levels. In C. M. Renzetti & C. Harvey (Eds.), *Violence in gay and lesbian domestic partnerships*. New York: Haworth.

Merrill, G. S. (1996). Ruling the exceptions: Same-sex battering and domestic violence theory. In C. M. Renzetti & C. Harvey (Eds.), *Violence in gay and lesbian domestic partnerships*. New York: Haworth.

Nieves-Rosa, L. (1996). *Survey of same sex domestic violence among Latino gay males*. New York: HIV Center for Clinical and Behavior Studies, Columbia University.

U.S. Conference of Mayors. (1993). *Assessing the HIV-prevention needs of gay and bisexual men of color*. Washington, DC: Author.

Zemsky, B. (1990). Lesbian battering: Considerations for intervention. In P. Elliot (Ed.), *Confronting lesbian battering: A manual for the battered women's movement*. St. Paul: Minnesota Coalition for Battered Women.

15

A "New Kind" of Battered Woman

Challenges for the Movement

Martha Lucía García

The hotline worker in a battered women's shelter notices that sporadically yet increasingly calls are coming from women with particularly complex and difficult situations. She addresses this problem in a staff meeting because she does not know what to do with these calls. She gives examples of the calls and points out that although the situations presented are similar they are also very different.

The caller profiles she describes include women who speak no English and women who speak a little English or are fluent English speakers but have strong accents. Women from different parts of the world who have come to the United States for a variety of reasons. Women who have become U.S. citizens. Women who hold green cards, have complicated immigration status, or are undocumented. The common factor among the different callers is that they are all being abused by their partners.

AUTHOR'S NOTE: Reprinted from *NCADV Voice* (Summer 1996). National Coalition Against Domestic Violence, P.O. Box 18749, Denver, CO 80218; (303) 839-1852. Membership information can be found on the inside back cover of an issue.

Complicated enough? No! Sometimes, the abuser is a man, although the caller is in a relationship with another woman. Other times, the abuser is a woman. What to do? The advocate is confused.

The staff attempts to find solutions, but as the meeting progresses there is more confusion and emotions and tempers begin to rise. Some divisions emerge and the staff becomes more and more polarized—the women of color focus on the issue of race because most of the callers are women of color. The lesbians focus on the fact that some callers identify as lesbians while others are married to men but are in relationships with women. The director is concerned with liability and funding issues and asks questions about the consequences of serving undocumented women. Other staff members simply ask, "What is the difference anyway? If they are being battered, shouldn't we just get them out of the violence?"

The above scenario is not uncommon. The battered women's movement has not been able to escape the "white mind," which, as Anne Wilson Schaef (1995) points out, sees the world "in dualisms. It's either this or that. Black or white. Right or wrong." She further explains, "White minds reduce and isolate. They don't readily move into wholes and universality. They are hierarchical and mechanist, and see nature as a force to be tamed and used up with no regard for the future" (pp. 2-3). Anyone who lives in modern Western society can have a "white mind."

The battered women's movement continues to be dominated by the idea that to create unity we must focus on our commonalities and that the experience of being abused and being a woman is enough to create bonds. The underlying message is that we must be the "same" if we are to be united—the same in our perspective and philosophy, the same in our ideas about how to work with women. We are expected to share the belief that our focus is solely on the violence the women experience, that our function is solely to assist women with the issues of violence in their lives. These beliefs lead us to conclude that once the violence is resolved, everything else will fall into place.

In reality, this is not the case for many women who seek help from our organizations—battered women of color, battered lesbians, battered rural women, battered immigrant women. For them, domestic violence is not the sole issue they contend with, and they and their advocates have organized to demand that their multiple intersecting issues be addressed. Yet the battered women's movement continues to be polarized, and the multiple needs of many women continue to be unresolved.

Immigrant Lesbians and
Bisexual Women

Just as we cannot separate U.S. women who are experiencing abuse from the society they live in, we must also look at how immigrant lesbians are affected by globalization of the economy, war and political strife, and the widening gap between rich and poor that forces many to leave their home countries in search of work and a better economic life in the United States. In addition, many immigrant lesbians face the risk of persecution in their native countries for being lesbian, which affects their ability to live freely as lesbians or as immigrant women.

Many immigrant lesbians see the United States as a refuge. They have read stories of the gay liberation movement here. They believe that they will have an easier life in the United States. However, on arrival, what a lesbian may find is very different from what she imagined. If she is lucky, she will find a lesbian community that assists her and shelters her from an intolerant society. Most likely, however, the lesbian community is ambivalent about her and is not receptive to her "difference." She may feel "odd," as if she has nothing in common with U.S. lesbians, and may feel pressured to become like everyone else.

It is therefore not uncommon for an immigrant lesbian to end up living in a neighborhood or community where other people from her country live. Often, this community may have become very traditional after coming to the United States in an attempt to survive alienation in a hostile culture. As a consequence, the immigrant lesbian who escaped traditional constraints in her home country might encounter these constraints from her compatriots here, so that although she is surviving cultural alienation on the one hand, on the other hand she may end up living a closeted life that is not much different from her life back home.

Juggling Cultural and
Immigration Factors

The immigrant lesbian must learn as an immigrant woman how to juggle at least three different cultures: that of her country of origin, that of the lesbian community, and that of the dominant U.S. society. These three cultures are often at odds, and the places where they converge can be problematic.

For example, the lesbian's first culture and the dominant culture may converge on the construction of women's roles so that she ends up in a community that does not challenge these roles but, rather, replicates them. All of her cultural values may contradict what she knows in her heart is the truth about herself. This struggle is psychically, emotionally, physically, and spiritually draining, to say the least.

An immigrant lesbian's immigration status, whether it is legal or unclear, also places her in a precarious situation. The current anti-immigrant propaganda in the United States creates an environment in which immigrants are disliked, distrusted, and blamed for the economic problems of the country. Many politicians would have us believe that immigrants are overburdening our system and ought to be ineligible for most human services. An immigrant lesbian is not immune to these negative feelings against her people. Fear becomes an all-too-present emotion—fear that is heightened by the possibility of being sent back to her country, whether she is undocumented or not.

Contending With Class, Race,
and Sexuality

If she is visibly immigrant, the immigrant lesbian will have to deal with hatred against her race. Her class will determine entry into the work world and into the lesbian community. If she is poor or working class, she is more likely to remain in her immigrant community and to work in jobs that sap her energy. She is affected by substandard wages, fewer opportunities for employment, and undesirable working conditions.

Bisexual and lesbian women fall within a broad spectrum of acceptance or ambivalence about their sexual orientation. Some women clearly define as lesbians or bisexual, others are confused about their identity. Immigrant women are not different in this respect. In fact, for many immigrant women the word *lesbian* is a label that they don't identify with. Some immigrant women will not say that they are in relationships with women for fear of being shunned. It may happen that they feel they must maintain a heterosexual image within their immigrant community; to do this they might have a boyfriend or even marry.

For cultural or economic reasons, immigrant women also may be forced to marry but might end up falling in love with women. The ambivalence and confusion about being attracted to women must be taken into account when addressing the needs of an immigrant battered lesbian or bisexual woman.

Power and Control

If the immigrant lesbian is married with children, being in an abusive relationship may result in her feeling "bad and sinful" for being in love with a woman. Or she may be dependent on a husband because he is her green card sponsor.

If the abuser is a female lover, then the immigrant lesbian is likely to feel betrayed and hopeless because she came to this country to be free from oppression. One woman I worked with was constantly abused by her lover who knew she was attempting to pass as heterosexual in her community. The lover went into jealous rages and accused her of not being a lesbian and of wanting to be with men.

Isolation and shame are perhaps the most common emotions experienced by battered immigrant lesbian and bisexual women. These feelings of exclusion along with the belief that there is nowhere to turn keep the women from reaching out for help.

Whether an immigrant lesbian is part of a lesbian community or not, she may feel she deserves to be abused. She may not talk about the abuse because her abuser may be her only ally in this strange land. If she reaches out and is questioned or is not understood, she might not risk reaching out again.

Forced Sisterhood

The complexity of issues and needs of battered immigrant lesbians and bisexual women demand that we look at the inherent problems in forcing unity and sisterhood through sameness.

Valli Kanuha (1990) enumerates what she sees as the challenge presented by battered lesbians of color to the battered women's movement. Kanuha states, "For feminists, the existence of violence in lesbian of color relationships will represent the failure of the mainstream women's movement to adequately address the interface of sexism, racism, violence and homophobia" (p. 150).

The presence of battered immigrant lesbians and bisexual women complicates the picture even further because it becomes necessary to add to Kanuha's list of issues: xenophobia, ethnocentrism, and heterosexism. Xenophobia and ethnocentrism refer to the movement's inability to integrate an acceptance of different cultures and ways of seeing the world. Heterosexism speaks to the movement's difficulty in embracing women's sexuality and capacity to choose who they will relate to intimately.

The problem with not being able to interface these issues is evident in the staff meeting described at the beginning of this chapter. The women we serve are not seen as whole individuals with unique realities. Instead, for the sake of "manageability," they are fragmented into components that are simpler for us to handle.

A Stagnant Movement

The inability of the battered women's movement to accept that sexism and patriarchy are not the "only" problems facing women, plus our difficulty with integrating into our analysis and practice the issues mentioned above, creates a movement that has allowed our differences to destroy organizations and weaken our efforts to end violence against women.

Worse still, by failing to respond to the multiple realities of battered women we either provide inappropriate services or no services for battered immigrant lesbian and bisexual women, a failure that could lead to their deaths.

Self-Reflection for Advocates

If we in the battered women's movement allow ourselves to be aware of the issues facing battered immigrant lesbians and bisexual women, we will realize that there are internal contradictions that emerge when working with these women. On the one hand, our feminist commitment to all women will encourage us to do anything we can to help battered lesbian immigrants and to ensure that all of their needs are met. We might even become involved with organizing against anti-immigrant backlash.

On the other hand, we may ask ourselves the following: Can I get into trouble for sheltering her? What do I know about her culture, let alone all the issues she is dealing with? Can't she have her batterer deported? Why doesn't she just go back home?

We may also use rationalizations such as these: Our program does not have someone who speaks her language, so we would not be able to help her anyway. She just has too many needs and we just cannot help her. We do not have the money to cover her shelter stay.

What really comes up for us when we ask these questions and make rationalizations? Does the battered immigrant lesbian confront us with our own vulnerabilities? Does she confront us with our own prejudices? Does she in some way create a reflection that we would rather not see? The problem is that even when we write her off because she does not fit neatly into any of our categories we can still feel her pain.

So the question is, which side are you on? Will you take the risk of becoming a more humane advocate? Will you choose to do what is necessary to understand and work with a battered immigrant lesbian?

References

Kanuha, V. (1990). Compounding the triple jeopardy: Battering in lesbian of color relationships. In L. S. Brown & M. P. P. Root (Eds.), *Diversity and complexity in feminist therapy* (pp. 142-157). New York: Haworth.
Schaef, A. W. (1995). *Native wisdom for white minds.* New York: One World/Ballantine.

16

Battered Bisexual Women

Sarah Sulis

A lesbian friend once told me that she did not believe that bisexual women suffer from homophobia. "Straight men love the idea of two women together," she said. "So what's the problem?" The problem, of course, is that bisexual women's relationships are about loving women, not about pleasing men. Furthermore, when a bisexual woman leaves a gay bar with her female lover, gay-bashers roaming the parking lot don't stop to ask if she also sleeps with men. I'm reminded of what my father always told me about my being half-Jewish: "You would have been Jewish enough for Hitler."

When I came out as a bisexual woman in 1977, no community addressed the reality of my life. In my town, the lesbian-feminist community was still in its heyday and being bisexual was unacceptable. The closest connections I found were with bisexual men, who shared my understanding of dual attractions but who did not share my vision of feminism. Today, a feminist bisexual movement is visible and growing. I am grateful to many women, most of whom I have never met, who helped create an understanding of bisexuality that not only embraced, but depended on, a feminist analysis.[1] These women worked tirelessly on the national and local levels to raise awareness about bisexuality and to create a bisexual women's community. Discussions about domestic violence in the bisexual community are possible only because of their work. In addition, a growing number of lesbians have demonstrated not only support but a willingness to struggle with the difficult issues involved in bisexual inclusion.

Today, controversy rages in the battered women's movement about the inclusion of bisexual women in lesbian caucuses and task forces. As important as these discussions may be, they are far removed from the reality of the lives of many battered bisexual women. In one very real sense, such debates are the product of privilege. Those of us with the safety and the means to do so can travel to such meetings and participate in what we may see as cutting-edge work, but for many women, our efforts have little relevance. It may matter a great deal whether someone is lesbian or bisexual at our meetings, but to those in rural areas and small towns, such labels and distinctions are mean-ingless. The reality for these women is that they love other women and that this alone puts them in danger. Heterosexual privilege will not protect them, and they know it. These women can also be battered, and their voices have yet to be heard in the debate over inclusiveness.

To move from rhetoric to effective action, we must understand both bisexuality itself and the intersection between bisexuality and domestic violence. Only then can we design services that will effec-tively address the needs of bisexual victims of such violence.

Who Are We?

The bisexual women's community is not monolithic. It includes women in partnerships with women, those in partnerships with men, single women, celibate women, monogamous women, and those who have multiple partners. Some bisexual women feel confident and proud of their identity, whereas others experience internalized shame, self-hatred, and homophobia. Some bisexual women say that gender is irrelevant to attraction, whereas others note that gender is very much a part of how they relate to their lovers.

Researchers have developed several tools to evaluate the range of sexual orientation. Many bisexuals have pored over both the Kinsey Heterosexual-Homosexual Scale and the Klein Sexual Orientation Grid[2] in an effort to develop a sense of self, but such definitions remain a limited guide to the complexities of our lives. Bisexual literature contains a rich and diverse vision of these complexities and is useful reading for those engaged in this work. Most revealing in such literature are the stories about bisexual women who have been closeted in the lesbian community for years.[3] These women may have seemingly impeccable lesbian credentials and may even be activists and leaders in the lesbian and gay community. Yet even these women can be battered. Bisexual women living in partnerships with other women may seem just like lesbians, yet any discussion of the violence they suffer must include a look at how the dynamics of bisexuality play into the violence. A bisexual woman can be battered by any woman with whom she has an intimate relationship; the batterer may be either lesbian or bisexual.

The Intersection of Bisexuality and Domestic Violence

Although no research exists about the experiences of battered bisexual women, it is easy to see that the systematic use of power and control lends itself well to the complexities of bisexuality. Tactics may include threats of outing, verbal abuse about bisexuality, and extreme jealousy about both men and women. Outing is a particularly effective weapon against bisexual victims. The batterer may threaten to out her partner as a lesbian to family and coworkers, yet also threaten to out her as bisexual within the lesbian community. Such threats reinforce the isolation bisexual women already experience within both the lesbian community and society as a whole.

When bisexual women have children, outing becomes an even greater threat. The batterer may threaten to expose her sexuality to the children's father or to other family members. Battered women's advocates know well the powerful effects of such threats on battered women. Fear of losing one's children is one of the most common reasons women give for staying in abusive relationships. It seems unlikely that a bisexual woman who is actively involved with another woman would fare any better in a custody battle than a lesbian would.

Bisexual women battered by other women report that they are called sexually degrading names and continually threatened about their bisexuality. In the same way that homophobia is used by batterers in heterosexual relationships, biphobia is used against bisexual and even lesbian women. Lesbian victims report that their batterers accuse them of not being "real lesbians" and of wanting to have sex with men. The bisexual victim may constantly be accused of having affairs with both men and women. Verbal abuse may include comments such as

"I'm the only one who will have you" and "If people knew about you, they would take my side." For some bisexual women these tactics are particularly devastating because internalized shame may include shame about relationships with both men and women. In addition, bisexual women may experience the traditional tactics of batterers: eating and sleep disruption, property destruction, harm to pets, and physical violence.

When a bisexual woman is injured by her partner she may experience the same revictimization by service providers that lesbians do. At the emergency room, her batterer is introduced as a friend and allowed to accompany her throughout the visit. As with domestic violence in general, women of color and other marginalized women may experience even more extreme isolation and revictimization by these systems.

Attitudes about bisexual women in the lesbian community may help support the batterer's statements or actions. I have listened to lesbian friends verbalize extreme hostility about bisexual women while others in the group remained silent. As the only bisexual in the room, it then falls on me to interrupt and challenge the myths, lies, and half-truths that are being presented. For example, it is not true that bisexuals are really lesbians who are afraid to come out or for whom relationships with women are always secondary to men. However, it is true that some bisexual women become involved with men and that some have left female lovers to be with men. Regardless of the circumstances of a woman's life, violence against her is unacceptable. I know one bisexual woman who experienced just such violence. When she told her lover that she had slept with a man, she was severely beaten. Friends of the couple supported the violence as "understandable given the circumstances." No one acknowledged the woman's injuries or the ongoing threats to her safety. If a bisexual woman calls the police or attempts to use the legal system to protect her, she may be further ostracized by the lesbian community. For bisexual women who have lived for years in the lesbian community, such ostracism can be traumatic. In addition, homophobic reactions by straight friends and family members may further the sense of isolation.

The bisexual community must also recognize that bisexuals can be perpetrators of such violence. We must hold the batterers among us fully accountable and challenge the homophobia that may contribute to such violence. Furthermore, we must acknowledge that some bisexuals have heterosexual privilege and may use such privilege as a tool in battering other women. An example of this is economic control by a bisexual more able to work in straight society who plays on internalized homophobia: "You're the lesbian, not me." As with race and class, the use of heterosexual privilege makes such violence even more dangerous. It does not serve the bisexual community well to deny that such realities exist.

Recommendations for Provision of Services

Both domestic violence centers and programs serving battered lesbians should be prepared to address the needs of battered bisexual women. Bisexual women experience many of the same obstacles as lesbians when they seek services from mainstream domestic violence programs. These include invisibility, homophobia, and lack of understanding of the unique safety concerns in a closeknit community.

Programs for battered lesbians may also be limited in their ability to assist battered bisexual women. Questions of confidentiality and safety are of critical concern. Bisexual women may be afraid of being outed in the community or of encountering hostile attitudes from lesbians in their group. Although such groups already include closeted bisexual women, the presence of openly bisexual women in groups may make some lesbians uncomfortable. The battered women's movement has struggled for years over similar issues of diversity in shelters and support groups. The common thread is that the women are battered; in this case, the commonality is that they are battered by other women.

Although it is important to include the word "bisexual" in program literature, the attitudes of staff and volunteers are even more crucial in determining the ability of the program to serve bisexual women. Programs should consider the following steps:

1. Develop policies about the inclusion of bisexual women and do so at the beginning stages of program planning rather than waiting until a bisexual woman seeks services.
2. Note the policy on bisexual inclusion in your printed materials, mission statement, and service manuals.
3. Provide training about bisexuality for staff and volunteers.

4. Avoid making judgments about a woman's sexual identity and provide participants with the opportunity to identify as they choose.
5. Establish relationships with bisexual organizations and networks and use their expertise in policy development and training.
6. Subscribe to bisexual feminist publications.

Bisexual networks and organizations are now in their second generation and are useful resources for domestic violence programs. Bisexual groups vary in their philosophy, politics, and scope of activities. Some are social groups, whereas others foster activism and political analysis. Activities include social events, support groups, and newsletters. Battered women's advocates should seek out alliances with these groups and use their expertise in the development of strategies for services. Such groups may also offer a forum in which to provide education about same-sex domestic violence. Topics can include the dynamics of abuse, the legal system, and the services available for victims. In addition, bisexual groups should become familiar with safety and security concerns and be encouraged to develop policies regarding perpetrators and victims in their networks.

The development of specialized services for bisexual women will depend on the community and the resources available. In communities where there is an active and flourishing bisexual community, such services might make sense. In general, bisexual women's groups are supportive places for women with both male and female partners. A group for battered bisexual women could include both women battered by women and women battered by men. However, some lesbian-identified bisexuals may prefer to be in a group with lesbians. If a variety of services is available, the women herself is the best judge of which service will meet her needs.

In most areas, however, there is neither a visible bisexual community nor specialized services for women battered by women. The provision of services will depend on the sensitivity and training of existing agencies. These may include domestic violence shelters, lesbian and gay mental health providers, and women's organizations. Appropriate training is a first step toward the provision of services. What bisexual women most need from service providers is what anyone who is battered needs: to be heard and supported, to be treated nonjudgmentally, to have safety concerns taken seriously, to develop safety plans that are applicable to their day-to-day lives, and to have access to resources if they need to leave home.

Domestic violence shelters should include information about bisexuality in their antihomophobia trainings. This should be taught, if possible, by openly bisexual women who can appropriately address group concerns and answer questions. Lesbian women who need the opportunity to process their own concerns about bisexuality should do so before attempting to teach others. Training should include bisexuality, the dynamics of domestic violence specific to bisexuality, crisis intervention skills, and community resources. The inclusion of information about bisexuality is no easy task. Bisexuality calls for an examination of sexual orientation versus sexual preference, as well as a variety of other complex questions. It is tempting for organizations to use the "people can't help it that they are gay" argument to generate community support for gay and lesbian services. The need for services that are inclusive of bisexuals may change the nature of such discussions. Service providers should call on the bisexual community for assistance with such training.

The Future

As a young woman in 1977, I couldn't have imagined the revisioning of sexuality that has emerged from today's queer movement. Although their analysis of bisexual identity is often different from my own, I am heartened by the activism of the young women in this movement. Their confidence, refusal to accept labels, and insistence on being heard is inspiring. When they speak up in meetings and identify themselves as bisexual, seemingly without fear and trepidation, I am reminded that social change never quite looks like we think it will.

After the bitterness of the recent struggles about bisexuality in the battered women's movement, I'm left wondering if inclusion in lesbian groups is an appropriate goal. Perhaps it's too hard, too fraught with turmoil, or too disturbing to lesbians in the movement. It is tempting in such meetings to be silent, to pretend. Yet when I think of battered lesbian and bisexual women who are isolated and alone, I realize that silence is not the path to take. Keeping women who are battered by women on the agenda of the domestic violence movement will be a great challenge. Alliances between lesbian and bisexual women can only make us stronger.

Notes

1. For a full discussion of these issues, see R. E. Weise (Ed.), *Closer to home: Bisexuality and feminism* (Seattle, WA: Seal, 1992).

2. For further information on the Kinsey Scale and the Klein grid, see T. Geller (Ed.), *Bisexuality: A reader and sourcebook* (Ojai, CA: Times Change Press, 1990), pp. 64-81.

3. A number of these stories can be found in L. Hutchins and L. Kaahumanu (Eds.), *Bi any other name: Bisexual people speak out* (Boston, MA: Alyson Publications, 1991); and in R. E. Weise (Ed.), *Closer to home: Bisexuality and feminism* (Seattle, WA: Seal, 1992).

PART IV

PROVIDING SERVICES

17

An Argument for
Separate Services

Jennifer Grant, for the San Francisco
Network for Battered Lesbians
& Bisexual Women

"Do you think it's appropriate for you to be meeting with children alone?"

"Why don't you post the flyers just where lesbians go?"

"Have you made lesbian-related phone calls?"

"I'd like to know about the pink triangle on your car."

"We just don't think we need to mention it in our brochure."

"No, that's not homophobic!"

Is this the rural Midwest? The 1950s? The Christian Coalition? No, these are excerpts from conversations at various San Francisco Bay Area battered women's agencies in the 1990s.

In October 1992, a group of lesbian and bisexual women came together to address the issue of woman-to-woman battering. Each of us had worked in other battered women's or lesbian/gay anti-violence agencies. Many of us had used services as battered women ourselves. Some of us had been involved with prior, failed attempts at organizing around this issue. One thing was clear: We were fed up with the homophobia, the heterosexism, the lip service, the lack of real services, and the different treatment that battered lesbians and bisexual women encountered compared to the treatment that heterosexual battered women encountered. We were pissed off about a self-proclaimed "recovering" batterer running the only program specifically for battered lesbians. We were tired of hearing that there weren't "enough" women to start a support group and that a lesbian group (unlike others) really should be run by clinically trained "professionals." We were sick of hearing that our agencies needed to be "inclusive," that it wasn't appropriate to have "no batterers/recovering batterers" policies. We were determined to provide safer and more effective services than we had encountered in our prior experiences.

Hence, the San Francisco Network for Battered Lesbians & Bisexual Women was born. Our mission is the elimination of battering within our communities. Our goals are to support survivors, educate our communities, and empower ourselves. We are an all-volunteer group and rely solely on contributions from individuals. As a way to maintain our autonomy and social change roots, we are neither agency affiliated nor constrained by any funders. We offer trainings and educational presentations to the community; provide information, referrals, advocacy, and phone counseling through our voice-mail line; and have been facilitating a weekly support group since January 1994. We are currently the only organization in the Bay Area (and one of only a handful nationally) dedicated solely to empowering and supporting survivors of woman-to-woman battering.

The Network Model

Definitions of collective, members, and volunteers keep expanding. Originally, when we were limited to organizing and doing some community education, everyone was a member of the collective. Then we started a support group. So then we had Network members and support group members: two separate, distinct sets of "members" without any overlap. Then we started a survivors' support group for the network members. Now there were three different sets of "members." It became apparent that this separation was awkward and somewhat patronizing to the women in the support group. Therefore, our next step was to move toward self-facilitated support groups. We thought we would start a second community support group and have any new women be in that group as well as any interested survivors who were network "members." This arrangement started bridging the gap between "us" (network members) and "them" (support group members).

Unfortunately, shortly after starting this group, the network went through an organizational crisis. As a result, this second support group dissolved. At the same time, several longtime network members left because of burnout and life changes. At one point, there were only two active Network "members." The facilitator told the women in the remaining support group that the future of the Network and the support group was uncertain. The women—all of whom had been in the support group for quite a while and were not in immediate danger—immediately and unequivocally asked what they could do to help. So we split up the duties: the phone calls, the intakes for the support group, the presentations, even the mail. Together, we pulled the Network out of the hole it was in. That's when it became clear that our prior divisions of network "members" and support group "members" had been not only artificial but actually counterproductive to our mission. We were all parts of the same whole; we were all "the Network." Some of us only organize, some only come to group, and some do both. But we are all "members." Now, it seems so obvious.

Our support group has been one of our major successes. It began in January 1994, about a year after we founded the network. We started with five women in the group; we've had as many as nine women and as few as two. The group has been larger whenever we've done active outreach and smaller when we haven't. But as Ginny NiCarthy and colleagues (1984) have noted, it only takes two people to create a group. And for those two women, our group is a desperately needed safety net and support. As a result, we have no minimum number for our group. At our highest point, we set a maximum of eight but then never had everyone there at the same time. And because of women moving on, we've never actually had to turn anyone down because the group was too large. We offer the only ongoing support group for survivors of woman-to-woman battering in the entire San Francisco Bay Area. We have obviously filled a need and are very proud of this.

When we first started a support group, we had two facilitators each week; at least one was always a survivor. Four people alternated facilitation two weeks at a time in a chain structure: facilitators A and B did it one week, then B and C the next week, then C and D, then D and A, and back to the beginning. This created a safety net on several levels: Nobody was "on" all the time; if one person got sick or had an emergency, there was someone to take her place; and everyone benefited from the different styles, personalities, and experiences of the facilitators. The goal was to decrease burnout and increase quality, and it was quite effective while it lasted. However, after about a year and a half, we shrank to three facilitators, then, four months later, to two. The two facilitators have chosen to do sole facilitation, rotating every few months. Currently, a major issue is that neither of these two women is a survivor. We have checked in regularly with the group about this, who consistently say they prefer that the facilitator be a survivor but want the group to continue in the interim. The group has asked that we make a commitment to recruiting new facilitators who are survivors, which we're still working on.

As previously mentioned, we also tried a self-facilitated or unfacilitated group for awhile. When the women in the facilitated group were asked if they wanted to try this alternative, most of them said in a very outspoken way that they wanted a facilitator. They said they needed the guidance and expertise they felt the facilitators brought to the group; in addition, they were concerned about taking on the responsibility for the group themselves, worried that it might fall apart.

Network support group facilitators have all had some prior, relevant experience—either as group facilitators, as group participants, as survivors, or as peer counselors. Although some of the facilitators have had clinical training, our groups are peer support groups, so clinical training is not necessarily relevant. Although the facilitators developed the original group structure and ground rules, these have continuously evolved based on solicited feedback from the group participants. Facilitators meet to discuss issues that come up in group and either do intakes for group in teams of two or get second opinions from one another.

One of our major organizational problems is high burnout and poor recruitment. Although we seem to be able to recruit new members for our support group, we have a very difficult time recruiting new women interested in the organizational side of the Network. Our original vision was that women would move from the support group to organizing, education, and group facilitation. This has not happened. As is often the case in both grassroots women's and progressive groups, many of the original members poured their hearts and souls into the network when it first started. Most of us also have full-time jobs outside of the network, many of us in the field of domestic violence. As a result, many original members burned out within the first two years and left.

Another major issue for the network has been diversity (or lack thereof). We've continuously struggled with being a primarily white group. This is something we openly address at all our public presentations, making it clear that we are not representative of large segments of our community. Although we have made a strong commitment to changing this and have tried to make these efforts a priority, we've been unsuccessful. Although we do have a fairly diverse base of women who come to the support group, we realize that this privilege base makes us less accessible to women of color. We are planning to work with a consultant with expertise in multicultural and diversity issues to help us address this concern.

Outreach is another major task, one that we have had mixed results with. We have leafleted on many occasions both at women's and domestic violence events. We have created some attention-getting flyers as well as small, fluorescent cards with our name, services, and number on them. We have placed ads in various gay community papers. We marched in the San Francisco Freedom Day Parade, passing out hundreds of our cards; we got two phone calls from that effort. Recently, we sent out an introductory letter with sample flyers and cards to about 200 Bay Area social service agencies, including domestic violence, gay/lesbian/bisexual, women's, and counseling agencies and agencies whose focus is people of color. That resulted in 10 to 15 calls for information from service providers and several calls for services from survivors.

We've also passed out our flyers at several California statewide conferences, and we've presented at national conferences sponsored by the National Coalition Against Domestic Violence. As a result of this broader outreach, we get many calls for information and assistance from people just beginning organizing efforts and/or services in their local communities. This networking has been invaluable; it not only validates our work, but it is also energizing to know that the work is being done throughout the country.

We have done several types of community presentations, but most of them have been staff or volunteer trainings for other domestic violence agencies. We did one major community presentation sponsored by the Women's Action Coalition (WAC). WAC had unwittingly sponsored and benefited from a theatrical performance about woman-to-woman battering. Several members of the Network attended the performance and were shocked at the myths and stereotypes that were portrayed as well as the fact that the story was a *comedy*. The Network wrote a letter to both WAC and the performance group outlining our concerns. WAC offered to host a communitywide presentation and training on the issue and invited the Network to be the presenters. This forum was attended by about 100 people and presented by the entire Network. This was also the first time our no batterers/recovering batterers policy was made public and put into use.

This presentation was very successful on several levels. A communitywide debate was carried out in the local gay press for four months. Every single issue had letters to the editor that mentioned woman-to-woman battering and the Network—just think of all that increased awareness and discussion, not to mention the free publicity! We sparked a controversy about the safety of local domestic violence agencies for same-sex survivors. We got several calls about services, several requests for speakers, a new volunteer, and $70 in donations.

From the very beginning we've made it clear that batterers and "recovering" batterers were not allowed to be Network members, to participate in the support group, or to attend any of our community presentations. We feel that to truly support survivors—and empower ourselves—we must make every attempt to create a safe space for survivors. We realize that we cannot *guarantee* complete safety, but we believe that by stating our priority clearly, openly, frequently, and immediately, we can move in that direction. If it becomes apparent that either a member of the support group or of the Network collective is, in *our* assessment, a batterer or a recovering batterer, that person is asked to leave the group/collective.

Trainings and presentations are not as clear, not as easy. Whenever we are invited to speak, we request that the sponsoring group announce our policy beforehand. In addition, we announce the policy again and briefly explain it before we begin speaking. Again, we know that this will not guarantee safety at our presentations. However, by stating our policy up front, we have set a guideline that enables us to either ask someone to leave and/or to end the presentation and leave ourselves. On several occasions, survivors have approached us at the end of a presentation, telling us that hearing our statement gave them a clear message that, if necessary, we would help protect them and would prioritize their need for safety. They explained that this sense of safety enabled them to fully participate in the training.

This policy has at times been accepted without question and at times has created furor. As a result, some groups have changed their minds and disinvited us. Early on, we weren't always sure how to communicate this policy and made a few mistakes. In one instance, we had been invited to speak at a volunteer training for one of the major domestic violence agencies in San Francisco. We made the mistake of telling them we needed to know (by name) who would be at the training in advance. As one might imagine, this was met with some trepidation, and because we hadn't been clear about our purpose, the agency decided that they would just get someone else. It took us two years to start mending that relationship. However, we have not changed our policy, just smoothed out the rough edges in our approach. And we know that no matter what the reaction or outcome, we've forced someone to think about the issue and about our policy.

Another time, we were asked to speak on a panel at a workshop sponsored by the lesbian domestic violence program of a local agency. We explained our no batterers/recovering batterers policy. We were told by the organizers that they did not feel comfortable excluding anyone from a public workshop. They even claimed it might be illegal and could possibly cause problems with their funders. As a result, the network did not participate in the workshop. We wrote the sponsoring agency a letter, explaining that their decision excluded us—as survivors and as activists—from participating. We sent a copy of the letter to their city/county funder, who clarified that their monies were only to be used for survivors, not for perpetrators.

Although we explain the need and philosophy behind our no batterers/recovering batterers policy, we are clear that we aren't here to discuss batterers, their needs, or their motives. As a Network member once said, "That's someone else's workshop."

In many ways, our policy—and our constant publicizing of it—is a symbolic statement about community accountability: what it is and what it might or should look like. The battered women's movement was originally a grassroots movement that grew out of a need to protect women and end violence against women. It was started primarily by survivors. The key to the issues lies in those words: *the battered women's movement.* It's not called the battered women and batterers movement. It is supposed to be by, for, and about battered women. This concept seems easier when the batterer is not like us, that is, is a man. Maybe the confusion arises around the words "women's movement." But how can we, as a movement, as a community, create safety for survivors with batterers in our midst? Community accountability should be about prioritizing the needs of survivors and making a clear and public commitment to them. In the gay/lesbian/bisexual community, this is often referred to as "ostracizing the batterer." However, by not creating batterer-free space, by not making survivors our first priority, we are actually ostracizing the survivor. One way of interpreting this is that the batterer is now controlling both her victim and her community. Shouldn't privileges be earned? Does being queer entitle us to be abusive? Because we're gay and we've had a difficult life, we aren't really responsible for our actions? Sorry, but if this doesn't cut it for child abuse or rape or murder, why should it excuse the behavior of gays/lesbians/bisexuals?

We are often asked about screening out batterers. If the battered women's movement wants to truly support *all* battered/formerly battered women, every volunteer, shelter resident, staff member, visitor, and board member should be assessed for a history of abusive behavior. Admittedly, this is uncomfortable, it's awkward, and it probably violates some labor law. But this has never stopped us before. Most of our work in this movement is hard and involves asking difficult questions—and many of us have worked around legalities when necessary. So, why does this feel different? Because it's about tearing down the walls of what we thought, hoped, was one of the last safe communities: women, specifically lesbian/bisexual women.

At the Network, when we meet with a potential volunteer, we ask directly whether or not they have ever been abusive. We ask potential support group members more indirectly, in the belief that we don't want to take on the abuser's role of blaming the victim or not believing her story.

Our screening consists of looking at the patterns and context of a woman's story, paying special attention to any red flags such as blame, responsibility, and initiation of abuse. Ninety-five percent of the time we've had absolute clarity about who was being battered. The few times we've had doubts, we've chosen to err on the side of not mistakenly allowing a batterer into the group. We may have turned away a survivor but we know we have not compromised the safety of the group members. Other groups have chosen to ask more direct questions in their intake and take the approach of not turning away any potential victims/survivors. In San Francisco, a task force is working on creating standardized screening for volunteers, staff, and clients specifically around same-sex battering.

Conclusion

Overall, we believe we made the right decision in creating the network and making it autonomous from other agencies. This has given us political freedom without the constraints of funders, legalities, or a board of directors. On the other hand, we've given up the security and stability an agency could provide. We don't always know how long we'll be able to keep the Network going, but we do always know that we can honestly say we have prioritized the needs and safety of survivors of woman-to-woman battering. We've been both acclaimed and controversial, have gained and lost individual allies and community support. But remember, discomfort is what prompts people to make changes. The bottom line is we have started the discussion and provided at least one safe option for survivors.

Reference

NiCarthy, G., Merriam, K., & Coffman, S. (1984). *Talking it out: A guide to groups for abused women.* Seattle, WA: Seal Press.

18

Assessing the Lesbian Victim

Alma Banda Goddard
Tara Hardy

Determining who is abusing who in an abusive same-sex relationship presents a challenge that is generally not present in heterosexual abusive relationships. At Advocates for Abused & Battered Lesbians (AABL) we have developed an assessment model in which the focus on context and patterns are critical components in making an accurate assessment. The following is an example of the process of assessing who is the victim.[1]

The Initial Call

A woman named Blake contacted AABL, saying, "I don't know if this is the right place to call, but the court domestic violence advocate told me I should call you. I'm a dyke, and my girlfriend and I had a fight over the weekend and I was taken to jail. So can you help me?"

AUTHORS' NOTE: Reprinted from *NCADV Voice* (Summer 1996). National Coalition Against Domestic Violence, P.O. Box 18749, Denver, CO 80218; (303) 839-1852. Membership information can be found on the inside back cover of an issue.

We would like to know a few things right from the beginning of a phone call. Is she safe, and can she speak freely? To her knowledge is her girlfriend seeking or receiving services from us? Can she or is she willing to give us her abuser's name?

For domestic violence (DV) providers the importance of the first question is evident and necessary, but the rationale underlying the others may not be so obvious. It is our mission at AABL to work with the woman we can most clearly identify as the victim/survivor of the abuse. Before we schedule an intake appointment, we want to be somewhat sure that we are inviting the victim, not the perpetrator, in for further assessment. The initial phone screening tool has helped clarify who is who approximately 95% of the time.

Blake's Story

We ask Blake if she has a little time to answer some questions. The advocate tells her that we may be able to help her, but if not, we will do our best to refer her to someone who can. (There are currently services for lesbian batterers in Seattle.) After a few introductory questions, the advocate asks her who is abusing her. Blake says she doesn't feel comfortable giving her partner's name. The advocate explains our confidentiality policy and tells her that we need to know her partner's name to ensure that we do not schedule them both for appointments in the same location on the same day or have them both in a support group. The counselor also informs her that we will only be able to serve the woman who we can most clearly identify as the victim. If a caller does not disclose at this point, we continue the assessment. If she does not disclose at a later point, the advocate will bring it up again.

Next, we ask Blake specifically about the relationship. Is she your partner, friend, ex-partner, roommate, or other? How long have you been together and what is your current status? Are you living together, separated, having contact, separated with no contact? Did you end the relationship? Asking the current status can also assist the advocate to focus in on how the caller feels about the current status.

Blake's Story Continued

The advocate asks Blake what has been going on in the relationship. What are the dynamics? What happened recently? When did the abuse begin?

Blake explains that she and her partner had been together for five months and, for the most part, things seemed to be pretty good. They met at a party and were instantly attracted to each other. They dated that week and became lovers right away. They seemed to have a lot in common: both enjoyed kayaking, hiking, reading, and sharing a meal on romantic evenings. Blake had her own place and her lover shared an apartment with two roommates. After the first month, Blake gave her partner a key to her place because they were spending a lot of time together.

Blake describes how she felt the first time her lover joked about Blake being a "super butch" in front of friends and said she would have to make a real woman of Blake. She says this was when she first started feeling uncomfortable and notes that after this they often argued about how Blake should dress when they went out together. The arguments were loud and usually ended with Blake becoming silent or giving in to the demands and "toning it down a little." Occasionally, one of them would storm out and slam the door.

Blake describes herself as being bigger and weighing more than her partner and she always "knew" she could overpower her. But, she says, from the beginning she has been afraid of her girlfriend's temper, especially when she started throwing things.

The advocate asks Blake about the most recent event. Now beginning to use her partner's first name, Blake says that Trudy had been staying with her for a couple of weeks because she was tired of her roommates. Blake had gone out with a friend after work for coffee and when she got home Trudy threw a mug at her, just missing her head. She yelled at Blake, accusing her of being unfaithful. An argument ensued. Blake said she felt like she had to defend herself from these accusations, so she yelled back and, because Trudy "was in my face, I pushed her into the couch. I felt awful immediately and apologized. Trudy was irate, she began pummeling me with her fists. So I grabbed her wrists and yelled at her to stop." Trudy broke the grip and started breaking things. At this point, Blake says events happened so fast she's not sure of all the details but all of a sudden Trudy became very calm. Trudy walked to the phone and turned to Blake and told her that she needed to call someone for support. Blake, assuming Trudy was calling a friend, said she was going to go outside for a smoke. Before she knew what was happening the police had arrived and Blake was in the back of the squad car going to jail. Before they took her away Trudy came outside. She appeared to have a bloody scratch on her face. All Blake could figure was that Trudy was scratched in the scuffle. Blake was booked in the county jail on assault charges. Trudy bailed her out two days later. Blake apologized to Trudy, and Trudy asked if she could move in. Blake was not sure if this was a good idea, but Trudy said it will be great. Meanwhile, Blake was ordered to get treatment, and after telling her story to the court DV advocates, they recommended she call AABL.

Final Phone Screening

AABL's advocate asks if Blake is afraid of Trudy. The advocate asks her if there have been threats, weapons used, and about her safety now. Does she have a safe place to go should she need to leave? Are there children in the household? If so, have they been abused or witnessed the abuse? If yes, what kind of support do the children have or need? All these questions are important in assessing who is the victim. Trudy did not press charges. However, because of the DV mandatory arrest law in Washington State, there is now a protection order against Blake. Neither Blake nor Trudy is adhering to the order.

Can AABL serve Blake? Is she the victim or the perpetrator? Do we even have enough information to make this decision? The advocate must be able to make an assessment quickly because we try to let the caller know if we can serve her at the time of the call.

Complications

Blake expresses a lot of concern about her part in or responsibility for this incident. She feels she did something to bring it on and that she should not have pushed Trudy or grabbed her wrists. She admits she was very angry and tired of the hassles and this seemed to be the last straw. She wants to know if she is the batterer. She's very concerned about Trudy getting support and help.

The Advocate's Assessment:
Context and Patterns

The advocate knew pieces of Blake's story because she had taken a call from Trudy the day before. The story was very similar, but the differences made the advocate take particular care in moving into a second-stage interview with Blake. After the initial phone screening with Trudy, the advocate had scheduled her for a second-stage assessment and intake. Trudy talked about the arguments but not the content or what had precipitated them. She did say that she had never been with a "real butch" woman before and wasn't so sure she was all that comfortable with roles. She said she really loves Blake and wants to work things out. "In fact," she said, "we're talking about me moving in with her. I just know for me I'll be a lot happier living with her and knowing what's really going on with her."

Having this information while working with Blake leads the advocate to hear a silent but important "Oops!" in her head. So, taking a couple of slippery steps backward, she considers that she may not have assessed Trudy correctly. Therefore, she immediately starts the second stage of the assessment process with Blake over the phone.

The second-stage assessment tool consists of a list of behaviors and dynamics that may have occurred in the relationship. The advocate asks Blake whether certain things were done to her or whether she did them to Trudy. All the while, the advocate notices what Blake is taking ownership of, knowing that, in general, victims tend to judge themselves more harshly than do abusers.

The advocate also notes the context in which behaviors took place. For example, when Blake says that she has locked Trudy out of the house, the advocate asks her what happened just prior. She says that Trudy had been running through the house, tearing pictures off the walls and throwing them at Blake, who was in the kitchen crying. Blake bruised Trudy's wrists in the process of getting her to stop the abuse. Since then, Trudy has been calling Blake an abuser. This type of information—both the individual incidents and the context in which they took place—leads the advocate to rethink her original assessment.

Blake goes on to describe more violent episodes. When asked why Blake pushed Trudy out the door, she said she was afraid that Trudy would get more and more violent as she had done in the past. The advocate is identifying patterns of emotional and physical abuse on Trudy's part.

In response to a question about how they handle financial issues, Blake related that she has been supporting Trudy. She said that she encouraged Trudy to find work but that Trudy said that this is what lovers do for each other and that she just needs a break. She promised that someday she'll do the same for Blake. This had not been a mutual decision—Trudy came home one day and announced she had quit her job. Part of the pressure to let Trudy move in with her is that Trudy won't otherwise be able to pay her rent.

The advocate asks Blake what percentage of the time she is the first to initiate violence; she estimates 10% of the time; she knows she shouldn't but feels like sometimes there just isn't any other option. She feels horrible about her behaviors and knows that she needs help. (We have found that lesbians who batter often respond to this question by claiming that both partners initiate the violence equally, or by claiming their partners initiate 100% of the time.) It is clear that Blake has been affected by the controlling abusive behaviors. She says she spends a lot of time feeling guilty, shameful, sad, and confused.

The advocate is now fairly certain that Blake is the person who is being abused in the relationship, but because assessments can be complex, she discusses it with a coworker. She talks about how she had originally interpreted Trudy's reluctance to share information as anxiety about calling for help, but now she wonders if it is related to her fear of being "found out." They decide to call Trudy and do the same second-stage assessment process with her.

Trudy: Second-Stage Questions

True to predictions, several things in the second conversation with Trudy give us enough reason to think that she is abusing Blake:

1. Trudy identifies her own patterns of hurting Blake, but she consistently blames her, saying, "If Blake would only be more flexible these things wouldn't have happened!"

2. Trudy claims that they both initiate violence equally.
3. Trudy says that she wants sex after a fight because they make up and everything is fine again. Blake does not want to have sex after a fight because she feels tense. Trudy often insists, because she says "it always makes us closer."

Once the advocate is more sure about who's who in the relationship, she makes the appropriate referrals to Trudy, saying, "After talking with you, I have doubts about whether you are the person being abused or the person doing the abusing. Because I have such strong doubts, the services of AABL are not appropriate for you at this time. I would like to refer you to The Counseling Services to see if that is a better match."

The Group as the Final Test

Several weeks after Blake joins the support group, we are certain that we've made the right decision. Generally, if we have misjudged a situation the women in the group let us know very quickly. The abusive person will often begin to target individuals in the group or act out in the group. The group has welcomed Blake, and she has responded strongly to the experience. Although she is still involved with Trudy, Blake gets enough support from the group to not doubt her own perceptions or feel it's her fault quite as much. She is growing farther away from the abuse and closer to a self-directed, violence-free life.

Conclusion: Patterns and Context

It's important to remember when sorting out any situation of who's who that you can't make decisions based on flat reports of behavior. You must look at context and patterns. This is not to say that determining abuse is subjective. Rather, it is to say that context and circumstance are why we can experience a raised voice to mean something different from the mouth of someone who is not trying to control us than from the mouth of an abuser. The difference is subjective. A raised voice from an abuser is a threat because it happens as part of a pattern of intimidation and control.

The second most important thing to remember about assessments is that you do the best you can and sometimes you make a mistake. Because we feel that being disbelieved as a survivor is too damaging to treat the decision to exclude casually, AABL has an informal policy that it's better to screen an abuser into the group than it is to screen a survivor out.

Although the prospect of distinguishing between the abuser and the abused can be intimidating at first, it is essential that we challenge our fears through practice and develop the skills necessary to provide safe and appropriate services to survivors of same-sex domestic violence.

Note

1. The phone screening/intake described here is a compilation of the stories of many battered lesbians. The names of the women are fictitious and do not represent actual program participants.

19

1 in 3 of 1 in 10

Sexual and Dating Violence Prevention Groups for Lesbian, Gay, Bisexual, and Transgendered Youth

Gregory S. Merrill

That lesbian, gay, bisexual, and transgendered youth face a range of violence is no surprise. It is an everyday occurrence for these young people to be bullied into gender conformity by peers and adults alike, to begin using substances to cope with pain and isolation, to run away from or be thrown out of their families, and to commit suicide. And yet, in addition to these risks—and largely because of them—lesbian, gay, bisexual, and transgendered youth (hereafter referred to as *queer youth*) are also at high risk for sexual and dating violence. For the purposes of this chapter, sexual and dating violence will refer to a variety of coercive and unwanted acts, including emotionally, physically, and sexually abusive behaviors, that occur in the context of a

---

AUTHOR'S NOTE: *To Ely: Your spirit touched us, and you will always be remembered.*

romantic or dating relationship. Despite the frequency and impact of intimate abuse in this population, little has been written about it. More devastating, little is being done to prevent it.

In this chapter, I provide theoretical and practical guidance to those who seek to integrate sexual and dating violence prevention programs into already existing rap and support groups for queer youth. To that end, I will draw on my experience as both a domestic violence service provider and a facilitator of queer youth groups to provide suggestions and creative program activity ideas for integrating intimate violence prevention groups into programs for queer youth.

Facilitating Intimate Violence Prevention Groups

In my almost 10 years of doing sexual and domestic violence work, I have never facilitated groups more frightening or rewarding than queer youth groups. Here in San Francisco, I have worked with the Lavender Youth Recreation and Information Center (LYRIC), primarily facilitating young men's and co-gender groups. In this setting, every racial and ethnic group is represented, with young people of color comprising 70% of the youth served. Some of the group members come religiously every week and live a fully out, integrated life; others have anxiously come to a queer-identified meeting place for the first time. The same group might attract 16-year-old homeless youths surviving by "street behaviors" and 22-year-old suburban college students. Planning exercises and discussions that will prevent intimate violence in and be relevant to the lives of this diverse group is a rewarding challenge indeed.

Planning

When you prepare to facilitate sexual and dating violence prevention groups, keep several key learning objectives in mind. First, members should decrease denial and increase awareness about sexual and dating victimization. Second, members should be able to better identify their personal risks for perpetrating and experiencing intimate violence and to enhance their coping and prevention skills. Finally, group members should improve their ability to establish proper accountability for such violence and should discard victim-blaming misconceptions about asking for, provoking, and liking abusive conduct. This last objective is particularly important because, according to Bergman (1992) and Mahlsted and Keeny (1993), young people who are victimized are most likely to turn to their peers for support.

The scariest possibility for any would-be facilitator to consider is that a group member will disclose that he or she is being abused during a group session. This fear is completely warranted; youth have disclosed being involved with someone twice their age, being incest survivors, and being battered by a boyfriend/girlfriend in groups I have led. Although you can select program activities that will provide information without encouraging personal disclosures, they still may occur. Having a plan for how you will respond sensitively to the individual victim's needs while helping group members process their reactions to such a disclosure is critical. In most cases, the individual will disclose a past experience from which they have begun to heal; if the situation is current, be certain to talk to the person privately at the group's end to arrange for appropriate follow-up assistance. Moreover, I recommend that you investigate your mandatory reporting responsibilities by contacting Child Protective Services and that you make any such responsibilities known at the group's beginning.

If you are not the regular facilitator, become familiar with the group. Usually, I find out how it was formed, who sponsors it, what purposes it serves, and for whom it is intended. In addition, you can interview the regular facilitator(s) and some of the members about what they think of the group. Consider the composition of the group in terms of gender (men, women, or both), age range, ethnic and socioeconomic backgrounds, and the varied reasons why members come to the group. Similarly, consider your own identity and experiences: How might they be similar to and different from those of the members, and how might they affect the dynamics of the group? If there have been prior groups during which abuse issues have arisen, find out what they were. Also, because teenagers are especially sensitive to authority, find out what power and control issues are operating among group members and between members and facilitators. It is also useful to identify problematic group members in advance so that you will know how to handle them.

When you prepare your outline for the group, consider the amount of time available and identify the primary learning objectives.

Then try to choose engaging and interactive exercises that prevent the necessity of excessive lecturing, a teaching modality that young people get near-lethal doses of at home and school and one that burdens you with having to be "the expert." Below, I describe a series of discussion and program activity ideas that have worked particularly well for me. They should be adapted to suit your style as well as the group's needs. Enough exercises are presented to plan for a series of groups, if desired.

Getting Started

Most queer youth groups begin with personal introductions, a brief check-in, a review of the group's ground rules, and introduction of the topic. If the group is not familiar with me, I share something about my personal self and professional background so that its members know who I am, and I check in the same way that they do. Enlisting everyone's agreement to abide by the ground rules is important, especially confidentiality, respectful cross-communication (including use of "I" statements), the right to pass, and the acceptance of different perspectives and experiences as group norms. When I introduce the topic of sexual and dating violence, I emphasize that many people from all different backgrounds and sexual orientations have experienced violence. I suggest that some members of the group may have been victimized or may know someone who has and stress how important it is that all communities, including the lesbian, gay, bisexual, and transgender communities, begin to talk about these issues. Acknowledging that some of the discussion might be difficult and potentially painful, I emphasize that it will also provide them with knowledge and power. Because young people historically have not been given information about these issues, I state my commitment to changing that. I then provide members with an overview of what I have planned, including time set aside for a break.

Defining the Terms

Before beginning program activities, it is important to define the concepts for the group. I often ask those in the group to pretend they are the editorial board of Webster's and have been asked to brainstorm a dictionary definition of abuse. During this discussion, we usually arrive at a definition such as "harmful behavior committed against someone without their permission." I emphasize that intention (that is, whether or not someone intended to be abusive) is not a determining factor but that infliction of harm and lack of consent are. I explain that abusive behaviors lie along a continuum; some are obviously abusive, but others are more difficult to determine. I frequently give the group the following gray area scenarios to discuss:

Teresa and Janet are a couple. Teresa comes from a family in which yelling was a way people settled differences, but it was never threatening. Janet comes from a family in which yelling meant physical abuse was about to occur. When Teresa and Janet have conflict, Teresa often yells and Janet becomes intimidated. Is Teresa abusing Janet? How do you think Teresa and Janet should handle this?

Antonio and Cedric have been dating for about three months. Cedric wants Antonio to be monogamous with him, but Antonio prefers to remain nonmonogamous. Cedric's feelings are hurt every time he finds out Antonio has seen someone else. Is this abuse? How would you handle this if you were Cedric? Antonio?

In the first example, Teresa may be being emotionally abusive, especially if Janet has explained her feelings and asked Teresa not to yell and Janet disregards her. In the second example, Antonio has not agreed to monogamy and is not forcing Cedric to remain with him, so he has not "abused" Cedric (although it may be emotional abuse if he is flaunting affairs to deliberately hurt or humiliate Cedric). When I discuss examples, I emphasize the importance of communication and of forming agreements in relationships, particularly around sensitive, potentially hurtful areas. Because the opinions of group members are included, and because they become more sophisticated in their ability to distinguish abusive from nonabusive behaviors, this discussion works well.

I also ask them to brainstorm and provide examples of the specific forms of abuse that the group will be focusing on, usually sexual violence, dating violence, or both. As soon as I feel that most of the group members understand the basic definitions, I ask them how common they imagine sexual and/or dating violence to be among their peers, provide them with brief statistics, and then ask them about their reactions to this information (some will be surprised and others will not). I also address from the outset the common misconception that most violence is perpetrated by strangers and ask members why they think we are taught to fear strangers when loved ones are more likely to harm us. Once this groundwork has been laid, we move into one of the program activities.

Program Activities

Continuum of Values About Violence

This program activity is designed to get group members moving, interacting, and discussing their core values about violence. Because it relies on a variance of opinion, it works best with groups of over eight members. I designate one side of the room as "strongly disagree," the other as "strongly agree," and the middle as "neutral/don't know" (premade posters labeling each of the polar opposite ends reduce confusion). I then read a value statement about violence (examples are provided below) and ask members to align themselves in the room according to their degree of agreement with it. After everyone has positioned themselves, usually after some degree of shifting around and noticing where everyone else is, I ask members to share why they chose their particular spot in the room, selecting people from different sides of the room and the middle. Great discussion of the issues will often ensue and when discussion seems complete, I read the next statement and have people reposition themselves.

The statements can all pertain to a certain theme, but I have found it particularly effective to vary the themes and types of violence addressed. Some of the statements are deliberately vague to allow for different individual interpretations that will add to the dialogue. Members will often ask me to further clarify the statement, but I simply repeat it and encourage them to interpret it in their own manner. Statements I commonly use during this exercise are as follows:

- Spanking a child is a form of child abuse.
- Sometimes when people say no to sex they really mean yes.
- Women are less likely than men to be violent.
- People cannot give meaningful consent for sex if they are drunk or high.
- Victims of domestic violence should always leave their abusers.
- If someone is going to be violent to you on a date, there is always a prior indication.
- It is always abusive when an adult has a sexual relationship with a minor.
- You should not go home with someone unless you plan to have sex with them.
- If somebody cross-dresses in public they should expect to be harassed.

After each statement, I may respond to some of the members' comments with factual information or with further questions. For example, after some discussion of the "Some people really say no when they mean yes" statement, I usually ask people what they think constitutes "teasing" and how they deal with this behavior. It is not uncommon for victim-blaming attitudes to evidence themselves, particularly in response to "You should not go home with someone unless you plan to have sex" and "Victims of domestic violence should always leave." Although it is important to address and explore these attitudes and to gently offer another perspective, it is rarely effective to become preachy or confrontational.

Members can be surprised by the range of values expressed, so this is an excellent opportunity to discuss how we deal with differing points of view. Often, I ask the people who are standing apart from the rest of the group how it feels to be out there by themselves. When I notice people shifting from their original position to be more in line with peers I point this out and ask them about it. I also underscore that even though people may be standing in very different positions, they can usually understand and respect others' opinions and values.

Sexual or Dating Violence Scenario

In this exercise, I read aloud a prewritten scenario of sexual or dating violence that is based on either a real or a potentially real incident. I change the names and identities of the characters to be reflective of group members and make it relevant to them by naming

208 SAME-SEX DOMESTIC VIOLENCE

places I know they frequent. I generally make parts of the scenario deliberately ambiguous as a discussion-generating device. Although the example I am about to provide is a sexual violence scenario written for a young men's group, other versions more applicable to young women or about domestic violence can easily be written.

Jim and Pablo

Jim is 23, Pablo is 19. They met on the dance floor at Club Universe after catching each other's eye earlier in the evening. Jim bought them both several drinks.

After dancing and working up a sweat (not to mention a sexual appetite), Pablo accepted an invitation back to Jim's apartment. Before doing so, however, he made it clear that although he'd like to fool around he wasn't into anal sex.

Back at the apartment they had another drink before beginning to fool around. They kissed and gently explored each other's bodies for a long time before Jim grabbed some lubricant and stimulated Pablo's anus with his fingers. Pablo felt uncomfortable, but he didn't think it would go any further so he didn't say anything. Almost before he realized it, Jim was on top of him, inserting his penis. When Pablo flinched and said, "It hurts," Jim said, "That's okay, it'll feel better in a few minutes." He continued to penetrate Pablo harder and harder. After he reached orgasm, Jim kissed Pablo, told him how hot the sex had been, and then rolled over and fell asleep.

After reading the scenario aloud, I lead a general discussion about people's reactions and ask the following questions:

- Was this rape? Why or why not? If not, what would make you think of this as rape (physical force, a reiterated "no," etc.)?
- How would you have felt if you had been Pablo? Jim?
- What factors contributed to this situation occurring? Do you think the age difference had any effect? The alcohol?

- What could Jim and Pablo each have done differently?
- How often do you think something like this happens?
- If you were Pablo's friend, how would you have reacted to his feelings?

Most members react strongly by blaming Pablo for not reiterating his original "no" and for "letting it happen." When these attitudes arise I ask why it is easier to blame Pablo for not reiterating his no than to blame Jim for failing to respect the original no, for not asking for permission to advance the next level of sexual intimacy, and for not responding to Pablo's obvious discomfort. Group members tend to become very animated and actively involved with the scenarios, so I highly recommend this exercise.

Talk Show

In this exercise, I invite guest speakers to come and talk about their own lives and experiences. For one group I invite a panel of speakers who identify as survivors of sexual and/or domestic violence. The panelists simply talk to the group about what happened to them and what impact it had on their lives. So that common misconceptions can be addressed, I encourage group members to ask survivors why they stayed so long or whether or not they feel they "provoked it." Members are usually able to relate to the survivors' stories and to feel a connection with them that informs their understanding of the problem.

In another group, I invite two couples to come and talk about their relationship—that is, how they met, how they came to be committed to one another, how they work through conflict, what some of their relationship agreements are, and what their strengths and challenges as a couple are. Group members learn something about the maturity and work it takes to build a solid, intimate relationship. Equally important, they are able to see healthy relationships being modeled that is just as important to prevention as is becoming aware of abusive ones.

The facilitator's role during "talk show" is perhaps the most fun of all: You get to be Oprah. In terms of selecting panelists, I am careful to choose people I know and trust and prefer panelists who are only slightly older than the group members and who resemble them in other dimensions (gender, sexual orientation, and ethnic background). For example, I deliberately invited a bisexual female-male couple and an interracial couple because I knew their experiences closely mirrored those of some of the members. As facilitator, I pose questions I think members want to ask but are afraid to, but I also forewarn panelists that they may be asked very difficult questions and give them permission to pass. After the panelists leave, I continue to lead a discussion by encouraging members to relate their experiences to those shared by the panelists and by pursuing themes that emerged. This exercise will easily occupy all of the group's time, it maintains interest, and it is very easy to facilitate.

Why People Stay

The following exercise that is intended to create empathy toward survivors of domestic violence is an old standby that works well with both adult and youth groups. I ask everyone in the group to take a minute to identify a relationship they have been in that did not work out for them. They do not have to have been abused, but they do have to feel that they were disrespected or that their needs were not met. The relationship could be with a friend, family member, partner, teacher, counselor, employer, or anyone. After participants have identified the "problem relationship" (and it is helpful to acknowledge that almost everyone has had at least one), I ask them to think about when they realized this relationship was not good for them and when they actually left it, if they have left it. Then I ask them to identify all the reasons why they stayed longer than they now think was beneficial. After a minute or two, I make a "Why We Stayed" list on posterboard, asking everyone to contribute one or two of their reasons. Although people may want to share extensive information about the relationship or may want to discuss why they think battered people stay, I try to focus them on briefly revealing their own personal reasons for staying.

Once everyone has contributed to the list, I often add a few reasons of my own, especially if they are ones that the group has not yet identified. I then acknowledge that most of the reasons listed are the same reasons why victims of domestic violence find it difficult to leave their partners. I also use this as an opportunity to talk about how difficult it is to leave someone you love or care about even if they are abusing you and to describe the impact that fear has in preventing battered people from leaving. If time permits, I teach the group Walker's (1979) cycle theory of violence to provide a deeper understanding of the psychological complexities of being battered. Other times, I simply ask people how they know when they need to end a relationship, how they go about doing so, why it is especially difficult to leave your first relationship, and other related questions.

Communication Skills Training/Role Plays

This exercise can work in a variety of ways, depending on the size of the group and the degree to which they enjoy drama (which, for queer youth, is usually a lot). The exercise begins with me providing a short explanation of the difference between passive, aggressive, and assertive responses to conflictual situations. In a passive response, the responding party surrenders their negotiating power and simply does what the other person wants; in an aggressive response, they are rude, disrespectful, and overpowering; and in an assertive response, they negotiate a fair compromise. When I explain these differences, I demonstrate them by asking a group member to briefly role-play a situation with me. For example, I have a member pose as a friend who wants me to go to a movie that I do not want to see and use this scenario to demonstrate passive, assertive, and aggressive responses. I then inquire about the perceptions of group members of the different response styles and the contexts in which each might be appropriate as well as contexts in which each might be detrimental. I also acknowledge that communication styles are often products of gender and culture socialization.

After this initial explication and brief demonstration, I split the group into smaller groups of two or three persons. Each group is asked to work together to prepare a short, creative skit involving a conflictual dating or sexual situation. If the smaller groups ask for help, I provide them with suggestions for scenarios (for example, one person wants to pay for their date's dinner but the date would prefer to "go dutch"; one person wants to be monogamous but the other prefers to date several people; or one partner wants to have sexual involvement but the other is not ready or interested). Each subgroup should be prepared to perform its skit twice, modeling two different response styles, while group members guess which style each skit is attempting to demonstrate. We then discuss the scenarios and opinions of the members about the response styles demonstrated. Actively praising members for taking risks and encouraging group members to practice being assertive in one real-life situation during the next week is a great way to close. Although this activity is excellent for teaching concrete coping skills, it tends not to work as well with extremely shy or extremely unruly groups.

Discussion Topics

Although I usually use program activities to get members talking, generating a discussion by posing interesting, relevant questions is always a standby. Often, I ask members what behaviors they have noticed early on from people who have later disrespected them and what qualities they imagine are indicative that someone they are dating might harm them. By charting and discussing these group-identified "red flags," members develop better partner assessment skills and are able to bond around their common dislike of being mistreated. It is also useful to entertain discussions about why they think people commit sexual and dating violence; how they would help a friend who had been victimized; what kinds of assistance they would want from friends if they were victimized; what difference, if any, it makes in who pays for the date; and other related questions.

Wrapping Up and Checking Out

At the close of any group, it is important to sincerely praise the members for their cooperation and for their strengths. I acknowledge that the topic may have been a heavy one but emphasize again how important it is that everyone be more aware of these problems so they can protect themselves and one another. During check-out, I ask members to share their impressions of the group and if they thought the group was helpful I offer to do another. I always make myself available afterward to members who want to talk, and I provide a phone number where members can either reach me or another sensitive provider. Whenever possible, I debrief with my co-facilitator or supervisor.

Conclusion

Because of the psychosocial stressors that lesbian, gay, bisexual, and transgendered youth face, they are an isolated population that is extremely vulnerable to sexual and dating victimization. Unfortunately, queer youth currently inherit a legacy of communitywide silence, denial, and ignorance that permits this violence to flourish. Although there are certainly risks involved with discussing these issues with queer youth, the risks involved with the status quo of not discussing them are far more serious. As these teens begin to date and become sexually active, they will inevitably be exposed to potentially abusive and exploitative situations. The discussion and program activity ideas described here provide community educators and group facilitators with concrete tools to begin preparing these youth for the unfortunate risks that await them. There is no debating the fact that queer youth need and could benefit from access to this information. The only question that remains is this: Are we prepared to give it?

References

Bergman, L. (1992). Dating violence among high school students. *Social Work, 37*(1), 21-27.

Mahlsted, D., & Keeny, L. (1993). Female survivors of dating violence and their social networks. *Feminism & Psychology, 3*(3), 319-333.

Walker, L. (1979). *The battered woman.* New York: Harper & Row.

20

Groups for Gay and Bisexual Male Survivors of Domestic Violence

Robb Johnson

Support groups for battered gay and bisexual men are among the services needed for survivors of same-sex domestic violence. To help those who wish to start such a group, this chapter describes my experience with groups at Fenway Community Health Center in Boston, Massachusetts, and relates it to experiences from existing groups in three other U.S. cities.

Support groups provide an opportunity for participants to focus on a specific issue that all members have in common, strategize ways to cope with feelings and manage new situations, and work with life issues as they are related to the focus of the group. They can be limited or long-term and may be led by peers, trained advocates, counselors, educators, or therapists. Support groups have been a fundamental element of the battered women's movement and have played a key role in empowering women to help recover from abuse. I believe that support groups are likely to offer similar benefits to male survivors as well.

Where Groups Are

Although people in many regions have attempted to provide support groups for gay and bisexual male survivors of domestic violence, I was able to learn of formal groups only in New York City, San Francisco, Columbus (Ohio), Minneapolis, Denver, St. Louis, Los Angeles, and Boston. There are likely other groups that have escaped my attention; any omissions are unintended.

For the purposes of this chapter, I interviewed individuals involved in running, or attempting to run, groups in San Francisco, New York City, and Los Angeles.

Presenting Needs

Central issues presented by most participants seeking a support group include grief over a lost or failing relationship, self-blame for causing the violence or not being able to stop it, shame about the abuse or about not leaving a relationship sooner; a need to understand why the abuse happened and why it happened to them; difficulties trusting others; fears or concerns about dating; and pessimism about achieving a healthy relationship in the future. Some participants have real fears about being harmed or harassed by their abusive partners or ex-partners. Others may present significant needs for housing, employment, financial assistance, legal advocacy, and other practical concerns related to establishing safety and independence from an abusive partner.

Support groups are structured to provide a safe space in which to explore these questions through education about battering and process-oriented discussions among group members. Safety planning and other practical issues also are discussed. As groups progress, members tend to acquire a better ability to recognize the abusive dynamic in the relationship, an increased ability to place accountability for the battering with the batterer, and a decrease in self-blame and shame.

Issues in Forming a Group

Forming Mixed-Gender Groups

Domestic violence survivor support groups have traditionally been for women only. In beginning to provide groups for men, a primary question is whether or not to continue that model of gender segregation. Most groups that I learned of were men-only groups, though the group in Los Angeles was mixed gender from the beginning, Boston's group became mixed-gender in its second year and New York was planning to start a mixed-gender group for Latino/a victims. In each case, groups are described as serving lesbian, gay, bisexual, and transgender victims.

Mixed-gender domestic violence groups are a new phenomenon. Decisions about whether to try them should be made at the local level and both clinical and philosophical factors should be considered. Philosophy and clinical opinion may hold, for example, that levels of bonding, safety, and validation are higher in a gender-segregated group. Concern about men dominating group processes may also arise.

On the other hand, local opinion may be that a mixed-gender forum is the optimal way to reach underserved communities. In New York, mixed-gender groups have been chosen for Spanish-speaking clients. The rationale for this is partly that men and women in New York's Latino community are less segregated than men and women are in the Anglo lesbian and gay community and partly because a mixed group is a strategy to achieve the critical mass necessary to run a Spanish-language group. (Many bilingual individuals currently join groups provided in English.)

Although he expresses confidence in the success of this mixed-gender approach, Roberto J. Font (1996) encourages attention to gender dynamics. He observes that men in groups tend to be more task oriented than women and focus on solutions more than women are and less inclined toward in-depth discussion of feelings. He also noted that women tend to come together in groups more easily than men and, although women may want a group to continue beyond its scheduled end, that men are more likely to feel fine about a group ending.

Font (1996) also cautions that gender socialization can influence how men internalize supportive messages related to domestic violence. He speculates that men may need more help than women in differentiating feelings from actions once they get in touch with anger toward their batterer. Noting that being a victim in one relationship does not preclude abusing in future relationships, he suggests that accountability education is an important ingredient in domestic violence support, especially for men. It is vital that our work not feed a sense of entitlement that could encourage anyone to make abusive choices in the future.

Although she upholds the effectiveness of mixed-gender groups in Los Angeles, Susan Holt (1996, 1997) reports that some of the challenges encountered include the tendency of men to be more task oriented than women; the occasional need for women to educate men about the dynamics of sexism; and concern that disclosure about sexual abuse and other sexual issues may be somewhat inhibited.

Although we have encountered similar challenges in Boston, we have also found that gender differences in a focus on tasks versus a focus on feelings have in many ways complemented each other in the group. Those who have participated in our mixed groups thus far have generally reported that they did not feel a need for gender segregation, that they valued the members of the group of the opposite sex, and that they benefited from seeing how the dynamics of abuse cut across gender lines.

Transgendered individuals also need consideration because they have typically encountered as much or more difficulty accessing domestic violence services as have gay and bisexual men. Roberto Font (1996) described efforts to try to integrate male-to-female (MTF) transgendered clients into New York's support group for men. At one point, when five MTF survivors were being seen over the same period, the agency weighed integrating them into the previously all-male group versus offering a transgender group. When they were asked their preferences, clients chose the "men's" group. Font (1996) cautioned that the wishes of this small group of MTF survivors is not necessarily representative of other transgender people.

Mixed-gender groups certainly warrant further study. My feeling is that they can work for many survivors but are not for everyone. Perhaps the optimal long-range strategy is for each community to provide choices so that victims can access the service that best meets their needs.

Achieving Critical Mass

A fundamental challenge in running groups for survivors is finding enough people able and willing to commit to participation at the same time. Many of those who have tried new groups agree that filling a group may be the hardest part of running it. For this reason, most cities were initially able to provide only one or two short-term groups per year, with frequency increasing as referrals to the group increased.

Boston and San Francisco group leaders have each set a guideline that groups will begin with a minimum of five people. In all four cities, most group members are identified from the counseling and advocacy caseloads of the sponsoring organizations, all of which have offered advocacy and counseling services to individual survivors of same-sex domestic violence for several years. Additional referrals have come via fliers, word of mouth, or trainings and publicity to providers and the community.

Ambivalence About Participating

Not surprisingly, individuals who already had an established relationship with a sponsoring organization were the most likely to join. However, even within an active caseload, many men are not interested in joining a group. Reasons for this include anxiety or discomfort about a group milieu, shame or discomfort with acknowledging the abuse experience before peers, inability to commit the time and emotional energy required (or resistance to making such a commitment), or concerns about a group facilitator or sponsoring agency (for example, "My partner knows him," "I know too many people who work there," "I'm attracted to him," "I don't feel at ease with her").

Some men have alluded to concerns that they will not be able to identify with other group members. In some instances, this might be related to the survivor's stage of coming out or level of comfort with and integration into the gay/bisexual community. Negative perceptions of gay men (generally related to internalized homophobia) sometimes are associated with a decision not to participate. Others may choose not to attend because of the perception or reality that their HIV status, racial, ethnic or cultural background, or gender identity will not be reflected among group leaders or other members.

Timing also impacts the ambivalence of participants. Boston, New York, Los Angeles, and San Francisco, to varying degrees, all use individual counseling as a tool for "holding" an individual until the next group is available. Some facilitators observed that the more time that passes between active individual counseling and the availability of a group, the less likely the person is to participate.

Several men have indicated a concern that the group experience will dredge up difficult emotional material at a time when they are trying to move on with their lives. The decision not to enter a support group may reflect an adaptive empowerment in the survivor. Although an effort can be made to explore and resolve hesitation in someone who might benefit from a group, enthusiastic leaders who are trying to fill groups must respect the knowledge and instincts of survivors about what is best for them.

Sometimes, survivors express ambivalence through poor attendance after admission to the group. Timely follow-up calls should be made to participants who miss sessions without notice. An unexplained absence can create doubt or worry among other group members; in addition, absences tend to interrupt the development of a group bond that fosters support. Group leaders have set varying guidelines for addressing absences. In one city, clients who miss the first two weeks are encouraged to wait to begin the next group. In another, clients who miss four sessions are asked not to return.

Diversity

Obviously, group members will have much in common simply by identifying as gay and bisexual survivors of same-sex partner abuse. Ideally there will be enough overlap among issues that each individual will receive some degree of validation, mirroring, modeling, support, and learning. Group leaders must pay attention to differences, however, because they will affect the group experience and the level of validation that individual members derive from the experience. Partner abuse can take many forms and survivors can be affected in various ways depending on their personality, culture, and life experience. The current impact of the abuse will also vary depending on whether they are still in the relationship and, if they are not, on how long they have been out of it. Members may have differing goals for group participation: Many will be focused on how to stay safely away from their abusive partner, although others may hope to resolve the abuse and remain with their partner.

Diversity of race, class, and culture can also be significant. Roberto Font in New York has found that a lack of diversity negatively affects participants of color; if only one group member is a person of color, that member is more likely to drop out of the group. For that reason, Font (1996) has made a commitment that at least one facilitator for each group be a person of color. He also says that socioeconomic class diversity can adversely affect group bonding.

Safety

Those who are living in abusive relationships or who have recently left may be in danger if their batterer learns they are seeking help or speaking out about their abuse. For this reason, some group leaders hold groups in a confidential location where participants feel secure and are not likely to be seen or observed by their abuser or his associates. Group ground rules are then set for maintaining the secrecy of the group's location. Other groups have been held within the offices of a widely known sponsoring agency or in another location that is not secret. The leader of one such group noted that, although he knows of no individual who has refused to attend a group simply because of its location, on occasion a batterer has shown up at the agency before or after a session or at another time during the week. At such times, batterers have been warned by the staff to leave or police will be called; when necessary, escorts have been provided to group participants to assist them in getting safely home.

It is important to discuss the feelings and concerns of applicants about the meeting place during the intake sessions. Meeting times and places should not be revealed to applicants until *after* they have been screened, reviewed, and accepted. Challenges can arise when group members vary in their definition of a safe location, their concerns about secrecy, and their ability to honor secrecy ground rules or when the secrecy of the location is accidentally breached.

Screening

The group leaders I interviewed agreed that the importance of safety makes group screening a necessity. All groups require an in-person intake as a follow-up to an initial phone intake; coordinators strive to have all intakes conducted with both group facilitators present. The intake is used to establish that the applicants are indeed abused and not themselves the batterers in their current or most recent relationship; that they can commit to attend all sessions; and that they are not suffering from severe mental health problems, suicidal idea-tion, substance abuse, or other problems to a degree that might jeopardize the group experience. The San Francisco program attempts to screen out men who are actively abusing substances, although the New York and Boston programs require participants to come to the group clean and sober and may make concurrent referrals to substance abuse treatment programs.

One of the most difficult dilemmas in screening arises when there is ambiguity about the applicant's own abusiveness. When they are trying to assess abusiveness, facilitators find that there are limitations when they rely entirely on one party's self-reported assessment of the relationship. In some cases, group leaders may actually be approached by both parties to a relationship, each claiming to be victims. The converse also occurs—victims have been mistakenly screened *into* batterers groups.

In Boston, each applicant is asked about his own threatening, violent, or controlling behavior in his current and past relationships. Great attention is also paid to narrative, tone, affect, and attitude to seek confirmation of a screening judgment. Screening challenges that arise include applicants who acknowledge significant episodes of "fighting back" or past relationships in which they were abusive to partners.

When there is doubt about whether an applicant might actually be a batterer himself, both Boston and San Francisco leaders noted that gut feelings among screeners and clinical supervisors about the intake process determines whether the individual is invited into the group. Leaders added that another tool for resolving doubts may be to ask the applicant to sign a release to allow the leaders to talk with his individual therapist or other counselors, if there are any.

None of the interviewed group leaders invites members into the group on the spot; acceptance into the group is finalized with a follow-up phone call after screeners have had a chance to discuss the screening in private and consider the needs of each applicant in the context of all other applicants. Nevertheless, one of the most uneasy realities in this work is that there are no 100% foolproof mechanisms for identifying a batterer.

Timeliness

One of the factors that makes it hard to achieve critical mass for a group is the fact that men may feel a more pressing need for group support at one point in their recovery than they will at another. When a closed, short-term group is all that is offered in a community and it is offered only once or twice a year, some victims of domestic violence may have to wait several months before they can access group support. This is frustrating for group leaders who believe in the value of their groups; it is undoubtedly also painful and frustrating—and perhaps even life-threatening—for potential members.

The issue of timely access is one that must be weighed by prospective group leaders who are facing a choice between offering a closed short-term group, an ongoing group that is periodically open for new members, or an ongoing group that is always open for new members. Counterbalancing this concern is the importance of building group cohesion, trust, and safety through consistent and dependable attendance. Group process and "curricula" will also vary, depending on which group format was chosen. In Boston, we chose a closed short-term group model, believing that men would make maximal progress if they moved through a certain progression of discussion topics with a cohesive group in which trust could develop over a span of weeks. We are conscious, nonetheless, of the trade-offs in terms of timely access. There is nothing quite so dismaying as learning that a client who was waiting for a support group to open has returned to an abusive situation. Staff at the San Francisco, New York, and Boston programs have also discussed hopes to initiate a monthly or weekly drop-in group as a complement to the short-term group to provide a more timely support resource. San Francisco staff have discussed monthly groups that are co-facilitated by an experienced group leader and a trained survivor.

Facilitation Models

Group Models

Although they evolved independently, groups in Boston, New York, San Francisco, and Los Angeles are very similar in structure and content. All are short-term closed groups that meet for 12 to 14 weeks, generally for 90 minutes per session. In most cases, groups were initially offered at a frequency of once or twice per year, with frequency increasing as capacity and referrals increased. In most of the cities, some participants have chosen to do the group again after their first group was finished.

All four groups use two facilitators, in part to provide varying perspectives for group members and in part for the mutual support of the leaders. Groups use a combination of process/discussion and psycho/socioeducation; leaders facilitate the support discussions and periodically assume an educational voice. Leaders are not required to be survivors of domestic violence themselves, although facilitator pools do include survivors of past domestic violence. Both male-female and male-male teams of facilitators have been used, but mixed-gender groups were always conducted with male-female teams. No differences in the success of groups for men were reported on the basis of the gender of facilitator teams. Group leaders have all been experienced counselors with training and experience in working individually with domestic violence survivors. Some were licensed psychotherapists; many were not. Some group participants, but not all, were or had been in individual counseling with one of the co-leaders prior to joining the group.

The Boston group was developed in 1995 for the Violence Recovery Program of Fenway Community Health Center. The group was initially for gay and bisexual men only but was opened to lesbian and bisexual women and transgendered individuals in 1996 and is currently a mixed-gender group. The group is offered free of charge. A schedule of topics provides structure for the 12 weeks. Each session begins with a brief check-in, followed by topic discussions that sometimes include exercises to facilitate participation. On some topics, group leaders provide brief educational information about domestic violence dynamics or resources. Flexibility is maintained to suspend the agenda if one or more participants has pressing issues that require the group's attention and support. Each member also "checks out" about how they're feeling at the end of the group. Discussion topics are provided in the Appendix.

The San Francisco group was developed as a collaboration between Community United Against Violence and Operation Concern, a community mental health agency. Participants pay a fee on a sliding scale, $0 to $20 per week. At least one facilitator is generally a trained therapist; an effort is made to use facilitators from different ethnic backgrounds.

The group uses a three-phase structure. Participants each write goals for their participation at the beginning of the group. In the first phase, each member takes a turn telling his story, and the group gives undivided attention. Each generally takes a full session to tell his story and receive feedback from other group members. In the second phase, facilitators introduce more educational content (for example, the nature of abuse, the cycle of violence, warning signs of abuse, and connections to childhood history). Content emphasis is driven in part by group needs revealed in the first phase. The third phase is devoted to closure, managing loss and loneliness, revisiting goals set at the beginning of the group, planning next steps, and writing self-addressed follow-up letters that leaders mail back to them two to three months after the last session. Participants fill out an evaluation form at the conclusion of the group.

The New York City Gay and Lesbian Anti-Violence Project (AVP) began its group in the early 1990s. Its goals are to reduce isolation, provide support, and increase the understanding of the participants about battering and about relationships that are more egalitarian. The AVP's domestic violence coordinator has recruited and trained a pool of facilitators, including peer counselors, clinicians, and clinical interns, to offer the group more frequently. Content is strongly influenced by a model that examines abuse through an analysis of patterns of domination and subordination, including all the "ism"s, both in society as a whole and in the specific cultures of participants.

The group follows a content outline and groups unfold uniquely depending on the styles of facilitators and the needs of participants. Some groups have used the first half-hour for discussion and the last half-hour for socioeducation. Some facilitators use a "check in" and "check out" go-around, although experience has shown that lengthy check-ins make it difficult to get to issues of concern to the full group.

One discussion exercise used in the group involves the Equality Wheel, a pie diagram that illustrates aspects of healthy intimate relationships. Participants are asked to brainstorm some of the things they like and look for in a relationship and are encouraged to reflect on and critique the roots of these ideals. They are then asked to highlight items from this list that mark a respectful and balanced relationship and those that do not. They then compare and contrast their abusive relationships to the list of healthy relationship markers.

Somewhat in contrast to groups in other cities, New York groups sometimes go over the 90 minutes allotted per session. Roberto Font (1996) explains his feeling that a domestic violence group should be flexible enough to respond to individuals in crisis.

The Los Angeles Gay and Lesbian Center initiated that city's first domestic violence group open to men in 1996. The group is actually a mixed-gender group, made up of approximately equal numbers of men and women. It is led by a female licensed marriage, family, and child counselor and a male mental health intern who is trained in domestic violence issues. Like the others, this group combines support, discussion, and psychoeducation.

The Meaning and Usefulness of Groups

All group leaders I interviewed shared the opinion that support groups were valuable and provided a level and type of support that one-on-one counseling rarely provides. The interviewees also agreed that group participation addresses some of the primary issues of gay and bisexual male domestic survivors: shame, invisibility, and isolation. Participants gain strong validation from knowing that they are not the only ones to have faced this problem. Because of the relative invisibility of battering among gay and bisexual men, this validation in itself is powerful. Participants are likely to encounter a degree of understanding and validation not previously available from others who have not been through a similar experience. Groups also may provide a level of interpersonal nurturing not available in individual counseling.

A specific benefit of group participation is more creative problem solving. For example, when a group of survivors strategize together for safety planning, members can garner a wide range of options for responding to situations and choose those that fit them best.

Gregory Merrill (1996) believes that groups also provide a strong "mirror effect." Hearing the stories of others can put survivors in touch with their own sadness and anger. By empathizing with others, they may be better able to acknowledge and accept their own feelings. Positive peer pressure also may empower them to move beyond places they have previously been "stuck" in while they are trying to understand or recover from abusive experiences.

However valuable groups may be, though, Ned Farley (1996), a Seattle-area psychologist, offers a caveat by distinguishing between batterer and victim services. Although he holds to a widely agreed-on position that group treatment is a pivotal ingredient of batterer intervention, he believes that the paths to recovery may be more varied. Although many survivors certainly benefit from group participation, joining such a group should not be viewed as a required element of any one survivor's recovery process.

Participant feedback offers valuable insights into the effects of these groups on the men who participate in them. Overall, feedback to facilitators in all four cities has been very positive. Although a small number of participants have dropped out, most have completed the groups and have spoken appreciatively about their participation.

Some written comments from participants from the San Francisco group (edited for syntax and spelling errors) are representative. In the words of one participant, "I was able to see that I wasn't alone with the violence that happened to me. . . . [The group] helped me regain my self-esteem and to set boundaries that will guide me in my next relationship." Another man said simply, "The more I came to the group the less I felt like an idiot." Another stated, "I saw the situation with [another group member] and now I realize more about the problems I'm dealing with." Participants also offered important constructive feedback concerning the content of group discussions and conduct of the group.

Conclusions and Future Directions

The need for domestic violence groups for gay and bisexual men is clear. When groups have been offered, they have been helpful in providing men with education and support that will help them in current and future relationships. Expansion of these groups is needed—expansion into parts of the country where they have not been offered and expansion of group frequency in those cities where they have been offered.

Those of us concerned about how domestic violence affects individuals of every sexual orientation and gender identity will be well served by sharing our increasing body of knowledge about issues and service models for survivors. In the interest of providing the most effective, survivor-centered forms of support in years to come, I encourage comment, critique, and elaboration on the information I have shared here.

References

Ned Farley, Antioch University, Seattle, WA. Coordinator of domestic violence programs at Seattle Counseling Services for Sexual Minorities, 1982-1991 (personal communication, March 20, 1996).

Roberto J. Font, Coordinator of Domestic Violence Services, New York City Gay and Lesbian Anti-Violence Project (personal communication, March 26, 1996).

Susan Holt, Training Coordinator, Los Angeles Gay and Lesbian Center (personal communications, August 6, 1996; July 28, 1997).

Gregory Merrill, Gay Men's Domestic Violence Project Coordinator, Community United Against Violence (personal communication, February 14, 1996).

APPENDIX

Model Support Group Outline

Week 1: Introductions. Facilitators introduce group and ground rules. Members take 5 to 7 minutes to summarize the relationship that brought them to the group. Members take home this outline to review.

Week 2: Feedback on proposed outline for group. Is there anything I would like to add? Which topics interest me most? Which topics interest me least?

Timeline exercise. When did I first recognize/label my relationship as abusive? Power and control wheel: What are characteristics of "abusive" relationships? Validating our experiences.

Week 3: Common reactions to trauma. Different ways of coping or dealing with trauma. Safety planning: How can I reduce the chance that my current or former partner will threaten, hurt, or control me again? What are the resources available to help people in my situation? What are the realities of dealing with police? courts? service agencies?

How does being in this group affect me? How have I felt after leaving the group? If stuff gets stirred up, what are some ways I can deal with that?

Week 4: How did I get into this relationship and why did I stay? If I left more than once, what led me to go back? A closer look at emotional abuse: Biderman's Chart of Coercion. The cycle of violence. To what extent do these models describe what I experienced? If not, how was it for me?

If it's over now, do I still sometimes find myself wanting to get back together? When does that tend to happen? What thoughts or ideas can we offer ourselves/each other about such times?

Week 5: Who, if anyone, knew/knows about the abuse? Did it all happen in private, or was it witnessed by others? How was it to disclose it to them? Have the reactions of friends, family, coworkers made it easier or more difficult?

What has been the influence of gender and sex roles on abuse dynamics? Family history? Homophobia, racism, or disability? Has HIV status been a factor in my abuse?

Week 6: What was the interplay between trust, emotional intimacy, and sex in the relationship? Was I getting what I wanted/needed in each of those areas? Did our sex life affect my staying in the relationship? Was sex (or unsafe sex) used as a form of abuse? What is a "safe" sexual/intimate relationship for me?

Week 7: Midpoint evaluation, check-in on agenda for remaining weeks. What makes someone abusive? Do I/did I feel I could have helped my partner change or get better? Did substance abuse play a role for either of us? Did most of the abuse happen when one or both of us were drunk or high? How did being together affect each of our patterns of alcohol/drug use? Is there any such thing as early warning signs of abuse? Did I see any?

Week 8: Future relationships: How does it feel to think about dating again? When/how will I disclose past abuse to a new partner? What do I want for my life, and what kind of person do I want to share it with? What does a good, healthy relationship look like? Where would I need or want to be for a healthy relationship to develop?

Week 9: How do I feel/respond to the anger of others? How has anger been expressed in my life? Which of these feels safe? Which feels unsafe? What distinguishes the two? What is the difference between anger and abusive behavior? What are sensible boundaries for me? Do I ever blame myself or feel guilty for contributing to the violence in the relationship? Did I ever hurt my partner? What feelings does that raise? Is there such thing as mutual abuse?

Week 10: Moving on: How do I gain a sense of closure with this relationship? How do I deal with feelings of grief, loss, nostalgia over losing a relationship I once had high hopes for? What role, if any, does forgiveness play? How has the relationship affected me in lasting ways? How can I deal with what "baggage" remains, so I can move ahead in my life? How far have I come already? Sharing about an object or symbol we brought in to mark closure.

Week 11: What are things I do to take care of and nurture myself? What fosters my self-esteem? How do I build/rebuild a sense of self, independent from how my partner defined me or made me feel about myself? What is my personal sense of myself, my center? What are my strengths? What are some of the things I've done for myself since I left (or despite) this relationship? Talking about how to end the group.

Week 12: Closure and next steps: What are my next steps in dealing with what I've been through? How can I support myself and/or others in the long run? Letters to ourselves. Feedback about the group experience. Saying good-bye.

21

Running Batterers
Groups for Lesbians

Susan Cayouette

Founded in 1977 by a group of men to address male violence, Emerge, based in Cambridge, Massachusetts, is the first batterer intervention program in the United States. In 1995, Emerge began its first lesbian batterers group.

When we decided to offer the group, we first had to reaffirm our mission of working to stop violence against women, which includes heterosexual and lesbian women.[1] We also decided to start a batterers group only if the grassroots organizations that were developing services for battered lesbians and gay men in our community supported the idea—within the feminist domestic violence community, there has been a long-standing reluctance to develop services for lesbian batterers before completing the first priority of developing services for lesbians who are battered. The Network for Battered Lesbians and Bisexual Women (Boston) and Emerge worked together to formulate a plan to implement services for lesbian batterers.

Emerge initially saw several lesbian batterers individually, with the ultimate goal of starting a group. However, as with heterosexual male batterers, we discovered that individual counseling did not work well and that most batterers dropped out after unsuccessful sessions in which they either avoided responsibility for the abuse, lied, or tried to use the sessions to focus on their personal problems instead of

234 SAME-SEX DOMESTIC VIOLENCE

their battering. We quickly realized that if we were going to have a successful program, both for the batterer and her partner, we had to use a group intervention model.

Pros and Cons for Partners

Batterers groups often afford the partners several important things. The most basic is that there is a two- to three-hour time period each week that the partner is away from her batterer and may be able to make safety plans or contact important people in her life. The batterers program may also offer her the opportunity to work with an advocate (or at least get a referral to one) who will help her find resources to develop a long-term safety plan, which may or may not include leaving.

The batterers group may offer the battered partner her first acknowledgment and validation of the abuse. This validation often happens when our "partner contact" advocate, who serves as a combination information bearer/safety advocate to the abused partner, schedules the first telephone interview. Batterers programs often find that they are the first outside contact that a battered woman has, because her batterer has either isolated her from the outside world, or in some cases, has convinced her that *she* is the batterer.

Other benefits for the partner are that the partner can see whether the abuser will attend an available group; she can assess the batterer's likelihood for change with the group leader; and she can monitor how the batterer reports her current behavior in the group, which gives the partner a baseline about how her batterer is perceiving and presenting the abuse. And, finally, the abused partner can work with the program to spell out a plan of accountability for the batterer in whatever terms the abused partner is comfortable with.

Some of the "cons" for partners are that batterers often use a batterers group as a bargaining chip to get back into the house or into the partner's life in some way. The batterer's participation in a program may convince a partner that she should give it another try or give her false hope that her partner will change. If an abused partner is contacted by a program, she usually will be told that total cessation of abuse is very rare and that it is more likely that she might see more limited changes and a change in typical abuse patterns. However, that limited hope may keep a woman in a relationship she was ready to leave.

Batterers also may use groups as a way of "credentialing" themselves with courts or probation authorities. Mere attendance at a group does not indicate true work toward change. However, batterers often try to use minimal attendance in groups as proof of positive changes.

Another drawback is that a batterer may use the knowledge gained in the group against her partner. For instance, a batterer may tell her partner, "My group leaders told me that when you interrupt me, that's controlling." Of course, what was said in the group was that it is controlling when the *batterer* interrupts her partner in an effort to dominate the conversation. The partner may *have* to interrupt a batterer who continually dominates the conversation.

Finally, giving batterers services will give them added weapons to use against their partners. An unfortunate result of groups is the opportunity for batterers to share tactics of control. Thus, batterer groups should only be done when the partner is offered the same information as the batterer and is prepared for the possible consequences of the batterer's participation.

What Makes a Safer, Better Batterers Group?

A bad batterers intervention program is worse than no treatment at all. More damage can occur if batterers get "credentialed" for completing a program when they really have done little or no work. A bad program offers the courts only attendance reports, so people sometimes falsely believe that a participant has "successfully" completed a program when she has merely attended.

The focus of a good batterers intervention program should be on safety and advocacy for the person(s) being battered. Helping the batterer to grow comes second. Programs need to hold batterers accountable for their actions, refuse to accept excuses and justifications, and refuse to accept the abuser's characterizations of her partner and the history of events without substantiation from the partner or outside authorities. One of the ways to do this is by prioritizing partner contacts. Partner contacts are designed to give the partner the opportunity to talk to someone who will believe and validate her experience of abuse and direct her to shelter or other advocacy services. Group leaders should also do periodic partner contacts to inform the partner of the batterer's progress and for guidance in constructing the batterer's goals in the group.

One of the other main reasons that Emerge does partner contacts is that many batterers lie or minimize the circumstances of the abuse. It is important that programs verify the reports of abusers when possible because they are often inaccurate. However, it should be clear to partners that their participation in the partner contact is optional. We like to at least offer them information about what will happen during the process so that the partner's information from the program is at least on a par with that given to the batterer. This is because information is power to the batterer. One way to equalize that power is to share information with the partner when possible. That does not mean, however, that a program shares information with the batterer that was gained from the partner. Often, we share nothing, although in 25% of contacts we share some of the information gained from the partner but only with her permission.

A good program will try to keep the partner's involvement as information-giver to the extreme minimum. One way to avoid the batterer's attribution of information to the partner contact is to use every other avenue available to get reports about the batterer's behavior. Regular contacts with probation officers, child welfare workers, or therapists will offer valuable information that cannot be blamed on the partner.

How Do I Know Who Is the Batterer?

Assessing who is battered and who is the batterer is a vital task of the therapist, advocate, or batterers counselor who works with lesbian/bisexual batterers. What makes identification of the batterer difficult is that often the battered woman will definitively identify herself as the perpetrator. She may also describe an incident in which she yelled or physically fought back. This still does not mean that she is the batterer—someone who is battered has the right to respond verbally and physically to abuse they are experiencing.

Emerge's work with batterers for the past 20 years has made us aware of patterns of behaviors that batterers frequently exhibit. Therapists, counselors, and advocates should watch for some of the following behaviors when they assess whether the person they are seeing is the victim or the perpetrator.

I'm the Victim

Batterers usually identify themselves as the victim of their partner, the courts, their family, or coworkers. Much of their energy is usually taken up avoiding responsibility—blaming others for their behavior, blaming others for instigating their behavior, or excusing their behavior with a laundry list of reasons why "she deserves x, y, or z."

The lesbian batterers we have worked with thus far have tended to acknowledge much more abuse than heterosexual male batterers, initially *admitting* to the acts but without accepting *responsibility* for the behavior.

Denial, Minimization, and Sidetracking

We tell every batterer who begins our program that three things may get in the way of her making progress in the batterers group. The first is *denial,* which often happens when batterers refuse to acknowledge what they've done. In doing so, they may contradict the victim, police reports, and eyewitness accounts. Usually, this is the initial response to coerced batterers' treatment. After several weeks, the cloud of denial usually lifts and some more sophisticated forms of avoidance appear.

Minimization occurs when batterers acknowledge parts of the abuse but underplay the full extent of the violence or control. For instance, they may say "I hit her, but only with an open hand, not a closed fist," or "She wasn't bleeding and didn't require hospitalization," or "She bruises easily."

When *sidetracking,* the abuser avoids full responsibility for the abuse by focusing on other people or events. For instance, she may say, "Yes, I hit her, but it's because I was abused as a child," or "Yes, I hit her, but I'm very stressed by my job and I'm having medical problems that make me tired and cranky."

Coercive Patterns of Control

The batterer is usually the person in the relationship who exercises control over her partner's life in various ways. For instance, the abuser frequently determines directly or indirectly who the battered partner gets to see, confide in, or socialize with. The batterer may believe that she also deserves to control the money and important decisions in the relationship and may set the emotional tone, determining which feelings are acceptable and unacceptable.

Entitlement

Abusers frequently feel entitled to delivery of certain services and behaviors from their partners (although each abuser's list may vary). These behaviors may include caretaking, sex, maintaining possessions and the household, and child care. They may expect protection of their image so that friends and relatives continue to view them positively. They may require the victim to devalue herself in the relationship and to herself, her friends, and her family.

Jealousy and Ownership

Batterers often believe that their partners do not have the right to make independent decisions, particularly if those decisions diverge from those of the batterer. They often believe they have the right to continue a relationship long after their partner has decided to end it and often will not accept the partner's statements or pleas that the relationship is over. Group members frequently describe monitoring partners through phone calls, following them, or checking up on them through friends and relatives long after the relationship has ended.

The Batterers Group

There are several different models for batterer groups, many of which share a similar philosophy but use slightly different methods. Emerge groups are 2 hours per week for 48 weeks, with rolling admissions. Because of limited membership, the lesbian group is not divided into intake and ongoing groups, as is the case with heterosexual men. This means that the one ongoing group must integrate new members and repeat the core education units. However, this may be positive, because experienced members demand a higher level of participation of new members than is true in a nonintegrated group, and the experienced members seem to learn things on a deeper level when units are repeated.

There are three main components of these groups: educational presentations by group leaders, in which members participate; "check-ins," during which group members describe abuse; and "turns," during which one group member is given time to describe her abuse and the group analyzes the underlying negative thinking and effects of the abuse.

We follow a curriculum designed at Emerge that features educational units about abuse-related topics: the effects of violence on partners; the effects on children; positive and negative self-talk; respectful and disrespectful communication; the continuum of abuse and control; and later-stage educational units on jealousy, lying, and topics tailored to each batterer's particular patterns of abuse.

In check-ins, group members are asked to report what they did and said to their partner that was abusive and controlling. They are not allowed to drag her into the story, blame her, or characterize her in negative ways. They are asked to take responsibility for what they did without sidetracking to what she was doing or saying or to other issues such as whether or not the police were biased, or why the batterer's bad childhood or tragic life circumstances were responsible for making her respond abusively.

We also ask them to imagine responding nonabusively in circumstances in which they are not treated fairly. We want to remind them that at various times in their lives they will encounter abuse, unfairness, or cruelty. The question becomes, can they still respond nonabusively without retaliating or seeking revenge? We want batterers to have a more realistic sense of what they might encounter because it is easier for them to be nonabusive when things are going their way.

Groups also ask batterers to give feedback and constructive criticism to other members. We expect them to not bond around negative remarks about each other's partners, to expect that respect for others becomes the norm, and to work on recognizing and changing the negative thinking in their heads (negative self-talk) that both fuels their rage and gives them permission to escalate their abuse. This self-perpetuating hate-talk can and must be stopped by them—otherwise they are likely to continue to abuse in the future. We ask them to explain their negative thinking and offer nonabusive alternatives. They may be asked to describe the effects of the abuse and to reenact the incident in a role play and then redo the role play to model respectful behavior.

After going over basics with each group member, the goal is to then work on outlining their particular relationship history with different women, highlighting abusive behaviors with each prior partner to try to see a pattern over time. We then ask the batterer and group members to develop a set of goals based on her history, prior group participation, and the expressed desires of the partner. These goals should help the member work toward a cessation of violence and toward controlling behavior and the development of respectful behavior toward her partner (or ex-partner) and others. For instance, a goal might be that Jane (the batterer) does not attempt to contact Jill by phone or letter unless first contacted by Jill. Or, if they are living together, that Jane allow Jill to initiate discipline of their children and that Jane not physically reprimand the children. On a more positive note, a goal might be that the group member develop self-care habits, such as keeping a regular job and taking responsibility for her emotional health; or if she is depressed, taking action in some positive way without burdening her partner with her negative moods.

Differences Between Lesbian and
Heterosexual Male Batterers

There have been some notable differences between heterosexual male batterers and the lesbian batterers in our groups. An additional tool of control that lesbian batterers have at their disposal is the use of homophobia against their partner by threatening to "out" them to friends, family, or coworkers and inflicting the self-hatred of the batterers' internalized homophobia onto their partners.

In a heterosexual male batterers group, there is usually a tendency to have participants whose violence ranges along a continuum. However, our experience so far is that those lesbians who are court ordered or forced to come by their partners are usually on the more extreme end of the spectrum of violence: they have threatened or attempted to kill their partners and use extreme cruelty or emotional abuse against their partners. One explanation for this is that lesbians are less likely to use the homophobic court system to defend themselves, so mandatory sentencing to batterers programs is far less likely unless the batterer has been extremely violent or has been arrested repeatedly.

Group members often are, or have been, in therapy and are well versed in therapy jargon and psychological language. They often use this language as both a weapon against their partner and as a way to avoid taking personal responsibility for their abuse in the group.

We have also seen a much higher frequency of acknowledged depression, suicidal ideation, and the use of antidepressants than with heterosexual men. This raises our level of concern about the potential for homicide because batterers who are suicidal often kill their partners, not themselves.

Differences in Lesbian Versus Heterosexual Groups

Thus far, lesbian groups have been smaller than heterosexual male groups at Emerge; 3 to 6 versus 8 to 12 members. This allows us more time to focus on individuals and to provide more educational units because check-ins take up less time. Because our group members have been more psychologically attuned than the average male batterer, there has been more of an effort on our part to keep the group focused on the abuser's *behavior,* and the partner's *feelings.* This has been difficult because the batterers have come to the group expecting to be allowed to talk about their feelings.

The group is run by and for lesbians. Because group members are themselves victims of oppression as women, lesbians, and/or members of other oppressed communities, we can validate their experiences of oppression. However, we must still demand accountability for their oppression of their partners and work with them to model and use nonabusive and respectful behaviors in the future.

Conclusion

As with heterosexual male batterers groups, we must hold ourselves to a high standard of accountability when running batterers groups. Areas that need to be attended to include screening procedures we use with applicants; ensuring that groups focus primarily on abuse, not other issues; and ensuring that contacts with partners to allow them to share information (or at least know what happens in a group) are responsibly done so that they will not have false expectations of change or about their own safety. A poorly run batterers group is dangerous to battered women. However, even well-run groups must exist with an organizational climate that addresses multiple levels of oppression or else issues such as homophobia, racism, and classism will undermine any positive work being accomplished around battering.

Note

1. Our next goal is to provide services for gay male batterers. That shift in our thinking occurred only after our participation in the broader focus of Boston's Same-Sex Domestic Violence Coalition. Although Emerge is experienced in working with male batterers, we have not worked with gay men in separate groups and have, in fact, prevented gay men from joining heterosexual groups because of our fear of the homophobia of other batterers.

Index

243

About the Contributors

Advocates for Abused & Battered Lesbians (AABL) was founded in 1987 by lesbians for lesbian victims of domestic violence. Today AABL's staff of two provide assessment and intake, individual counseling, legal advocacy, and support groups for lesbians who have been or currently are in an abusive relationship. Additionally AABL conducts outreach and education to lesbians, domestic violence service providers, and social service agencies regarding lesbian battering/ abuse and antihomophobia.

Charlene Allen has been working to end violence against women for more than a decade. She has provided training on domestic violence and sexual assault throughout the nation, reaching members of the judiciary, law enforcement officers, medical professionals, private individuals, and diverse organizations. She was a contributing author and member of the editorial board of *For Shelter and Beyond,* a nationally distributed training manual for domestic violence advocates. She also wrote "Defending Women in the 21st Century," a training curriculum for domestic violence legal advocates in Massachusetts. She now holds the position of Executive Director of the Boston Area Rape Crisis Center, where her mission includes integrating services for sexual assault survivors who are also survivors of domestic violence.

Bradley-Angle House believes that everyone has the right to be safe from physical, sexual, and emotional abuse and the threat of violence. Its mission is to end violence while simultaneously working to end all oppressive behaviors. Rather than judging what is right or wrong, the staff at Bradley-Angle House help women and their children who are emotionally or physically abused to make informed choices about their lives. They educate the community about domestic violence, its causes, and its consequences, and they encourage the community to help prevent abuse by making changes in the conditions that make it happen.

Andrea Cabral is an Assistant District Attorney and the Chief of the Domestic Violence Unit of the Suffolk County District Attorney's Office. In addition to maintaining her own domestic violence caseload in superior court, she supervises a superior court staff of 8 and a district court staff of 9. She is also author of the book *Obtaining, Enforcing and Defending 209A Restraining Orders in Massachusetts*, published by Massachusetts Continuing Legal Education, Inc. in July 1997. Prior to this position, she was an Assistant Attorney General in the Trial and Civil Rights Divisions of the Attorney General's Office from 1991 to 1993 and an Assistant District Attorney in the Cambridge Division of the Middlesex County District Attorney's Office from 1987 to 1991. She is a graduate of Boston College and Suffolk University Law School.

Susan Cayouette is the Clinical Director at Emerge: Counseling and Education to Stop Domestic Violence, located in Cambridge, MA. She has worked in the battered women's movement for 15 years and has spent the past 10 years at Emerge. She received a doctorate in education at Boston University and is a licensed Marriage and Family Therapist. Currently she is the Co-Chair of the Same-Sex Domestic Violence Coalition in Massachusetts and co-leads a group for lesbian batterers.

Diane Coffey is the Deputy Chief of the Victim Witness Assistance Program of the Suffolk County District Attorney's Office. Her responsibilities include the coordination of victim services in the Domestic Violence Unit. She develops protocols and policies, supervises victim witness advocates and coordinates trainings and outreach efforts. Prior to her current position, she worked as a victim witness advocate in the Massachusetts Office of the Attorney General and the Middlesex County District Attorney's Office. Throughout her career, Diane has provided practical training to police, prosecutors, advocates, and community members.

Evan Fray-Witzer is an attorney in private practice in Boston, MA. A graduate of Northeastern University School of Law, he worked as a student intern with the Middlesex District Attorney's Abuse Prevention Unit and as a legal advocate for Casa Myrna Vazquez, a Boston shelter for battered women. His writing on domestic violence in lesbian relationships has been used by the Massachusetts Attorney General's Office, the New Hampshire Bar Association, and Northeastern University's Domestic Violence Advocacy Project.

Martha Lucía García is a Colombian woman who has been working on domestic violence issues since 1983. A formerly battered woman and a lesbian, she is currently a therapist working with immigrant women and women of color and also does organizational consultant work.

Alma Banda Goddard is the Director of Advocates for Abused & Battered Lesbians (AABL) located in Seattle, Washington. She has been working in the battered women's movement for the past eight years. She has been with AABL for three and one-half years and has also served as the community advocate providing direct services for survivors. Chicana/Rocky Mountain Indian, single mom, dyke, survivor, activist, she believes that we must find common ground and fight all forms of oppression and that each individual must move forward to identify and eliminate his or her own internalized oppressions and to find and embrace the essence of personal power and self-love.

Jennifer Grant has been a part of the battered women's movement since 1985. She is currently Director of the Riley Center: Services for Battered Women and their Children in San Francisco. She is a founding member of the San Francisco Network for Battered Lesbians and Bisexual Women.

Bea Hanson is a social worker, community organizer, and activist. She is Director of Client Services at the New York City Gay and Lesbian Anti-Violence Project, which provides counseling and advocacy to over 1,600 survivors of anti-gay/lesbian bias crime, same-sex domestic violence, sexual assault, and HIV/AIDS-related violence every year. She is also Adjunct Professor at the Fordham University Graduate School of Social Service in New York City.

Tara Hardy is the Community Advocate for Abused & Battered Lesbians. She has been an anti-violence activist for the past 10 years and she is a survivor of lesbian battering. She believes that the most challenging issue about addressing violence in lesbian relationships is that it suggests that women must examine our own behaviors and realize that our femaleness no longer provides us with impunity.

Robb Johnson has been a victim advocate with the Violence Recovery Program of Fenway Community Health Center in Boston. He received a master's degree in public health from the University of Michigan in 1988 and has since worked on health issues of gay, lesbian, bisexual, and transgendered (GLBT) people. The Violence Recovery Program, founded in 1986, provides counseling and advocacy to GLBT survivors of hate crime, domestic violence, sexual assault, and other violence. Johnson co-facilitated New England's first domestic violence support group for gay and bisexual men at the Violence Recovery Program in 1995.

KJ is an Alaskan Native woman, born and raised in Alaska. She has advocated for women and children who have the right to be safe. She is also active in the Native Sobriety movement and has been clean and sober for several years. She also does trainings on anti-oppression work.

Patrick Letellier is a counselor and a freelance writer and editor. He has written and edited numerous articles and manuals on domestic violence and is coauthor of the first book on same-sex male battering, *Men Who Beat the Men Who Love Them*. At Community United Against Violence in San Francisco he counsels gay, bisexual, and transgendered men who have been battered and/or sexually assaulted. He is a survivor of same-sex battering.

Beth Leventhal, a formerly battered lesbian, has worked in the battered women's movement since 1986. She is the founder and Coordinator of the Network for Battered Lesbians & Bisexual Women. She

is a founding member of Boston's Same-Sex Domestic Violence Coalition, and has served on the Boards of the Massachusetts Coalition of Battered Women Service Groups, Emerge, and the Massachusetts Older Women and Domestic Violence Prevention Project. She wrote and produced the audio program "Voices of Battered Lesbians" and provides training and technical assistance on same-sex domestic violence to legal and health care providers, battered women's programs, and GLBT groups.

Sandra E. Lundy is an attorney and writer living in the Boston area. As a solo practitioner, she specializes in family law for straight and queer families, with an emphasis on assisting victims of domestic violence. She has written and lectured widely and on the topic of same-sex domestic violence, and has conducted trainings on the topic for police departments, lawyers, health care providers, and judges. She has represented many victims of same-sex domestic violence, including Debra Reid, a battered lesbian and member of the Massachusetts "Framingham Eight" who sought commutation of her prison sentence for killing her abusive partner. Her poetry, short stories and review have appeared in many queer and arts publications. She obtained her Ph.D. in English Literature from Columbia University, and her J.D. from Yale Law School.

Jennifer Margulies is a Smith College Women's Studies alumna living in Austin, Texas, where she is grateful for her partner Jackie, her dog Chula, the Texas sky, and all the friends who teach her about risk, safety, and love.

Terry Maroney graduated from Oberlin College in 1989 and is currently a student at New York University School of Law, where she is a Root-Tilden-Snow Public Interest Scholar. Formerly the HIV-Related Violence Program Coordinator at the New York City Gay and Lesbian Anti-Violence Project, she has also worked at the NENA Health Center in New York's Lower East Side and at the Workplace Project, a center for Latino/a immigrant workers on Long Island. She serves as a law clerk for the Honorable Amalya L. Kearse of the United States Court of Appeals for the Second Circuit. Prior publications include "Psicología de la Oprimida: Un Estudio Psicosocial de dos Refugiadas Salvadoreñas en Costa Rica," *Estudios Centroamericanos* 480 (octubre 1988), pp. 911-925.

Gregory S. Merrill is a summa cum laude graduate of Bowdoin College who recently received his master's degree in social work from San Francisco State University. For his master's thesis, he conducted an exploratory study of the experiences of battered gay and bisexual men. The Director of Client Services at Community United Against Violence (CUAV) in San Francisco, he has also volunteered extensively for the Lavender Youth Recreation and Information Center (LYRIC) as a group facilitator and trainer.

Curt Rogers, a formerly battered gay man, is founder of the Gay Men's Domestic Violence Project, P.O. Box 9183 #131, Cambridge, Massachusetts, 02139. The Gay Men's Domestic Violence Project is currently working to provide services to gay male victims of domestic violence with a primary emphasis on establishing a safe-home network. He was also founding Secretary for the Same-Sex Domestic Violence Coalition, Boston, MA.

Ann Russo is a lesbian activist, writer, and educator who is currently an assistant professor of Women's Studies at DePaul University. She is coeditor of *Third World Women and the Politics of Feminism* and has written articles on feminist, lesbian, and antiracist politics in relation to violence against women for a variety of journals, including *Sojourner, Women's Review of Books,* and *Women's Studies International.*

The San Francisco Network for Battered Lesbians & Bisexual Women was formed in October 1992. It provides information and referrals for survivors and for service providers and community organizers. The Network facilitates a weekly support group for survivors of woman-to-woman battering and also makes educational presentations about this issue. It is an all-volunteer collective with a nonprofit fiscal sponsor.

Tonja Santos is a recent graduate of a small all-women's liberal arts college. She has interned at both the D.C. Rape Crisis Center, Washington, D.C. and the Network for Battered Lesbians and Bisexual Women in Boston. She hopes to one day integrate her work in sexual assault and battering into a career as a medical doctor.

Sarah Sulis is the pseudonym for a woman who is the director of a statewide domestic violence coalition. She has worked previously as a sexuality educator, women's health counselor, and director of a domestic and sexual violence center. In 1992, she organized the first bisexual delegation to the Gay Pride march in her small southern town and has facilitated bisexual women's groups.

José Toro-Alfonso is a clinical psychologist and Executive Director of Fundación SIDA in Puerto Rico. Communication can be addressed to him at P.O. Box 36-4842, San Juan, PR 00936-4842. He wishes to express his gratitude to the Prevention Department at Fundación SIDA and to its director, María Isabel Báez, for their support in the domestic violence project. Funding for this work was also provided by the National Latino Lesbian and Gay Organization (LLEGO) in Washington, D.C.

Jack Higgins

Jack Higgins lived in Belfast till the age of twelve. Leaving school at fifteen, he spent three years with the Royal Horse Guards, serving on the East German border during the Cold War. His subsequent employment included occupations as diverse as circus roustabout, truck driver, clerk and, after taking an honours degree in sociology and social psychology, teacher and university lecturer.

The Eagle Has Landed turned him into an international bestselling author, and his novels have since sold over 250 million copies and have been translated into sixty languages. Many of them have also been made into successful films. His recent bestselling novels include, *The Killing Ground*, *Rough Justice*, *The Khufra Run*, *A Darker Place*, *The Wolf at the Door*, *Confessional* and *The Judas Gate*.

In 1995 Jack Higgins was awarded an honorary doctorate by Leeds Metropolitan University. He is a fellow of the Royal Society of Arts and an expert scuba diver and marksman. He lives on Jersey.

ALSO BY JACK HIGGINS